ALSO BY CHRISTOPHER BROWNFIELD

Oil on Landscape:
Art from Wartime Contemporaries of Baghdad

SUB VERSION

SUB VERSION

A Shocking True Story of Corruption and Redemption in the Nuclear Submarine Force and the War in Iraq

CHRISTOPHER BROWNFIELD

Originally published in hardcover as
My Nuclear Family: A Coming of Age in America's 21st Century Military

Skyhorse Publishing

Skyhorse Publishing books may be purchased in bulk at special discounts for sales promotion, corporate gifts, fund-raising, or educational purposes. Special editions can also be created to specifications. For details, contact the Special Sales Department, Skyhorse Publishing, 307 West 36th Street, 11th Floor, New York, NY 10018 or info@skyhorsepublishing.com.

Skyhorse® and Skyhorse Publishing® are registered trademarks of Skyhorse Publishing, Inc.®, a Delaware corporation.

Published by arrangement with Alfred A. Knopf, an imprint of The Knopf Doubleday Publishing Group, a division of Random House, Inc. Originally published in hardcover as *My Nuclear Family: A Coming of Age in America's 21st Century Military*.

www.skyhorsepublishing.com

10 9 8 7 6 5 4 3 2 1

Library of Congress Cataloging-in-Publication Data is available on file.

ISBN: 978-1-61608-349-6

Printed in the United States of America

To the memory of
Captain Richard Gannon
United States Marine Corps
and
Haitham T. Yaseen
Ministry of Electricity, Republic of Iraq

To the perseverance of
my dear Iraqi friends throughout the world

To the hope and commitment of
Sergeant Larry Lloyd, United States Army,
who volunteered for duty in both
Afghanistan and Iraq, that he may better serve
the people of the United States
as their future president

You can always count on Americans to do the right thing—after they've tried everything else.

—Winston Churchill

Contents

Author's Note

Memory is the perfect liar. I did not begin my naval service with the intent of writing a book, which means that some of my account is based upon my imperfect memories and personal notes. Furthermore, a great deal of my experience was classified, which means that certain details of my story must remain absent out of respect for the law of the United States and concern for the security of my former colleagues. Wherever possible, I have listed open sources that corroborate the details of my account, and I have also sought advice and criticism from numerous colleagues who served alongside me in the submarine force and Iraq. For most of my friends and colleagues, I have altered their names to preserve their privacy, while allowing myself to be completely candid about what happened. Finally, I've listed the numerous works that have influenced my opinions and illuminated the contexts of the situations I've presented.

SUBVERSION

Introduction

In the twilight of my childhood, I swapped my mother for the navy. It was a clean break, made less painful by the uncanny similarities between the woman and the war machine. In the navy, it was, "Sir, yes, sir!" At home, it was, "Yes, Mommie Dearest!" My mother took me to the doctor when I was sick; the navy gave me free cough syrup and eye exams. There was no sex allowed as long as I still lived under her roof, and no sex allowed aboard their ships. Both my mother and the navy considered it their solemn duty to prescribe exactly what I would wear, and who was I to argue? I knew my place in the pecking order, and besides, they both had pretty good taste.

"I'm glad you picked the navy," Mom confided after I joined. "Their uniforms are the nicest."

I never wanted to be a jarhead or SEAL or Ranger or Delta Force or Batman or anything else that the local beer-bellied wannabes claimed they were gonna be when they grew up. I wanted to be a naval officer, "a gentleman of liberal education, refined manners, punctilious courtesy, and the nicest sense of personal honor," as John Paul Jones described the profession. When I stood at attention during my sweat-soaked boot camp in the Annapolis summer, my trainers so frequently invoked the Father of the American Navy's words that to this day the ghost of John Paul Jones haunts me. Don't get me wrong; it's a very civilized haunting, bereft of any moaning or chains or spooky frivolities unbecoming of a gentleman. Instead, Jones haunts me with dignity, sporting a freshly starched navy blue uniform bedecked with gold buttons, a gleaming saber at his side. In his confident colonial British accent, Jones paints the naval officer as "the soul of tact, patience, justice, firmness, and charity." At first our relationship disturbed me, but that soon passed; now, after all we've been through together, we're practically family.

Over the years, I realized that instead of joining the navy, the navy had actually adopted me. At the beginning of the twentieth century, some of my real ancestors fled Eastern Europe, leaving behind the bulk of our heritage. I know very little about these people except that my mother's side of the family might have been Jewish, which would make me Jewish by default. The Roman Catholics among us were not particularly eager to upturn that stone, so I inherited a somewhat truncated family history. Regardless, a familial navy rabbi offered to "arrange the surgery" if I ever decided to convert. The gesture flattered me, but I declined; in the navy, there were plenty of surrogate ancestors who didn't require circumcision. It was these adoptive forefathers like Stephen Decatur, Oliver Hazard Perry, and, of course, John Paul Jones, who gave me a sense of pride and belonging in the service of my country.

My official nomination to the United States Naval Academy arrived from Spencer Abraham, a Republican senator who soon received his own nomination to the cabinet post of energy secretary. Everyone was moving up in the world. I loved the Naval Academy for its rigidity and its clarity in separating right from wrong. Three of my roommates were thrown out while I attended, one on account of "mediocrity." John didn't fail to make grades or physical standards, but he didn't exceed any of the standards, either. *What kind of draconian school treats people that way?* I knew full well, and I loved every minute of that draconian school from Induction Day till the day I shook President Bush's hand, swore "to support and defend the Constitution," and walked off the stage with my diploma.

I practiced what I vaguely considered to be "strong conservative values" and supported President Bush in 2000, though my absentee ballot was lost in the mail en route to Annapolis. During my training, John McCain—a graduate of the Naval Academy—spoke repeatedly to the Brigade of Midshipmen, recounting tales of torture at the hands of the Vietcong in the dreaded Hanoi Hilton. My heart swelled with pride over McCain's perseverance and the fact that he was a member of my extended naval family. When Oliver North waved from the stadium stands at the Army-Navy football game, the entire brigade erupted in applause and chanted his name in unison—*Ol-lie, Ol-lie, Ol-lie*. More than anything else, we kept unquestioning faith that those who had marched before us had done the right thing. An austere memorial in the central rotunda of our campus enshrines the names of our alumni who paid the ultimate price through their service. It is a large memorial, and the names are quite small. Like a half-filled family gravestone, blank space on the bottom allows room for future expansion.

It took me years to realize I had come of age in a world where energy and violence met, but it was at the Naval Academy that I cut my teeth on these principles. For years, my classmates and I pored over texts of strategy and thermodynamics, war doctrine and weapons systems, while between our classes we debated the ethics of combat. The question was never whether we were capable of killing; we simply explored the methods and rationales. While my civilian counterparts studied Karl Marx, we joked about "killing commies" and calculated the optimal altitude for detonating a nuclear weapon to maximize the effect on unarmored personnel. The latter was part of a three-credit course; I scored an A without much effort.

After those early years, my career progressed dramatically along the same lines. From nuclear power school to the sub-

Naval personnel in the individual augmentation program wait to depart for the Middle East. The grandma in combat boots is shown, wearing bifocals and reading a paperback novel. Both of us were headed to Baghdad.

marine force, I lived inside the physical embodiments of defense and energy policy. Instead of the invisible hand of capitalism, I became the highly visible hand of Americanism. New names like Hyman G. Rickover and Jimmy Carter became part of my nuclear family as I absorbed the sacred texts of atomic energy, submarining, and top secret missions. Even more than the navy at large, the nuclear submarine force became my strange aquatic home within a home.

After nine years of this patriotic American life, it came as a shock to me that my family was in jeopardy. It was a balmy day in South Carolina, August 2006, as I waited in an isolated airport terminal to depart for Baghdad. A grandmother in combat boots sat in a chair in front of me reading a novel, bifocals riding low on her wrinkled nose, M-16 in a hard plastic case at her side. A young sailor held court with an audience of older officers, explaining how to pirate music for their iPods. There were fifty of us in the terminal and twenty plastic seats. I sat on the floor, staring at some crackers wrapped in thick green foil and a miniature bottle of Tabasco sauce from the MRE I'd been issued for my in-flight meal. High on the wall, a plastic American eagle hovered like it was swooping in for the kill.

What the hell am I doing here?

It was a rare and well-concealed moment of self-doubt.

"Those things are a bitch to open, aren't they?" someone remarked, pointing to my crackers in their weatherproof wrapping. The expiration date was seven years out. I nodded slowly; the crackers were a bitch to open, but they were even harder to swallow.

What the hell am I doing here?!!! It was an existential identity crisis; instead of growing up like John Paul Jones, I was turning into a strange mélange of G.I. Joe and Jean-Paul Sartre! In a matter of weeks I had withdrawn my resignation from the navy, deferred enrollment at Yale, and volunteered for duty in Iraq. At the age of twenty-six, I had just written my third mandatory will. My mother questioned my sanity, and to top it all off, I looked ridiculous in camouflage: she knew it; I knew it; hell, even the navy knew it.

For years I had trained to become a nuclear submariner. In 2005 the Departments of Defense and Energy certified me to supervise an entire reactor plant aboard a nuclear warship. My ship had deployed across the Atlantic, Pacific, Mediterranean, and Caribbean in numerous missions. Submariners are warriors, but warriors of a distant and calculating sort of warfare, trained to conduct surveillance and to sight our targets through a periscope, not through the scope of a rifle. To me, the idea of killing another person face-to-face is reprehensible, unclean, distasteful. Yet on that particular morning, with a Beretta service pistol at my side, I pondered the possibility of having to do just that. Looking down at the embroidered submariner's "fish" on my camouflaged breast pocket, I shook my head; if my goal was to become a fish out of water, then it was *mission accomplished.*

My life was at a crossroads. A month before, with one foot out of the navy, I had the world before me. Headhunters had been calling me for years to set me up with jobs. "Say the word and I'll get you an interview with McKinsey . . ." Yale could have opened practically any door I wanted. Still, it seemed as though something was missing from my life. The United States had been fighting the Global War on Terrorism for five years, and up to that point there was little evidence that our world had become more secure. By most accounts, the world was becoming less stable. Despite my service aboard submarines, there was little I could show for having done my part. To me, the problem was worse than political— it was a family matter. The insurgency in Iraq, the criticism against the administration, and the conspiracy theories were getting worse by the day. I wanted to know the truth about what was happening in Iraq, but more importantly, I wanted to help fix something that my family apparently had broken. For the sake of my country, for the sake of my naval forefathers, and for the sake of my mother, who taught me to clean up after my own mess, I needed to do something good in the name of the United States.

According to the Department of Defense, the sailors who waited with me in that cordoned-off terminal were known as individual augmentees. To me, the group looked like a bunch of aging reservists who had come to the realization that they'd picked the wrong line of work to get free medical. The individual augmentation program evolved from a general shortage of personnel who could serve in Afghanistan and Iraq. Essentially, the program was an interservice draft that drew heavily from the inactive reserves. As the "army of one" commercials were dropped from television, the "support unit of one" was born. There were doctors, pilots, dog trainers, explosives experts, and many others called to do their part by leaving behind homes, civilian jobs, and even regular military units to go to war. When I learned of the program, I was floating somewhere below the surface of the ocean in the belly of a steel beast, the USS *Hartford*.

But before we dive into this tale and I share with you the lives of men who served aboard that billion-dollar fast-attack submarine, I must issue a warning. Diving deep into the sea is a perilous act; one is never quite certain where it will lead, what it will reveal, or whether the same man will make it back to the surface. That is the chance we must take.

1

In the Belly of the Beast

"Awoooooogaaa! Awoooooogaaa! Dive! Dive!"

That was what I heard in my head every time we dove the USS *Hartford* below the waves. I pretended to hear that sound with a sense of wistful nostalgia as I surveyed the seascape through my periscope, cherishing every last second of sunlight before the optics dipped below the water and we descended into the utter darkness of the ocean. The real sound of the *Hartford*'s diving alarm, however, was no cause for nostalgia. Rather than the unmistakable tone of World War II Klaxons, the *Hartford*'s aural signal to "take her down" more closely resembled a wounded chicken. *"Baawwkk! Baawwkk!* Dive! Dive!" was the sonic reality in this modern marvel of engineering. And so it came to pass that I settled for driving a nuclear warship that executed its primary design feature with the undignified sound of common poultry. It was this sound that first clued me in to the fact that life on a submarine is decidedly not what it used to be.

"Smith! Put your balls away! How many times do I have to tell you to keep your dick in your pants while you're on watch?" I yelled across my small elevated desk from the stool where I sat, supervising the men who controlled our ship's nuclear reactor.

"But, sir, it's hot in here . . . and besides, you know you

like it," replied Petty Officer Smith, the overweight, smelly, and highly intelligent sailor who knew exactly how far he could push it before getting fired (and liked to prove so on a regular basis). The fat-ass winked at me.

"Whether I like it or not is *iiii-fucking-rrrelevant*! Stow your cock! End of discussion," I growled, slamming the heavy Reactor Plant Manual I was reading down on the metal desk. I said "End of discussion," but my rant was just getting started.

The Maneuvering Area, as it is formally known, is a room the size of a walk-in closet where more than five hundred gauges, meters, indicator lights, switches, and every other bell and whistle imaginable reside. It is the principal location from which three highly trained nuclear operators and one supervisor keep constant watch over the most important parameters of the ship's nuclear reactor plant. The late Hyman G. Rickover, Father of the Nuclear Navy, to whom *The Simpsons'* Montgomery Burns bears a remarkable resemblance, believed that the Maneuvering Area was sacred. The Reactor Plant Manuals use the word "inviolate" to describe Rickover's expectation of formality within Maneuvering's boundaries. And yet this was a typical day in Maneuvering, when a watch-stander, tired and hot, decided to unzip his trousers and brandish his genitals. Let's get something else out in the open—*none* of us actually enjoyed Smith's awkward testicular presence, but it *was* unusually hot in there and we couldn't really blame him for wanting to air out. Somewhere in nuclear heaven, Rickover was beginning to vomit.

"Listen up, fuckers." I continued my rant, annoyed. "I used to be a fucking gentleman before you pricks corrupted me!"

The ghost of John Paul Jones was nowhere to be seen.

"Did you say you were *fucking gentlemen*?" interrupted Jenkins, another petty officer (and petty wit), who never missed an opportunity to make someone else look stupid.

"No, shit-scrap!" I shouted, eliciting chuckles (any novel

permutation of basic vulgarity was enough to make them giggle). I was still annoyed, but they'd found the chink in my armor. With my momentum fizzling, I recommenced my rant. "As I was saying, I used to *be* a gentleman, and I'll be god-damned if I let you knuckleheads wag your dicks around in Maneuvering on my watch! Let's have some fucking professionalism!" I breathed deeply while dismounting my soapbox, but the bastards had done me in. I choked back a laugh but was unable to conceal my smile. The troops spotted my break in character and howled with delight. Smith zipped up his pants, sheepishly admitting defeat.

"Does it get any lower than this?"

"Technically, sir, we can go down another four hundred feet."

"Shut up, Jenkins."

"Aye, aye, sir."

The first time a sailor wagged his testicles before me as I knelt to read an instrument gauge, I completely lost control. It quite literally flew in the face of every example of professionalism that the Naval Academy had trained me to uphold. I was so angry by the overt harassment and the indignity of stumbling face-first point-blank into another man's balls that I threatened to have the pervert taken to captain's mast, the navy's version of a court-martial at sea. While morally and legally correct in that course of action, I know in hindsight that it was the wrong way to handle things aboard a real submarine.

When the hatch of a submarine shuts, the vessel becomes its own little universe, with a very different set of rules. Bollocks to Einstein—the modern submarine redefines relativity. In that universe one should never admit one's weaknesses. Aboard a submarine, to reveal that a particular thing irritates you is to invite repeat occurrences of that irritant ad infinitum. It was a mixed-up maxim, a Kantian kerfuffle that promised, through the miracle of socialized military medicine, to make our lives nasty, brutish, and long. For example, when our ship's executive officer (XO) divulged that he was "somewhat of a homophobe," our fellow officers responded by taping pictures from gay porn magazines onto the ceiling above his stateroom bunk. The first time he lay down to read and looked up at the pictures, he ran screaming through the door in his skivvies. The man's public display of hairy near-nakedness opened the field for more comments—nothing was off limits, except the captain himself. Days later at sea, several members of the "all-balls" crew sent the man anonymous love notes and signed pictures of shirtless male models posing on sports cars, all graced with loverly terms of endearment and XOXOXs. One envelope was even sealed with a lipstick kiss. I don't know which man brought the lipstick aboard, and it's probably better for some questions to remain unasked.

But just as the XO had erred in admitting his fear of homosexual behavior, it was my mistake to admit that the sight of another man's penis in close proximity to my face was . . . well, odious.

"You should have just grabbed it," my colleague Jake opined after my first encounter. Jake was always the pragmatist.

"Or pretended that you liked it or something—that would have freaked *him* out. Now every enlisted man on the ship knows that you can't abide cock."

I thought about it for a second and agreed that Jake's tactic of *carpe scrotum* was indeed a better alternative than threatening the sailor with penal action. A thorough hand-washing would've been required, of course.

"Think about it, Chris," he continued. "If you had simply grabbed his sack and dragged him around the ship like a fleshy little puppet, nobody would have ever fucked with you again—you would have been a *god.*"

Jake was right. I could have been a god. We paused for a moment, lamenting the lost opportunity for ultimate respect, albeit respect bounded in the nutshell of that horribly finite space. And so it came to pass that instead of being a god among the sailors of the *Hartford*, I writhed within my mortal coil, a prick supervisor, irritated by the sight of other men's schlongs. From that point forward, in accordance with standard submarine practice, I saw, unwillingly, more schlong than any other officer aboard the ship.

Please recall that this is a family story. It's true that I've seen more of certain tiny things than I'd ever hoped for in life, but every family has its quirks. I don't recall my less gentlemanly shipmates with any particular fondness, but I can no more divest myself of their underwater antics than disown my brothers. The experience was all part of growing up in that strange watery world. Welcome to my home.

The modern nuclear submarine is the most extreme machine on the face of the planet. By comparison, space shuttles and fighter jets and even armored tanks are fragile and basic. The vacuum of space is nothing compared to the cold, crushing pressure of the deep. The thrust of an afterburner is nothing compared to the silent force of atomic engines. It is a well-known fact that a nuclear submarine is capable of traversing the depths of the oceans to strike practically anywhere with lethal precision. It is far less well known that the nuclear submarine can create and maintain its own atmosphere. Now, at the dawning of the third millennium, it is strangely novel to recall that the nuclear submarine—equipped with a hundred-ton backup battery—was the first hybrid vehicle that could sustain its environment and mission independent of oil.

Energy has always sharpened the cutting edge of violence, especially in the world's navies. In the first millennium, Greek Fire swept the Byzantine navy toward stunning victories. At the beginning of industrial modernity, Roosevelt's Great White Fleet circumnavigated the globe on coal. But the greatest shift in the forces of violence that energy brought to the world came in the discovery of oil. More than any other source of power in history, oil—the most efficient, mobile, and useful energy source—empowered nations to seek and maintain control. It was a legendary American admiral, Alfred Thayer Mahan, who coined the term "Middle East" in his monumental geo-strategic book of 1890, *The Influence of Seapower upon History.* But it was the British who learned seven years later the influence of oil upon empire.

By dint of capitalist zeal, a British prospector unearthed the massive oil reserves in "petroliferous" Persia. Like an explosive gusher of crude, the discovery of oil propelled the ancient homeland of the Zoroastrians (who worshipped burning oil seepages) to the forefront of the twentieth century's greatest power struggle. American captains of industry like John D. Rockefeller had been building empires of capitalism for thirty years, and the British saw controlling Persia as a strategic step toward controlling their own massive energy supplies. The grand secret was out: with oil came wealth and power.

By 1913 Winston Churchill, at the helm of the Royal Navy, changed the course of his empire with the historic decision to shift the British fleet from coal to oil. At the time Churchill feared the rising power of Germany. It was this fear that finally convinced him to agree with the founder of Shell Oil that change was necessary—even before a steady oil supply could be secured. The switch to oil gave Her Majesty's fleet a fighting edge, making Britain's ships more fuel-efficient and faster than the steamships fired by coal. The switch was more than tactical—it was a matter of evolution or extinction.

Ironically, Churchill's move encountered considerable resistance at home. Sheffield had plenty of coal, but nary a drop of oil. Thus Britain faced the choice of forgoing a reliable supply of coal and basing its naval supremacy upon a single, enormous question mark. Conservative parliamentarians and admirals argued against foreign oil in favor of energy independence. To these men, homeland security meant keeping coal alive as a reliable and profitable source of energy. The switch to oil flew in the face of conventional wisdom by necessitating an unprecedented level of global interdependence. Yet even more critically, Churchill's progressive switch to an oil-based navy encountered tremendous resistance at home because it required the Britons to embrace a changing world.

Despite the resistance that Churchill faced in moving his country forward, the Great War had a way of forcing Britain to grow up. As Daniel Yergin explained in his history of oil, "Many would look back upon those spring and early summer days of 1914 as the dusk of an era, the end of a childhood." By the end of World War I, the strategic importance of oil had proven itself beyond all doubts. The mechanization of militaries and the introduction of the Tank (a secretive project that got its code name from its liquid-fuel tank), broke the hopeless stalemate of trench warfare. For England, oil had been crowned the new king. And for the soon-to-be prime minister, Churchill, the thirst for oil was all too clear: "Mastery itself was the prize of the venture."

After World War I, England's need for foreign oil was obvious, though as Yergin explains, "explicitly pronouncing Mesopotamia as a war aim would seem too old-fashionably imperialistic." Thus British Foreign Secretary Balfour succinctly explained the required evolution of imperialism: "I do not care under which system we keep the oil, but I am quite clear that it is all-important for us that this oil should be available."

For the next several decades, the Anglo-Persian Oil Company (later British Petroleum) exploited the unsophisticated Persians with the legalistic power of oil concessions, becoming one of the most profitable companies in the history of the world while driving the Royal Navy at full speed ahead.

For America, World War II began and ended over the pivotal forces of oil. It was not the temptation of power but the fear of dwindling energy supplies and the American oil embargo that spurred the Japanese to strike at Pearl Harbor before seizing the oil fields of Borneo. It was not the bravery of the Allied forces but the critical shortage of gas that stopped the tanks of Nazi field marshall Rommel literally in their tracks; the Desert Fox died of thirst for oil.

For postwar America, energy security meant engaging the Middle East in developing its oil. The war's last secretary of the navy and America's first secretary of defense, James Forrestal, led a concerted effort to shift American dependencies to Middle Eastern oil, effectively putting an end to America's energy independence. While the major oil companies faced antitrust lawsuits at home, the U.S. government gave them carte blanche to collude in Saudia Arabia, ushering forth the greatest oil discoveries in history and an era of unmitigated consumption.

While profits of multinational oil companies soared and the coffers of petrol states began to fill, the people of the Middle East slowly awakened to the reality that they'd been bought and sold by the West. The spark of nationalism was fanned into flame in Tehran when a brilliant secular lawyer, educated in France, surprised the world by having the audacity to stand up to the British. Mohammed Mossadegh vowed to rid his homeland of the exploitive British concessionaires and restore what he believed to be the birthright of all Iranians. Nationalizing the Anglo-Persian Oil Company in 1951 and reclaiming Iran's oil for its own people was an earthquake that sent a tidal wave of strident self-determination around the globe. England was too weakened by war to break its addiction to foreign oil; the ravages had been enormous. Without Iranian oil at her disposal, the last remnants of the British Empire were doomed to collapse.

A plot was formed.

Churchill, desperate to salvage his country's strength, implored President Truman to help overthrow Mossadegh and reinstate the Shah of Iran. Truman rejected the proposal flatly; to replace an elected leader of a democratic country with a monarch was insultingly backward for a world that was supposed to have been "made safe for democracy" by the terrible sacrifices of two world wars. Truman, however, did not remain president for long. When Eisenhower took office, Churchill found his ally for the plot against Mossadegh, overthrowing the elected leader in a secret CIA-led coup.

Ironically, Eisenhower supported the coup not because he wanted Iranian oil but because he feared that the nuclear-armed Soviets would engulf Iran if the West did not intervene. At the onset of the nuclear age, the paradigm of energy and violence had split into two. For energy, Oil was still King, but for warfare, the Atom had been crowned Emperor.

In the same way that oil empowered the armadas of the world to speed forward, so did atomic engines sharpen the swords of the world's navies. Between 1949 and 1955 the United States embarked upon one of the greatest industrial, scientific, and engineering feats in the history of humanity. By employing the brightest minds, the most dedicated engineers, and a unique fusion of disparate institutions, the United States conceptualized, developed, built, and deployed the world's first modern war machine capable of sustaining its environment and mission without fossil fuel. In this context, in 1955, the world's first naval nuclear reactor came to life in the belly of the USS *Nautilus*. Science fiction had become science fact as nuclear-powered warships reignited the race for mastery of the seas.

And so it came to pass that just as Alfred Thayer Mahan had pondered the influence of sea power upon history, I sat upon my small metal stool, deep within the bowels of my submarine, pondering the principles of energy and violence. My ass hurt. I had been sitting there for three hours, barely moving as my four-man team in the Maneuvering Area slowly went insane. We'd joined the navy in search of Homeric odysseys, only to become Homer Simpson. The clock struck zero-three. Smith lifted his clipboard and jotted some numbers in the hourly logs. Jenkins belched. *Three more hours to go*, I thought. *That's one hundred eighty minutes—ten thousand eight hundred seconds . . .tick, tock . . . ten thousand seven hundred ninety-eight . . .tick, tock . . . ten thousand seven hundred ninety-six. . . .*

Once again, Maneuvering is the inviolate nerve center of the ship's nuclear power plant. A colleague once described an officer's job in Maneuvering as follows:

[with gravitas]

"Imagine a man standing in a closet-sized room. A panel of meters lies before him. None of the meters move . . . but if they did, it would be really, really bad. But they don't move . . . for six hours."

His civilian friend then inquired, "*That's* what you do?"

"No. I sit in a desk behind that man, and I watch *him.*"

Outside Maneuvering, there are stacks and stacks of electronic equipment: control systems, circuit breakers, and panels with blinking lights. Unlike a car, where the inner workings are concealed from view, a submarine crew lives among the inner workings. In some ways the men actually *are* the inner workings. The ship is a maze of piping, cable conduit, and machinery. Pumps, steam turbines, and valves lie everywhere in a weave of steel so convoluted that calling it byzantine seems reductionist. The temperature varies widely as air-conditioning ducts blast cold air between hot, steam-filled pipes. Everything is kept immaculately clean, much to the annoyance of the junior enlisted personnel who are required to scour, sweep, and swab regularly. The sound of whirring machinery and steam flowing through pipes creates a constant din that would be bothersome to the operators were it not for the fact that they've already lost some of their hearing. Only a few conscientious youths bother to wear the required earplugs.

There's a laboratory for analyzing nuclear chemistry, a welding bench for at-sea repairs, and various other makeshift office spaces with laptop computers crammed into nooks and crannies wherever the designers could afford to spare a cubic foot or two for humans. Steel bookshelves hold innumerable Reactor Plant Manuals, each bound in hard plastic and dirty from frequent use by hundreds of unwashed hands. A few scattered exercise bikes and rowing machines lie in disrepair, strapped to the deckplates. A small toolbox holds some dumbbells. There is even a "smoke pit," where the crew is permitted to relax and tell jokes about the officers while exhaling smoky carcinogens into our small enclosed atmosphere.

In the center of the ship lies the nearly unlimited fuel of the modern nuclear vessel, where billions of atoms shatter into fragments every second. Within the reactor compartment's shielded bulkhead, the invisible neutron flux and gamma rays are so intense that they could deliver a lethal dose in a matter of minutes. Outside, where the crew lives and works, the highly sensitive Geiger counters barely even register a blip as we steam full speed ahead. I was inherently skeptical that our Geiger counters seemed not to detect our own reactor, but later amazed to learn that the reactor really was that well shielded. Over time, I could tell the depth of our submarine by the ship's background radiation level; higher levels meant that we were closer to the surface and detecting the sun's radiation. For a time, I was in charge of monitoring and documenting the crew's exposure to radiation using a device called a dosimeter. The crew was exposed to higher levels of radiation in the months when we were home in New England than while we were under way on nuclear power. Regardless, the fear of cosmic rays didn't stop us from hitting the beach as soon as we pulled into port. Most of us looked pretty pasty from our sub-aquatic lifestyle, and we considered the threat of skin cancer an acceptable alternative to looking like vampires in June.

For dining out at sea, the ship has a mess hall where up to

thirty people can sit at once. As the biggest "people space" on the submarine, it is frequently commandeered for training, lectures, briefings, and watching movies on a plasma-screen television. The galley is a small industrial kitchen where a team of culinary specialists work round the clock to prepare upwards of five hundred meals every day. I have a love-hate relationship with the galley, but it's mostly hate. I hate the food aboard submarines, not because of the quality or the skill of preparation, but because after the first week at sea, nothing fresh remains. Of course, this lack of produce doesn't dampen the sanguine spirits of the cooks. In a naively nautical way, two weeks after leaving port the cooks still try to spruce up the same putrid brown lettuce for a meal or three before bidding farewell to freshness and tossing the compost overboard.

There are other reasons why I hate the food aboard submarines, not the least of which is the colorful history of our galley. One day, the ship was in the process of pumping its septic waste overboard. This common practice with submarines at sea doesn't usually involve creating a biological hazard for the entire crew, but the *Hartford*, in many ways, liked to be exceptional. On that particular day, while the *Hartford*'s septic tanks were being pressurized to force out the hundreds of gallons of waste, something terrible happened that I will never forget. It started with a low gurgling sound in the galley sink—a primordial monstrous groaning and bubbling from deep within the ship. The cooks, working on preparing Philly cheesesteak sandwiches, looked up with alarm. Knowing from experience what was about to happen, the most senior of them, Bill, grabbed a lid from a large metal pot and leapt across the galley counter toward the sink—*too late!!! WHAM!!!* An explosion of noise and stench spewed forth as the sink erupted with a pressurized stream of liquefied human shit.

In the army, an act of conspicuous gallantry and intrepidity in the face of danger is worthy of at least a Bronze Star, or

maybe even the Medal of Honor. But covered in his shipmates' piss and shit, poor Bill fought nobly with no prospect
of any medal, deflecting the lumpy column of fecal matter,
clutching his pot top tightly in hand, trying his best to look
away and keep his mouth closed. A poop mist descended
upon the galley like volcanic ash upon stunned islanders, as
the crew gaped motionless at the devastation, paralyzed by
the fear that they had somehow offended the submarine gods.
The Waldorf Astoria is famous for its salad. Burger King is
famous for the Whopper. After the Night of the Poocano (as
it came to be immortalized in legend), the *Hartford* was
famous for its filthy cheesesteak.

If that weren't enough to whet our appetites, we could
always arrange for an at-sea surgery on the wardroom dinner
table. Of course, clearing the three-forked, two-spooned table
settings and sterilizing the tablecloth for an appendectomy
wasn't exactly normal, but it was the way the Doc did things
in the case of a medical emergency at sea. The Doc was not an
actual doctor or a nurse, but the equivalent of an emergency
medical technician. If ever there was a surgery aboard, it
would likely be his first, with scalpel in one hand and instruc-
tion manual in the other. To this day, I consider myself
blessed that I never needed to consult him for anything other
than Dramamine or foot powder.

The rest of the submarine has pretty much what one
would expect to find. There's a torpedo room where sailors
invent new phallic metaphors, a sonar room where people listen to stuff in the ocean, and a control room that isn't too different from the one on *Star Trek,* except for the videophones
and aliens. Last, but certainly not least, are the bunkrooms,
where the 140 men aboard the submarine sleep. Despite what
the rumors may say about 140 men going down and 70 cou-
ples coming up, these bunkrooms are relatively straight and
innocent. My stateroom—a luxurious officer's suite—measured six by eight feet and boasted two fold-up desks, lockers,
and a fold-up sink. These quarters slept three, each of whom

had his very own "rack" measuring six feet by two feet by eighteen inches. This Lilliputian living space was where I spent an uncomfortably long part of my life, hitting my shoulder on the bunk above me every time I rolled over and waking up to the disturbing surprise of another man's flatulence. Little did I know that shortly after my years aboard the *Hartford*, I would awaken to the surprise of somewhat louder and more deadly explosions after swapping my submarine sneakers for combat boots and heading into the desert. *Oh, the fleeting bliss of ignorance!*

2

Nuclear Family Life

"You're *dink*, Brownfield. Un-fuck yourself."

The words reverberated in my head like depth charges in a swimming pool, spat from the deadly launcher of my fearless leader's mouth. *Direct hit, asshole. You sunk my battleship.* The engineer officer, Dale, frequently used his words as a weapon against the weak and lowly of rank. I naturally fell into the latter of these two categories, and in the face of a formidable superior, assumed the demeanor of the former. "Dink" was submarine-speak for being professionally delinquent. Halfway through my first year at sea, I was two months behind in my nuclear qualifications. My illustrious ball-baring brethren had yet to introduce themselves to me, and for the time being my virginal idealism remained intact.

The *Hartford* was out to sea for the first time that year after a long overhaul in the shipyards. The work left the enclosed atmosphere of the submarine reeking of synthetic paint, cleaning solution, and unpronounceable chemical vapors. Because of the fumes, my head felt somewhere between a migraine and a drug trip for the first two months aboard. By the third month, I had either gotten used to it or enough brain cells had died that I could no longer tell the difference. As Dale's verbal depth charges plunged toward me, what little resistance I had built up to our marginally toxic atmosphere quickly vanished and my head felt ready to split. My aural assailant was the most talented submarine driver I'd ever met. Dale was a young lieutenant commander with chiseled features, a sarcastic wit, and a beautiful trophy wife. Among the junior officers of the wardroom, Dale was also the most hated man on the ship. As long as I knew him, every junior officer aboard dreamed of having the opportunity to drop a pipe wrench on his head and make it look like an honest accident.

"You've been aboard my ship for five months, and you can't even pass your basic qualification exam," Dale lectured me condescendingly.

The Formica-covered steel door of Dale's stateroom was shut, isolating the two of us from the rest of the ship. The Germans in *Das Boot* couldn't have felt more trapped.

"What the hell am I paying you for?" Dale demanded, acting as though he owned the ship and I was his hired help rather than a commissioned government official like him. The idiosyncrasy irked me, but I was more concerned with the guilt I felt for failing to meet my boss's expectations.

"I don't know why *you're* paying me, sir," I mumbled. Dale glared at me, catching on to my criticism. I may have been a nuclear neophyte, but by God, I had words on my side! Sadly, I couldn't pass the nuclear qualification exam. Dale had a good reason to "counsel" me, as he so eloquently put it in our euphemistic professional parlance; I had just failed my fourth basic qualification exam in a row. On a submarine, one is not allowed to stand watch until after completing a lengthy and detailed qualification process. For nuclear officers, this training pipeline takes nearly two years from commissioning to the completion of initial training aboard a sub. Until that point, one is merely a trainee, barred from operating any equipment aboard the ship. This prohibition is so strict that some ships even bar the newbies from "operating" the galley's self-serve ice cream machine. Thus, until qualified, a new crew member is functionally useless, a freeloading oxygen breather ("FLOB" for short). The nuclear exam I had just failed was a critical part of my qualifications and a major obstacle to my usefulness. I sat next to Dale's fold-down desk, cringing, keenly aware of my first-class flobbery. My colleagues were standing watch in grueling shifts, working over one hundred hours a week while managing their divisions of enlisted personnel, and I couldn't even pass the basic nuclear competency exam. *What the hell am I being paid for, anyway? Were years of Academy training and hundreds of thousands of dollars wasted upon my pathetically non-nuclear brain?*

Before submarine officers report for duty on a boat, they complete a twelve-month stint at nuclear power school. For my classmates, this consisted of a six-month academic course of study followed by six months of practice on a real nuclear power plant. Since I was an English major, the powers that be forced me to attend a one-month nuclear "preschool" before matriculating in the full-fledged course. My classmates appeared universally smarter, or at least better prepared. If there had been a short-bus, I certainly would have ridden it to

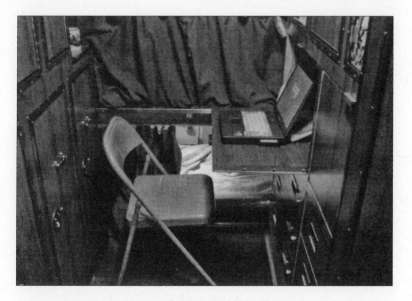

My quarters aboard the USS *Hartford*. This closet-sized stateroom berthed three officers, each of whom was lucky enough to have his own footlocker. The junior enlisted crew frequently "hot-racked," sharing their bunks in shifts.

the base. I sat next to a rocket scientist who was married to a medical doctor. My mostly older classmates introduced themselves by name and college major, nearly all of which were engineering disciplines.

"I'm Jeff, a Double-E" (electrical engineering).

"I'm Matt, a Mech-E" (mechanical engineering).

"I'm Steve, a Systems-E" (systems engineering).

Needless to say, I felt a bit out of place.

"What was your major, Chris?"

I stated confidently that I was a Single-E. They shook their heads in acknowledgment, thought about it for a second, and then asked, "What kind of engineering is that?"

"English."

Condescending smirks. "How did you get into nuke school?"

After becoming the butt of a few jokes, I changed majors retroactively to grammatical engineering, which seemed to hold more weight.

Nuke school was a brutal and intense course of study. My academic advisor thought it best for me to be placed on mandatory study hours, landing me in the classroom for more than sixty hours a week. At this school, unlike a normal school, all of our books and notes were classified. In order to study anything at all, one was required to sign in to the building with an electronic access card, pass through several armed security checkpoints, and unlock the sacred nuclear texts from an impressive steel locker. Students' study time was tracked down to the minute and tallied up at the end of each week to ensure they followed orders and kept up their grades. I scraped by, eventually passing all of the required exams. My grades were not spectacular by any means, but my work and efforts were honest. The rocket scientist who sat next to me ended up setting the school record for the highest grades ever. I felt smarter just from having sat next to him, though my advisor was quick to note that my grades in no way reflected this.

Back behind the closed door of the engineer officer's stateroom, I sat bruised and rattled, his chiseled face leering over me. It seemed that everything I had learned in nuke school had abandoned me. But strangely, the basic qualification exam was anything but basic. To me, it seemed so ridiculously hard that it looked like a foreign language, even after spending a year in nuke school and several months studying aboard the ship. The first time I failed the qualification exam on my boat, it was devastating—I worked very hard, but the results weren't even close to passing. When my fellow junior officers asked me what happened, they were surprised that I hadn't been given the unofficial "study guide" before the exam.

"Sorry, Chris. Somebody dropped the ball."

Before my second exam, the study guide mysteriously appeared in my in-box. To my surprise, the document was no study guide at all, but the answer key to the exam I was about to take. I immediately walked up to the officer assigned to proctor the exam and handed him the document.

"I beg your pardon, sir, but somebody dropped the ball."

The proctor looked at me intently, wondering whether I was serious. He shook his head in disbelief, then huffed, "Fine, but you'd better pass next time."

My heart sank. It was such a disappointment that my colleagues were encouraging me to cheat on a nuclear qualification exam; my impression of them was permanently tarnished. I had never cheated before in my life and wasn't about to start on something this important, where it seemed that cutting corners could have serious consequences. When I quietly protested, several other junior officers confided that they had cheated as well. I was floored. *How could this be possible in my navy, where honor was considered a core value?* Somewhere between the theory and the practice, there had been a serious breakdown aboard my ship.

I stuck to my guns. The second exam fried my brain like a rock of radioactive crack. With a score of 1.9, I felt sick and somewhat dizzy; it wasn't even a high F. When the results from my third and fourth exams came back, Dale started documenting my failures to make the case for firing me. A fellow junior officer who had been aboard for almost two years attempted to come to my rescue. Hugh, a fully qualified officer who was universally respected, offered some friendly advice.

"Chris, I know the system is bullshit. Practically none of us could have passed that exam at first—hell, half of the guys who are qualified can't pass it now. But we need you to check the box."

Like every other newly reported crew member, I had been under constant scrutiny from the time I stepped aboard. They knew that I could handle what was expected in the job, but the administrative part of my qualifications was paramount. I implored Hugh to help fix our broken process, but he demurred.

"Chris, we're not going to change it. I hate it, but that's the way it is."

I felt abandoned. Hugh was the smartest of the junior officers and the most respected by our chain of command. In my estimation, Hugh was the only one of us with enough political capital to fix the corrupt system, but he refused even to try. Everyone respected Hugh for his ability to accomplish difficult things, but his unwillingness to help me face my moral dilemma left a bad taste in my mouth. It reminded me of the time he stole someone else's parking ticket to put on the windshield of his illegally parked BMW. He thought it a victimless crime until I pointed out that the guy whose ticket Hugh stole probably found out about it when a penalty notice for late payment came to him. To Hugh, it was easier to do the right thing when it involved his personal benefit. Having exhausted my other options, I studied like crazy and took my fifth exam alone. The spirit of Rickover spurred me on like an engineer version of Mickey, that cranky old boxing trainer who growled at Rocky to get back up. After all the exam failures and verbal depth charges and brain cells killed by toxic fumes, I simply refused to quit. When my final test results came in, Hugh broke the news.

"3.21—you passed. If this weren't your day job already, I'd tell you not to quit it."

I was elated, but the race wasn't quite over. The last official part of my qualification was a two-hour interview with the captain, a department head, and the ship's engineer. The oral cross-examinations were notoriously difficult. Some of the smartest officers before me had failed their first attempts after having rushed through the facade of administrative readiness. Interviewees were expected to recite procedures verbatim, to draw detailed schematics from memory, and to explain the complex interactions of various nuclear systems. My interview didn't last two hours; the captain made up his mind well before that.

"What took you so long, Chris?" The captain laughed. "It sounds like you were ready a while ago!"

I made no excuses for my delay. I was never a nuclear genius, but it was clear that I had met the minimum standards for joining the team. My stubborn refusal to cheat was justified. Two years after my graduation from Annapolis, I was finally permitted to stand my first watch in the nuclear navy. As I stepped into the engine room, a gust of dry heat blew through the portal. Petty Officer Smith stood by the reactor compartment, clipboard in hand.

"Did you qualify, sir?"

"You bet your ass I did."

"Oh, good," Smith chuckled, his stomach wobbling inside his greasy, stretched uniform. "We needed some fresh meat."

The nuclear cheating scandal aboard the *Hartford* was but one instance of a fleet-wide problem. Universally, my colleagues from other ships regretted the situation but went along with the dubious practice for fear of impeding their ships' progress. When I reported the cheating problem to my ship's engineer officer, Dale feigned concern before sweeping the whole matter under the rug. Ironically, the nuclear cheating was an administrative way to prove competence and safety that generally *did* exist. Due to our considerable training, robust management, and solid system designs, there was never any significant danger in the way we operated our nuclear reactors. Nevertheless, the administrative requirements careened out of control to the point that they were unattainable, even by the best and brightest among us. This divergence between expectations on paper and the requirements of reality caused me great consternation as I continued to grow up.

For now, it's worthwhile to discuss how the submarine force evolved into its present state. In the aftermath of World War II, the military-industrial complex was born when Congress passed the National Security Act, establishing the CIA, DoD, and NSC in 1947. Defense budgets soared as President Truman implemented NSC-68, the defining strategy of the Cold War that sought to shape a new world order upon liberal capitalist values. After Truman left office, President Eisenhower shifted the military away from conventional weapons and toward a nuclear-based arsenal. Eisenhower believed that nuclear weapons would allow the military to downsize while still defending against total war. Nervous and eager for defense dollars, Congress overrode Eisenhower's vetoes on excessive defense budgets, continuing the avalanche of spending that deeply entrenched the military-industrial complex. A tremendous buildup of nuclear weapons ensued as the air force expanded its bomber fleet and developed intercontinental ballistic missiles. Russia followed suit, and the race was on for nuclear dominance.

Over the decades, arms limitation talks attempted to rein in the escalating risks of nuclear war, but the nuclear genie was out of the bottle. While the SALT I treaty placed a limit on the number of missiles, both the United States and Russia put multiple warheads on each missile to circumvent the treaty. When the SALT II treaty was passed, limiting the total number of warheads, both countries shifted their focus to the only "survivable leg" of the nuclear triad—the submarine force.

By placing more and more missiles aboard submarines, the United States and Russia created the most dangerous arsenals in the history of the world. It is an important fact of geography that the shortest flight path between the United States and the Soviet Union went through the arctic circle. For this reason, a new battleground for the submarine force appeared in the icy aquatic caves of the Arctic Ocean. Only submarines could go undetected into the arctic circle, surface through the ice, and launch a secretive first strike in a nuclear war. The hunter-killer submarine assumed a position of prime importance. Only fast-attack subs could defend against the threat of submarine-launched ballistic missiles.

Fortunately for humanity, the Cold War ended and total nuclear annihilation was recognized as a generally bad idea. The looming threat of nuclear war evaporated and the Russian submarine force dropped off the face of the earth. Suddenly, fast-attack submarines of the U.S. fleet found themselves chasing the ghosts of an outmoded ideology; the mission was over. American subs were retrofitted with cruise missiles, but little could be done to reconfigure the massive, highly specialized ships for contemporary warfare.

Under President Clinton, the enlargement of NATO encroached upon Russia's comfort zone. After 9/11, President Bush withdrew from the Anti-Ballistic Missile Treaty to pursue Reagan's dream of a missile defense shield. While purely defensive in technical scope and ostensibly useful only against "rogue states," a successful missile shield program began to tip the strategic scales in favor of the United States. The predictable response to this was a Russian threat to develop countermeasures to confuse the intercepting missiles and negate the shield. Also, the rogue states saw the U.S. move as a step away from dialogue on nuclear matters. North Korea restarted its nuclear weapons program in its initial bid to join the axis of evil. Iran announced that "civilian" nuclear power was a domestic goal. The harmonious balance of brinksmanship became a wistful memory.

Overall, the history of the global nuclear regime is one of lofty expectations on paper followed promptly by categorical cheating. In the shadow of this history, it was no wonder that my ship's crew was only a small part of a much grander problem. The fleet-wide cheating scandal had less to do with my tiny little submarine than with the uncontrollable duality in the swirling atoms of Pandora's box.

As I worked through the trials and tribulations of submarining, a different sort of conflict put my nuclear family in the backseat. Thousands of miles away from New London, Connecticut, where my submarine lay berthed, a newly acquired U.S. ship was setting sail. The skipper took command before he ever saw the ship. The vessel was old and severely damaged and needed a great deal of work before it could sail fast. The skipper brought with him a brand-new crew, replacing the men who had known her like the backs of their hands. It was a ship that ran on oil. And so it came to pass that the USS *Bremerstan* set sail on her maiden voyage up the murky waters of the Shatt al-Arab. The Coalition Provisional Authority, under the supreme executive power of L. Paul Bremer III, was underway.

The news of Operation Iraqi Freedom took me by surprise. Our crew was spending a lot of time on the sub, and reports from the outside world were limited. Without being chained to a television, I somehow missed the seriousness of the buildup to war. I believed that Iraq had once possessed chemical weapons, but thought that the real objective of the aggressive posturing was to convince Saddam Hussein to disarm peacefully.

The nuclear question, however, was more important to me. Colin Powell's immense credibility convinced me that Iraq had acquired uranium from Africa (which was later proven to be false). Even so, merely having uranium didn't mean that Iraq was close to having a nuclear weapon. Uranium requires an extremely high amount of enrichment before it becomes useful enough for weaponry, and this sort of enrichment takes an enormous amount of time and resources and facilities that Iraq simply didn't have. Alternatively, nuclear weapons can use plutonium, which is not enriched but is produced inside an operational nuclear reactor. Iraq's only nuclear reactor had been long since bombed to smithereens by the Israelis, which meant that producing plutonium in Iraq was out of the question. Even if Iraq was trying to build a nuclear weapon and had the resources, the world had a long time to act on the matter before it became dangerous. While it's true that Saddam was playing games with the International Atomic Energy Agency (IAEA) by banning nuclear inspectors, this seemed more like a poke in the eye of international authority than evidence of building atomic weapons.

To many people, Colin Powell was at the center of this storm. Years before, when then General Powell spoke to my classmates at the Naval Academy, he recounted a story of losing his service pistol in Korea as a young lieutenant. It was a serious offense, punishable by court-martial; a soldier must be held responsible for his weapons. A few days later, Powell's captain returned the pistol and remarked, "It's a good thing that the kids who found this only fired it once—and nobody was hurt." Powell was shocked and embarrassed by his own irresponsibility. *How could he have let a dangerous weapon fall into the hands of children?* Several days later, the officer counted the bullets in his weapon and realized that none were missing; the captain had lied to scare Powell straight. When Powell was told that Iraq sought weapons of mass destruction, a strange and more serious parallel emerged. *How could he let a dangerous weapon fall into the hands of Saddam?* I'm no psychologist, but something tells me that Colin Powell actually believed what others told him about weapons of mass destruction, the lies that scared the American public into accepting the cause for war as the truth.

At the naval academy, my class motto was *Novum Millennium Fabricari*—we forge the new millennium. But for my country's leaders in 2003, *Casus Belli Fabricari* would have been more appropriate. Strangely, the haste of Operation Iraqi Freedom was a break from the well-respected Bush family precedent. After Saddam invaded Kuwait in 1990, President Bush took his time and built a strong international coalition before liberating Kuwait. Invading Iraq without an international coalition and without a UN resolution seemed brash. In other words, the United States seemed to behave as though its intentions exempted it from following international law. The UN resolution approving an international war effort soon followed, but it seemed as if the resolution was merely an attempt for the UN to save face at the risk of being marginalized. My position was the same as that of the UN: *Now that we're there, I guess I'll support it.* I wished the good captain and crew of the USS *Bremerstan* fair winds and following seas as I walked along the pier toward the *Hartford*, saluted her flag, and climbed down the hatch. I had my own ship to sail.

3

Damn the Torpedoes!!!

When David Glasgow Farragut sailed aboard the original sailing sloop *Hartford* into the Civil War's Battle of Mobile Bay, he uttered the famous words "Damn the torpedoes! Four bells! Captain Drayton, go ahead!" In the parlance of our times, Farragut's words translate to "Screw the mines, we're going in anyway!" Fortunately, Farragut is regarded by history as heroic because his ship didn't get blown out of the water. To his perpetual credit, the bastard lucked out, managing to capture the last seaward Confederate stronghold and all its okra-laden secret recipes for the Union. Two years prior, Farragut had intrepidly sailed past Fort Jackson and Fort St. Philip to capture New Orleans in a surprise attack. For the first admiral in the United States Navy, intrepidity seemed a profitable way to do business. Another intrepid historical example comes from an obscure Civil War general at the battle of Spotsylvania. Rushing out in front to rally his Union soldiers, General John Sedgwick cried, "Come on, men! They couldn't hit an elephant at this dist—" whereupon he was promptly shot in the face by a Confederate sharpshooter. Intrepidity also has its downside.

It was October 2003, and while standing on the deck of an aircraft carrier, my commander in chief challenged the insurgents in Iraq to "bring 'em on." *Strange*, I thought, *he must have missed the footnote about Sedgwick.* But I didn't have time to worry about what President Bush didn't learn as a history

The officers and crew of the original Civil War sailing sloop
Hartford. Admiral Farragut is standing, right of center.

major at Yale; the modern-day *Hartford* had its own problem
with intrepidity.

Having earned my nuclear sea legs, I began to learn how to
drive the warship. Throughout my training, several experienced crew members offered the same brotherly advice: "If
you can't be right, at least be confident." Confidence before
the enlisted men was the minimum standard, perhaps even
more important than actually doing the correct thing. Confidence reinforced the authority of the chain of command, our
sacred order of being. Of course, it was preferable to do the
correct thing, but if one were to screw the pooch, then the
pooch ought to be screwed boldly and with confidence.
Other themes of this ilk surfaced from time to time. The
most telling of the crew's maxims was "Never let knowledge
stand in the way of your qualifications." Together, these atti-
tudes formed the *Hartford*'s unwritten but standard operating
procedure: *Look good on paper, make confident orders, and
(right or wrong) move forward boldly.*

My ship's modus operandi managed to work in the nuclear division, where top-notch training and unsurpassed system design were always on our side. And even if the nuclear division inflated its own performance on paper, what did it matter? The training and personnel were solid, and no bureaucrat ever died from blowing smoke up his own ass. Still, I was unnerved by the crew's tendency to emphasize appearances over reality. Cheating on nuclear exams to inflate Washington's perception of our performance was one thing, but driving the warship on a mission of national security was another matter altogether. A captain at sea cannot afford to be a bureaucrat. And unlike our robust reactor plant, the real world simply wasn't equipped with backup systems to keep the ship safe.

The *Hartford* suffered tremendously when our confidence cycle hit critical mass in the navigation department. Our navigator—third in command—had just been passed over for his last chance at promotion. Despite this news, several months remained before he would transfer off our ship and take command of his shiny new desk. In the meantime, our crew was stuck with the lame-duck officer. The nav was a bold, competent leader, at least as long as he was pretending to drive a Federation starship.

"Light speed wouldn't actually look like that," the nav declared with gravitas as Captain Kirk ordered the *Enterprise* forward on the wardroom's television screen. My officer brethren blinked in silence. Sadly, this naval leader with a master's degree in physics couldn't muster the same level of savoir faire when Klingons and photon torpedoes weren't involved. In the summer before our deployment, our ship failed to meet the minimum standards for navigation when the buffoonish navigator recommended that it turn the wrong way in shallow waters. If the conning officer had followed the advice, the ship would have run aground in a matter of seconds. Our captain's boss, the visiting commodore, was so angered by the mistake that he stormed down from the bridge, pulled out a Magic Marker, and inscribed the letters "L" and "R" on the navigator's hands.

"Left. Right. *See?* If you fuck this up again, I'm firing you on the spot."

Eventually the replacement arrived and the crew began the process of recertifying the ship to voyage out to sea. Our six-month deployment was fast approaching, and we had a lot of work to do before we could boldly go where no man is at liberty to discuss. The new navigator was a nice guy who seemed to know more about the U.S. Navy than about Starfleet, but he still had a lot to learn in a very short time. Despite the fact that he made a few important mistakes of his own, our inspectors gave him the benefit of the doubt since he was new and learning so fast. We checked the administrative box and set sail.

It was a glorious fall morning in the archipelago of Sardegna, Italy, where our submarine lay berthed. We had crossed the Atlantic and into the Mediterranean quickly, uneventfully, and completely submerged. Our first port of call was the tiny island of La Maddalena, where the Peroni flowed like waterfalls, for a stolen week of revelry. A few wayward sailors got arrested for skinny-dipping by the downtown piers, but most simply took sanctuary in a vacation home that the navy rented for us. The plan was to continue our voyage after recovering our nudist miscreants and taking on a load of fresh vegetables. Our final destination was the Persian Gulf by way of the Suez Canal and the Red Sea. We had "missed" the first strike in Operation Iraqi Freedom, and some of the crew lamented that we wouldn't get to launch our missiles. As if to exacerbate our unrealized warrior machismo, the boats that had "shot their load" of Tomahawks were passing us on their way home to the States. Our lofty expectations deflated from becoming war heroes simply to visiting some good foreign ports and maybe getting laid. The crew joked about the unplanned port calls we could make if the right pieces of equipment were to "break" at the right time, but such audacious hopes never actually resulted in sabotage for the pursuit of happiness.

One night our ship received orders to vacate its parking space. A returning sub that had shot its missiles into Iraq needed our berth to reload its arsenal. It was an unusual situation; most ships that deployed overseas returned to the States to replenish their implements of destruction. Nevertheless, our submarine was in the way of another's missiles and we had to move. Parallel-parking a submarine is never a simple maneuver, and the navigable harbor space was severely limited by our deep draft. To simplify the whole tangled mess, the commodore decided to send us all the way out to sea while the other sub docked and loaded her weapons. There was no pilot available in La Maddalena that day, so the commodore took charge himself and boarded the *Hartford* for a jaunty little three-hour tour.

Everything seemed in order. Our energetic captain decided to use the opportunity to conduct "man overboard" drills, which the crew actually considered to be fun. The drills involved a floating cardboard dummy affectionately nicknamed Oscar. In the drill, Oscar was tossed overboard, catching the bridge team unawares. At that point, the mission was to recover the unfortunate floating cardboard box with a painted melancholy face before it became soaked enough to plunge into Davy Jones's locker. (A side note: I never mentioned this particular detail of submarine life to my older brother, who caused me great consternation by naming his first child Oscar. When I approached my mother about how to handle this delicate diplomatic issue, she simply reminded me that "kids are like waffles—it's better to throw the first one out.")

It was time to head out to sea. I climbed up into the bridge with my waterproof charts and a hefty pair of binoculars, snapping awake in the crisp October air. The natural harbor of La Maddalena was strikingly beautiful, complete with sparkling waves and the exact same rock formations that Homer once described in epic form. *This is why I joined the navy!* I thought, standing silent as the breath of the morning rose from the water and my own breath eluded me.

"Up ladder," a voice shouted from below. It was Adam, the officer of the deck, climbing through the hatch into the bridge. I moved aside, sitting on the edge of the cockpit while Adam gained his footing.

"Hey, Chris."

"Hello, sir."

"Wow! Nice day out!" Adam grinned. "Just keep your eyes open and your mouth shut today. You'll get your chance to drive next time," he ordered indifferently.

I nodded. The directness wasn't offensive, it was simply the way we talked to each other. Besides, on a day as beautiful as this, who could complain about being the ship's official sightseer? The captain and the commodore joined us atop the bridge, and the ship was ready to sail.

A large tugboat came alongside and towed our 7,000-ton ship away from the berth. The ship spun in place, pointing the bow toward the harbor's channel. Adam ordered the main engines to life. "Helm, all ahead one-third." We pressed ahead slowly and deliberately, impelled by our massive nuclear propulsion train. The commodore, a senior officer bound for admiral, leaned over my shoulder, whispering in a fatherly voice, "Hand me those charts, will you, son?" I handed him the charts. The captain and the commodore spoke with cordial formality, chatting about the things that salty sea captains chat about, while I enjoyed my sightseeing thoroughly.

After the ship steered away from one island and turned toward another, the intercom crackled to life: there was an equipment problem belowdecks. The ship's ring laser gyro and electromagnetic speed log were indicating different speeds. The glitch was equivalent to having a car with two speedometers that didn't read the same number. The commodore remarked that it was not a big deal, and it wasn't. On the surface, it was easy to see how fast we were going, and the meters were of little use. Adam dismissed the report and increased speed. A moment later, our computerized charts went dead, but that wasn't particularly important either—we had paper charts in our hands. Even so, it was unusual for this many things to be going wrong, even if they were not critical on their own. The atmosphere grew tense. The confidence cycle demanded that the captain know what was happening at all times, particularly when his own boss was watching over his shoulder. Faced with these equipment failures, the captain had two options: focus on navigating the ship or focus on the equipment problems and keep the confidence cycle running.

The captain chose the latter, snapping into the mic, "Is anything working down there?"

While the question sounded like an impatient nuisance from the bridge, everyone who has ever worked in a hierarchy knows that shit rolls downhill. In a matter of seconds, the captain's impatient question caused an avalanche of expletives below as the executive officer tore into the navigator. Embarrassed and inexperienced, the nav lost all ability to function. The navigator's enlisted assistant, an aggressive man with no patience for the officers' facade of confidence, took matters into his own hands by storming out of the control room to fix the equipment himself. The navigator suddenly found himself alone, floundering as he struggled to determine the ship's position on the chart.

When a ship drives through shallow waters, the only way to keep it from scraping the bottom is to follow the chart. There are no painted road lines at sea. Most ports have dozens of buoys marking boundaries of deep water, but even buoys are no substitute for the most important part of navigation—knowing where you're going. Minutes later, the captain slowly realized that the navigation team was overdue for a position report and raised his voice in alarm.

"Nav, we need that position report!"

The intercom remained eerily silent.

A hint of nervousness crept into the captain's voice—never a good sign in a force built on intrepidity. Our ship, surrounded by tiny islands, had to thread the needle through the invisible natural channel below the waves. It was a maze of submerged rocks. I started to sweat as the tension grew. Until that moment, it never seemed possible that a captain might not know where his ship was going. The fatherly commodore scrutinized the charts but said nothing.

"I think we've missed our turn," the captain declared with growing alarm. Still the intercom remained silent. Unable to bear the wait, the captain seized control,

"Turn the ship—TURN NOW!!!"

The rudder swung to port, steering the ship away from the closest island. A long stretch of open water lay before us. The whole team breathed a sigh of relief, calmed by the confidence of the captain's order. The ship steadied on the final leg of its seaward trek. On either side of us now were two small islands, and the vast Mediterranean lay ahead. Having regained his wits, the navigator made his overdue report, but it was not what we expected.

"Sir, our last fix plotted off the chart . . . we're investigating the cause!"

Oh, shit . . . we're off course! The captain and the commodore whispered hurriedly to each other.

Seconds later, the intercom crackled once more with a terse declaration: "Yellow sounding!"

The water was getting dangerously shallow! My heart raced. I looked up at the officer of the deck, who was listening to the captain and the commodore—he hadn't heard the report!

"Sir, did you just hear that?"

He looked at me, puzzled. "Hear what?"

The speaker crackled to life again. "Red sounding!!!"

Too late!

At that precise moment, our crew attempted to drive a warship with a thirty-foot draft over a well-charted rock that was five meters below the surface. Needless to say, the laws of physics proved equally effective in English and metric units. The bow of the ship heaved upward as cold American steel crashed into old Italian stone. We rolled hard to port and I nearly fell over the side as the bow dipped back again with a mighty splash. The topside decks plunged below the surface, swallowed up by the churning water.

"What the fuck? Shit! Fuck!! Oh, FUCK!" was all the poor captain could manage. Eighteen years of training crumbled into a handful of curses.

Then, like a reincarnation of Farragut at Mobile Bay, the commodore took control, demanding, "SPEED ON!"

I was dumbstruck by the chaos and the inscrutable order as I clutched the railing for dear life. But amazingly, there was method to the commodore's madness. Having read the charts numerous times, he suddenly recalled exactly where the ship was—it was a tiny outcropping, only a few meters wide, and surrounded on all sides by deep water. The ship was grinding to a halt and teetering upon the small peak. The last thing the commodore wanted was for the sub beneath his feet to become a beached nuclear whale, so he ordered the final surge.

"Helm, all ahead flank," the officer of the deck shouted into his microphone. It was the modern equivalent of "four bells"—the fastest speed we could muster. Fourteen million pounds of steel leapt forward with such force that the spirit of Rickover himself seemed to impel our vessel. The reactor peaked above the redline as the hull scraped away from the rocks . . . *the surge was working!!!* But it wasn't over yet. The entire ship jolted backward as the tapering hull slid off and the rudder bit the rocks. We rolled once again—even harder to port—and I struggled not to fall overboard into the thrashing water. Our atomic engines and cold American steel prevailed, and with a final burst, the rudder broke through the stone.

As the *Hartford* came up in speed, the ship began to ride lower and lower in the water. A casual observer might have thought we were sinking, but I knew better. A distant memory from my Academy days sparked inside my brain. The ship was *squatting*, a little-known hydrodynamic phenomenon that pulls a hull down as a ship speeds through shallow water. This brief flash of logic from my naval architecture class grabbed hold of me, snapping me out of my stupor. I grabbed the officer of the deck by the sleeve, imploring him, "Sir, slow down!" Adam looked at me in a daze before snapping out of it himself and ordering the ship to a halt. The captain took the microphone.

"The ship has run aground! All hands report damage to Control."

I looked back over our wake, fading into blue waters of dazzling Homeric beauty. A sense of awe gripped me as the foam vanished, swallowed by the gentle waves.

The captain turned to me and gave an uncanny order. "Don't talk to anyone. Go below and write down the honest-to-God truth about everything you just saw."

A shiver crept down my spine. The captain turned to Adam. "That goes for you, too—as soon as we're back in port."

The captain's head would soon be on the chopping block, yet his only concern was finding out what had gone wrong. It impressed me immensely that our leader was so forthcoming—his immediate response to failure was the hallmark of integrity. At the same time back home, Enron and Arthur Andersen executives were shredding documents, covering their tracks to avoid responsibility for deliberate wrongdoings at the helm of corporate America.

Our ship remained in La Maddalena for weeks, but the waterfalls of Peroni had run dry. The officers and navigation team were confined to the submarine and formally investigated for various levels of misconduct in the incident. The captain and commodore were swiftly court-martialed for the offenses of hazarding a vessel and dereliction of duty, ending their otherwise distinguished careers. The executive officer, the officer of the deck, the navigator, and his enlisted assistant were either forced into early retirement or relegated to desk jobs before their contracts expired, without offers for renewal. Hugh and I were the only two officers who were investigated for misconduct and actually exonerated. A junior enlisted man who stared in awe at the Fathometer as the bottom approached our hull was also exonerated—he had felt too intimidated by the officers' confidence to question their decisions. My investigating officer was a senior navy captain in his late fifties who sported a neatly trimmed mustache, stark gray hair, and a Naval Academy class ring. Our interview wasn't long, but conversations have a way of feeling longer when they begin with someone reading you your legal rights.

After that formality, the investigator asked in a relaxing tone, "Eyes open, mouth shut—that's what they told you, *right?*"

"Yes, sir."

"And you're not qualified to drive yet, are you, Lieutenant?"

"That's correct, sir."

The gray-haired officer penned a few notes and smiled. "Navy's got a good team this year, don't you think?"

"I don't know, sir . . . I haven't been watching football."

"Well, it's a good one. Thanks for your time, Lieutenant."

A few days after the grounding, our captain called me into his stateroom. "Chris, I have to ask you a favor," he whispered in a soft, pleading voice. I could barely look him in the eye. We both knew that his replacement was inbound from the States.

"What can I do for you, sir?" I asked, swallowing and trying to keep my composure.

"I need some boxes, Chris. Could you find some for me?"

There were no boxes left aboard. When a submarine goes to sea, the boxes full of food and supplies are emptied out into every available storage space. The passageways become literal tin-can alleys and the cumbersome cardboard is thrown out. Without him saying another word, I knew why the captain needed boxes: he was mailing his uniforms home.

The officer who relieved our captain was temporary. He arrived only a few days after the grounding, but it was important to the navy to get rid of the broken skipper as soon as possible. The "Band-Aid captain" issued only one order publicly—he banned the crew from visiting the nearby island of Palau, to which our fallen skipper was promptly exiled. It was a travesty of punishment more surreal than reality shows to see our captain voted off the island. The banishment seemed even more strange in light of the geography; Napoleon himself had been exiled to a nearby island after his first failure of command. To make matters worse, our captain was as short as Napoleon—he was the only skipper I'd ever met who had to lower the periscope to see into the eyepiece.

Other humiliations followed. Italian newspapers printed photos of three-eyed fish and warned of a nuclear disaster in their waters. Radioactive fallout symbols covered the local press, and anti-American sentiments soared under the ignorant fear of the nuclear unknown. Of course, there was never any sort of nuclear problem with the incident. Aside from banging up our rudder, we had barely scratched the submarine's paint. But the broader context was no help to us either—the United States had been in Iraq for over seven months, and the international press seized upon the *Hartford*'s accident to exacerbate the public's fear and mistrust of the U.S. military.

Traditionally, nautical charts have followed a more formal method for humiliating grounded ships. For centuries, intrepid explorers who discovered shoal waters by scraping their vessels' bottoms irrevocably graced the rocks with their ship's own name. When the HMS *Valiant* ran aground in Long Island Sound, those shallow waters were christened Valiant Shoals. It was the nautical equivalent of "You break it, you buy it." Whether Italians followed that same convention doesn't really matter. To me, those rocks off the coast of La Maddalena, where seven men's careers and part of my soul remain, will forever bear the name of my fair ship.

4

Crush Depth

HY-80 is an alloy of naval steel that draws its name from its high-yield strength. An unusually specialized alloy, HY-80 can withstand 80,000 pounds of pressure per square inch before crushing inward. In the U.S. fleet, submarines are constructed with pressure hulls of HY-80 two inches thick. Even so, the modern submarine has a well-defined limit of how deep it can dive into the ocean. As a submarine descends, every inch of depth adds a bit more pressure to the massive steel hull, every foot takes her closer to the limit. Amazingly, the tremendous hull buckles infinitesimally inward as the ship sinks farther. The thick steel deckplates pop beneath one's feet as the diving officer of the watch eases the ship downward, farther and farther below the surface. "Conn, Sonar—detected hull-popping due to changing depth," the sonar supervisor reports over the intercom. There is no need for an announcement—the whole ship can hear it. When a submarine descends through the darkness, deeper and deeper, its hull groaning like a sickly elephant, cracking like muffled gunshots, it reaches a point where it can bear no more stress without collapsing. Any deeper and the hull would implode so violently, so quickly that the pressure wave from the implosion would kill every crew member aboard before he ever got wet. This is the abyss where the pinnacles of man and machine float upon the precipice of death; this is crush depth.

When the crew of the *Hartford* regained its footing from

the physical impact of ship upon rock, we began to sink into the depths of our own despair. Unlike the well-defined limits of HY-80 steel, our flesh and blood had no clear limits. The crew continued mothering the steel beast in the doldrums of stunned silence. For days, we walked through the passageways of the submarine like beaten dogs. Hugh couldn't take the tension any longer and suggested that we go out for dinner in La Maddalena, just to get off the ship for a while. The doomed officer who had driven the ship aground overheard us and poked his head out of the stateroom, catching us off guard.

"You guys going out tonight?"

"Yes, sir," Hugh confirmed. We tried not to look him in the eye. It was embarrassing to talk about going out while Adam sat pondering his fate.

"Oh," Adam responded, looking a bit dejected.

Hugh quickly offered, "Wanna join us, sir?"

"Sure, as long as I'm not *driving*."

Gasp. Hugh tensed, unsure of how to interpret the comment.

Adam grinned, breaking the tension. "Lighten up, guys— it's not the end of the world!"

The man's career may have been dead, but his sense of humor was still alive and kicking.

For the officers in the *Hartford*'s wardroom, it was definitely not the end of the world. Officers in the sub force are very well paid and well educated; they typically have little trouble finding jobs in the civilian world, even after crashing a nuclear warship into well-charted rocks. Our homophobic XO was the only man in the history of the world to run submarines aground in two of the five nuclear navies, yet he still ended up with a great civilian job after leaving the force a few months later. Unfortunately, financial prospects were much less certain for the enlisted men. While the enlisted men on subs are well trained and highly intelligent, few have the college degrees required to obtain jobs commensurate with their capabilities. Many sailors had fallen into credit card debt, and going out to sea allowed these men to spend less and save more of their income. Crossing into combat zones like the Persian Gulf exempted the crew from paying income taxes, but the grounding dashed our expectations of catching that financial windfall. Instead of sailing onward to the tax-free war zone, we would be limping back to America and paying our taxes in full.

Much of the crew was collapsing under the pressure. The nukes blamed the navigation department for crashing the ship. The men on the navigation team who hadn't been fired resented their harsh treatment. The crew became divided by different levels of training and education and sought release by laying blame upon one another. Several fights erupted, and friendships ended as accusations rattled around the narrow metal passageways. As the bitterness swelled, the bulkheads of the submarine seemed to close in upon us and the crew felt trapped.

There are ways to escape from sunken submarines. The Royal Navy trains its entire force to escape using a specialized exposure suit. The Brits trained me to use this orange cosmonautical life-jumper by "escaping" from an underwater tank, a hundred feet below the surface. When seawater is flooded into an escape compartment, the atmosphere compresses, becoming hot and moist. Eventually, the hatch flies open, the ocean fills the breach and the inflated sailor rockets upward like a balloon. It's an exhilarating ride, except for one minor caveat: if one holds his breath, his lungs will explode. If we were sunk in waters deeper than four or five hundred feet, an escape would still be possible, but much more difficult. In order to prevent the escapee from getting nitrogen narcosis or the bends, the escape trunk would have to be pressurized extremely rapidly. Inevitably, such rapid pressure changes would rupture the escapee's eardrums. To prevent the sudden pain and confusion during the actual escape, the sailor's eardrums are lanced with a needle before he enters the trunk.

While this seems like a horrific thing to do, the alternative of asphyxiating in a sunken hollow tube makes the choice somewhat easier. Sadly, after all this effort, real-life escapees would most likely spend a few days bobbing around on the surface, cold, disoriented, and in extreme pain before the sharks eventually eat them.

One of our sailors found an escape route slightly easier than getting eaten by sharks; he came out of the closet (metaphorically speaking—there are no closets on submarines). The homophobic XO was quick to administer the out-processing paperwork under strict privacy (i.e., inviting the entire wardroom to "witness" the pictorial "evidence" of the sailor's boyfriend). A week later, the young gay sailor was tossed out on the street (again, metaphorically speaking). I remembered seeing the sailor in the engine room, smoking a cigarette and looking distraught. At the time, I didn't ask if he was being thrown out and he wasn't about to tell me.

"What's up? Is everything okay?"

"No, sir. I've got some serious problems."

"Wanna talk about them?"

"Thank you, sir, but no. There's nothing you can do."

When the wardroom found out that the man was getting thrown out for being gay, a few of the officers were agitated. He was smart, a good worker, and everyone seemed to like him. Most, however, took the XO's position.

"Good riddance," they remarked.

"I don't want that faggot looking at me in the shower," one of my colleagues spat, disgusted.

"Don't be ridiculous," I chimed in. "You saw the pictures . . . that faggot's boyfriend is much better-looking than you. He wouldn't waste his time on your hairy ass."

Abrupt silence. A few blinks. If we hadn't been on a submarine, I'm certain we would have heard the distant sound of crickets.

"Just kidding, man," I said with a smirk.

"Fuck you, Chris."

"Sorry, I'm straight." I grinned, making an exaggerated wink. My colleague huffed away, nursing his ego only slightly more than his distended sense of homophobia.

After the grounding, the prospect of escaping from the *Hartford* seemed all the more appealing to the entrapped sailors. Despite our ship's complement of high-tech escape suits, the sailors invented escape devices of their own. Theirs were much smaller—a few square inches and paper thin. Theirs came in little cardboard sleeves with neatly written labels sporting the words "Submarine Escape Device." They were razor blades, intended not for beards or mustaches or cleanly shaven scalps but for sailors' wrists.

More than any other group aboard the submarine, the nukes were feeling trapped. Because of their valuable training, nukes were forbidden to transfer from the submarine force. The nukes started their enlistments at two ranks higher and with significant monetary bonuses over non-nuclear personnel. To top it off, they frequently became eligible for reenlisting as soon as they arrived aboard their ships, which encouraged many of them to re-up immediately for six-year contracts before they knew what life at sea was like. The problem with this was that as soon as they realized what life at sea was like, they wanted out. When the *Hartford* grounded, they wanted out like upwardly mobile nuclear rats fleeing a sinking ship. The money and marginal rank advantages were simply not worth the pain. The razor-blade escape devices quickly became their ostensible backup plan, though none of the nukes aboard were actually dumb enough to use them. Unfortunately, several of them were smart enough to pretend.

"What the hell are you doing, Fong?"

"I'm cutting my wrists, sir. Aren't you going to stop me?" Fong replied meekly, trying not to smirk as he made a small incision into his flesh with the razor blade. Fong's hand moved incredibly slowly as I looked on from my elevated metal desk in Maneuvering, shaking my head.

"Look, sir, I'm bleeding. Aren't you going to stop me?"

A single drop of blood had formed on Fong's wrist from the imperceptibly small cut that would in no way threaten his life.

"For fuck's sake," was all I could muster. I put down the reactor plant manual and picked up my microphone.

"Engineering watch supervisor, report to Maneuvering." The EWS was the senior enlisted man on my watch section. Fong fell silent and the razor blade vanished. Twenty seconds later, the EWS knocked on the door. I granted him permission to enter the inviolate metal gauge box.

"What's up, sir?"

"We've got another escapee," I explained, pointing to Fong, who avoided our glares, suddenly sheepish before the seasoned enlisted supervisor.

"Make them disappear," I ordered. "If I find another one of these damn escape devices, I swear to God I'll have the entire nuclear division scouring the ship until every fucking razor blade is in my hands."

"Yes, sir," the EWS replied, extending his hand toward Fong, who immediately turned over the razor blade without making eye contact.

Dale, the engineer, pretended that nothing was wrong. "Those are cute," he quipped when I showed him the blades with their ominously inscribed cardboard sleeves. Dale's indifference was not surprising: he ignored the cheating scandal; why would he care about suicidal gestures among his own men? In the months that followed, several of the crew would make real suicidal gestures and ideations. Fear of an unknown future and our collective sense of failure drove many of them to their own personal crush depths. A few non-nuclear sailors who made suicidal ideations were quickly jettisoned, setting a clear double standard between the men of different backgrounds. The cracks that formed when our steel struck rock had widened into a chasm as differing identities became a force for division. The fact that we still sailed aboard the same ship had long been forgotten . . . at least until our new captain arrived.

Captain William Stacia was a formidable naval officer. Having successfully commanded a fast-attack submarine, Bill brought a wealth of experience to our wardroom table. His colleagues at headquarters called him "the Colonel" on account of his marine-like discipline, and I was scared to death of the man. When I met Bill before our deployment, he audited my program for monitoring the ship's radiological controls. The program I inherited was nothing but paperwork without substance. I made a concerted effort to make it more substantive and useful, providing actual feedback and training value to the crew in my division. I encountered great resistance from the men, who simply wanted to check the boxes and move on, but Captain Stacia saw what I was trying to do and supported it. "You've got a lot of work to do," he began as he read a long list of deficiencies in my program. Bill had the eyes of a hawk and caught every little flaw in my efforts, but he ended with encouraging words: "Keep working at it—you're going in the right direction." When he left headquarters in New London to become our skipper, I thought to myself, *Good God! He's going to tear us apart!*

To my surprise and delight, I soon witnessed the most amazing example of leadership in action that I have ever seen up close. Instead of taking control with an authoritarian grip, noting every little deficiency in our crew, and directing corrective action, Bill simply talked to us. Amazingly, he seemed concerned only with what the crew had to say.

Hugh was puzzled. "This new captain sure asks a lot of questions."

"Yeah," I replied. "I think that he's up to something."

The new captain *was* up to something. Bill assembled the crew on the pier to address the entire ship, face-to-face— something that rarely happens on a submarine because of the lack of space. In the tone of a disappointed father, Bill explained that he was not there to "fix" the *Hartford* but to support us as we lifted ourselves up. The crew breathed a collective sigh of relief, and the new captain immediately gained our respect. Shortly after his speech, he invited the entire crew, one person at a time, to no-holds-barred discussions. Everything was on the table: financial problems, domestic issues, career concerns, health and fitness, quality of life on the ship, even whether or not sailors got along with their bosses and why. Some sailors discussed their monetary problems, some talked about promotions and reenlisting, and some talked about how to get "college qualified." A large number of sailors vented their anger toward a particular enlisted supervisor who had apparently been quite a tyrant behind closed doors. Whatever the topic, the effect of having candid discussions with every crew member was cathartic. A transformation had begun.

When a submarine goes down too deep, it has one final procedure for making it back to the surface—the emergency blow. An emergency blow uses high-pressure air to blast water out of the ship's ballast tanks, expelling the excess weight and causing the sub to shoot to the surface. Captain Stacia's leadership had that effect on our morale and our competence. Once every problem was out in the open and every concern was voiced in a serious forum, a tremendous weight was expelled from our hearts and minds. When our basic human needs started to be addressed by the command, our fear of the unknown vanished and our differences in training and rank and education became less important. Instead of being a force for division, our different backgrounds were seen as strengths that allowed us to accomplish something that was unthinkable a century ago—taking a nuclear submarine out to sea. In a short time, the crew of the *Hartford* actually felt good about the fact that we sailed together aboard the same ship. Instead of being divided by superficial identities, we were united by the overarching commonality of being submariners as we trained hard, learned from our mistakes, and ventured out to sea once more.

Perhaps the most solemn duty of a naval vessel is to honor the dead in the ceremony of burial at sea. On the morning of the *Hartford*'s first such burial in years, I happened to be driving. The captain ordered me to prepare the ship and alert the crew. It was a bit of a surprise, in part because we didn't know that there was a dead guy aboard, but mostly because we had never seen such a thing before—burials were much more common aboard destroyers or frigates. I surfaced the ship and directed the off-going watch-standers to man the bridge for the ceremony. In addition to the normal complement of driver and lookout, the captain and gunner headed to the bridge to pay their respects and give the traditional gun salute.

The XO entered the control room with a small cardboard container, the size of a shoebox for toddler-sized feet.

"What's in the box, XO?"

"Petty Officer Smith," the commander replied, reading the label and biting his lip to conceal a grin. "What were you expecting, a fucking *urn*?"

"I guess I didn't expect anything, sir . . . Never done this before."

The XO handed me the box, which seemed much lighter than I expected; it felt almost empty. I read the label—"Musician's Mate Second Class R. W. Smith."

"Musician's mate? This guy's a fucking landlubber," I laughed.

"Yeah," the XO said, chuckling. "Probably never been to sea in his life."

The quartermaster, who had been listening in on our conversation, butted in. "Hey, sir—can I see the box?" I passed the dead musician's mate over. The quartermaster hefted it, also surprised by the easily bearable lightness of not being. The quartermaster shook the box next to his ear like a child with a mysterious Christmas present.

"Quit fucking around," the XO yelled, seizing the package from the sailor's hands. "For fuck's sake! Have some respect!"

The ship's personnel were in place, and Petty Officer Smith ascended the ladder to the bridge. The XO took the microphone for the ship's intercom and began reading the ceremonial script.

"All hands, bury the dead."

The box was opened and the ashes of Petty Officer Smith were forever consigned to the deep. Unfortunately for the bridge crew, "forever" took a little while to begin. It takes about ten seconds for a single machine gunner to perform a three-volley gun salute. Following that, it takes about one minute and three seconds to play taps over the ship's intercom. To the bridge crew, this total time of seventy-three seconds seemed like an eternity. While modern satellite imagery and state-of-the-art Doppler radar can predict weather patterns across the planet, nothing in our power could have warned us that at the precise moment of dumping the box, the wind would absolutely stop.

"Down dropped the breeze, the sails dropped down / 'Twas sad as sad could be," is how Samuel Taylor Coleridge described the beginnings of an unnatural encounter with dead people. Lamentably, our experience was slightly less poetic than the *Rime of the Ancient Mariner*. George, a germphobic colleague, bore the brunt of the assault. Submarine life always made George squirm. The poor man barely kept his sanity when some of the sailors were found to have head lice and when the cooks started using Purell instead of washing their hands after scrubbing the toilets. This current indiscretion, however, would prove to be a whole new level of uncleanliness. As the last of the ashes fell from the box, a cloud of dead-guy dust formed below the sail. The captain and crew began their salute as the gunner fired the first round.

The cloud lingered and swelled. An updraft came out of nowhere. The music began, and Petty Officer Smith's remains surrounded the men of the *Hartford*'s bridge like a pestilent cloud. Jeff twitched nervously as flecks of man-ash settled upon his lips. He tried his best to spit silently while holding his salute rigid. It was useless—wetting his lips only made the ashes stick better—and he could taste them now. The captain firmly closed his eyes and mouth, holding his salute and counting down the seconds.

Belowdecks, the audience gawked in amazement through the periscope, growing hysterical over the horrors transpiring above. We took bets on how fast George would get relieved, race down the ladder, and jump into the shower. Two sailors even bet on whether poor George would bother to undress before turning on the water. Hundreds of dollars changed hands. Typically, the formal process of watch relief takes more than fifteen minutes to complete. But our colleague, speckled with ashes like musical notes across his gaunt white face, managed to go from bridge to shower *con presto agitato*, setting a new ship's record at two minutes thirteen. And so it came to pass that Musician's Mate R. W. Smith, having composed the most macabre of finales, ended his illustrious nautical life on the lowest of notes.

On the far side of the world, another life was about to end. On the outskirts of Baghdad, Captain Richard Gannon and his marines of the Third Battalion were on the move. Their convoy of Humvees patrolled the area, looking for mujahideen insurgents who had scattered from Fallujah after American forces arrived.

I knew Gannon from the Naval Academy, where he lectured on leadership and ethics; he taught both subjects splendidly. At Cornell, he had double-majored in political science and history. With command of the English language and a reputation for being as "tough as a $2 steak," Gannon epitomized the intelligent, honest, and fair military leader. My classmates and I admired him greatly.

As Gannon's men continued westward, they combed the desert near the Syrian border, but the insurgents found them first. The details are sketchy. An ambush happened. A gun battle ensued. Sometime during the fight, a mortar-round landed on Gannon and his men, or at least close enough to do the job.

Somewhere on the Naval Academy grounds, a monument was about to change. With Richard's death, a new name would be added to a wall of honor. When I walked into the ship's wardroom for dinner, Grant, a fellow Naval Academy grad, told me the news.

"Did you hear about Captain Gannon?"

"No. How's he doing?"

I forgot about dinner and the grounding of our hollow steel ship, went to my six-foot-by-two-foot-by-eighteen-inch rack, pulled the curtain shut, and tried not to think about or feel anything.

5

Gunboat Diplomats

A year of training, repairs, and paperwork passed between the grounding and the *Hartford*'s next deployment. Our new permanent skipper, Captain Frank Kattani, proved to be a very competent leader. In the spring, the ship set sail from Long Island Sound to the Caribbean before transiting through the Panama Canal and arriving at its first port of call—Panama City. The *Hartford* was the first submarine to visit Panama since the canal had changed hands, in 2001. After docking the ship, the crew rolled out the red carpet for President Torrijos-Espino, the son of the canal treaty's signatory. Twenty-eight years had passed since Jimmy Carter and Omar Torrijos signed the Panama Canal Treaty, returning the ownership of that tiny, strategic waterway to the Panamanian people.

The diplomat in me celebrates the treaty as a reason for pride in my country's history. While the canal had been designed and funded with American engineering and capital, equally important was the backbreaking labor of the innumerable Panamanians who toiled and died from malaria and yellow fever while building the path between the seas. It was fair for the United States to profit from using the canal *for a time*, but not forever. Though Roosevelt's imperialism paved the way for the canal to the benefit of all, Carter's relinquishing of control was an even grander service to the world. In that single stroke of his pen, President Carter showed how America could profit fairly from developing the Third World, without behaving like a perpetual empire. Thus one of the most amazing constructs of American imperialism was made benevolent by one of the most magnanimous feats of American diplomacy. And so it came to pass that the *Hartford*'s crew followed in the footsteps of Teddy Roosevelt and Jimmy Carter as a modern-day blend of benevolent peacekeepers and gunboat diplomats. Much to my chagrin, I was detained in Connecticut, forced to complete an advanced nuclear certification while the crew hobnobbed with President Torrijos and smoked Cuban cigars in Panama City without me.

"Captain, I don't want to go back to nuke school."

"My hands are tied, Chris; I was supposed to send you three months ago," Frank explained. "The nukes at headquarters are riding my ass."

"But I'm not staying in the navy, sir—I won't even use the skills."

"Sorry, Chris. It's not my call."

Theoretically, my argument was sound. There was no good reason for the navy to send me to a twelve-week school for advanced reactor plant supervision, but Rickover's jealous nuclear clutches were far too powerful for me to escape. For the *Hartford*, there was also the perennial problem of administrative readiness. By that time in my tour of duty, despite being a mediocre nuclear supervisor, I was actually one of the better tacticians aboard. A new department head arrived, just in time for our grueling predeployment certifications. The new officer had trained on ballistic missile subs, not fast-attack boats like the *Hartford*, which meant that he had a lot to learn about driving our comparatively tiny 7,000-ton ship. The captain needed me on the department head's team until we passed the administrative inspections. Ironically, the minute we passed the inspections, I jumped ship to hit the nuclear books and the crew set sail without me, all their boxes administratively checked.

Nuclear grad school was excruciatingly dull. For the first time in my life, the spirits of Rickover and John Paul Jones

After the grounding, I was the first officer aboard the *Hartford* to earn his warfare qualifications, symbolized by the golden submariner's "fish" that captain Kattani pinned on my uniform.

bickered, hovering above my head like caricatures of angels and devils arguing over what I ought to do. Eventually, Rickover won the argument on a technicality (he was always good at that). Jones sat in the corner, tapping his foot impatiently while I struggled to memorize the effects of xenon's macroscopic cross section for absorption of a thermal neutron flux. My final nuclear exams were a snap, since my academic advisor had administered an identical "practice test" to me a week before the formal six-hour written battery. I was disgusted by the pervasive dishonesty in the nuclear system but had long since given up on trying to fix it. In any case, I felt like I had attained the required level of knowledge, whether or not the official exam had any basis in reality. After the *Hartford*'s

grounding, I flatly rejected the maxim of "not letting knowledge stand in the way of qualifications" and silently held
myself to a higher personal standard.

At my final interviews with the National Nuclear Security
Administration, I bumped into Hugh once more. After his
tour aboard the *Hartford*, he had been selected for a prestigious position at nuclear headquarters in Washington on
account of his excellent performance record. Soon afterward,
he left the navy to attend Harvard Business School.

When he saw me, he offered his compliments. "Nice job
on your exam, Chris!"

"Thanks, Hugh . . . but do you realize I saw this exact
same test before it was supposed to be given to me?"

"Lucky you."

"Sure, Hugh . . . call it whatever you want."

There are times in life when your ship doesn't come in, but
rarely in life does your ship send you an e-mail explaining that
it will not be coming in and that you are nonetheless expected
to report for duty. By the time I left D.C. with my advanced
nuclear certification, the *Hartford*'s diplomatic visit to Panama was over and the ship had already set sail. To avoid the
hassle of contacting the Panamanian embassy for diplomatic
clearance, the captain refused to reenter Panamanian territorial waters to pick me up. I cursed the bureaucracy for choosing this particular time to cut out the paperwork, but John
Paul Jones was undaunted. *If your ship doesn't come in, rent a
banana boat!*

And so it came to pass that I boarded a decrepit forty-foot
motorboat, laden with fruits and vegetables, and set out upon
my first voyage into the Pacific. It was a gorgeous day, but the
puny vessel was not designed to travel so far from home. The
waves bounced us around for the fifteen-mile seaward trek. As
the coast faded on the eastern horizon, the sub appeared in
the west like the shadow of a cowboy riding into the sunset.

What happened next was part insanity, part standard operating procedure. The Panamanian banana boat pulled alongside, ever so slowly, nearly hitting the sub's underwater stern planes (which would have torn through its hull like paper). Both vessels inched forward, occasionally bumping together below the waterline with dull thuds and splashes. If anyone had fallen between the fruit boat and the 7,000-ton steel hull, they would have been crushed like a wet tomato in a life preserver. *Mind the gap*, I gulped, wide-eyed as the decks swayed in completely different rhythms. To be perfectly honest, I was horrified; at this very moment my prowess in the standing broad jump would either become a good story for posterity or a validation of natural selection. I took a deep breath, prayed to Darwin, and leapt. *Thud!* Ramon, a strong and competent sailor in my division, grabbed on to my life jacket, stopping me from sliding off the slick round hull.

"Welcome back, sir," Ramon said, grinning and slapping me on the shoulder.

"Thanks for the catch! It's good to be home!"

Ramon, an Ecuadorian American, turned to the banana boat captain, shouted a farewell in Spanish, and waved him off. The crew climbed down the hatch, and we didn't see the sun again with our naked eyes for fifty-four days.

Fifty-four days is a long time to be underwater—the longest stretch I'd ever done. As we sailed the depths of the Pacific, I marveled at how the crew kept balance in our small, enclosed atmosphere. With every breath, the level of carbon dioxide crept incrementally upward. With every smoke break that the sailors took, a tiny bit more oxygen got burned up as carcinogens filled the recycled air. When I led my team in driving the ship, it was my responsibility to keep the air breathable by monitoring every constituent of the atmosphere on an hourly basis. If there was too much CO_2, we turned on the "scrubbers." If oxygen was too low, we split water molecules with a massive electrolysis machine, pumping the excess hydrogen overboard. Amazingly, the ship was like its own little biosphere, but without a single plant aboard. We purified our own fresh water directly from the ocean. We turned off the water while showering, to be less wasteful. The shower heads even had special valves to shut off the flow without changing the temperature. We learned to live close together in relative harmony, walking about quietly, carefully shutting doors so as not to make a sound. The only thing that kept our environment sustainable was the seemingly endless stream of power from the ship's nuclear reactor. With sustainable energy, man and machine survived together in the precarious but manageable balance of our closely watched environment.

Sometimes, the precarious balance was not so closely watched. In one such instance, my shift seemed to drag on forever—there was little work to do and the crew was feeling lethargic. A few men complained of headaches. Toward the end of my watch, one of the ship's smokers came into the control room to inform me that he was having a hard time lighting his cigarette.

"Good for you," I quipped, half awake. "Maybe you'll live a few days longer."

The sailor looked at me with a big grin on his face—the kind of grin that screams *I know something you don't know.*

"With all due respect, sir, you'll kill the entire crew long before I have to worry about cancer. Check your atmospherics."

I started awake, then checked the instrument readings. To my embarrassment, the oxygen level was way too low and CO_2 was way too high—enough to have physiological effects on the men. It was my responsibility to keep the air breathable, and the conditions had become completely unacceptable right under my nose. I vowed never again to be so irresponsible, started up the full array of atmospheric control equipment, and restored the air to normal. Within a few hours, everyone was bright, perky, and happily chain-smoking packs of Marlboros in the engine room.

As far as secret missions went, this one was not particularly stressful. In stark contrast to my first years aboard the boat, our crew had become overmanned. Instead of the hundred hours per week that we had worked at the beginning of my tour of duty, we were barely pulling sixty. The new captain, Frank, was likable and talented, and the crew was well trained. Best of all, without any administrative inspectors aboard we focused on doing our job. Life seemed almost simple—perhaps *too* simple . . .

As I learned more and more about what was expected of our ship and our crew who had trained so hard, I couldn't help but wonder what value we added to the United States. What kinds of intelligence could a submarine gather that other methods couldn't get for pennies on the dollar? What kind of homeland security could the submarine bring that the Coast Guard couldn't provide with five times as many ships for the same cost? What terrorist threats could a submarine alone foresee through the towering vantage of a periscope? And what country threatened the United States enough that the possibility of total war at sea still loomed before us? I was perplexed by the range of questions that I was completely unable to answer, even after becoming extremely well informed by the vast array of top secret documents at my disposal. After the *Hartford*'s mission and after reading the highly classified mission reports of dozens of other submarines, I couldn't help but think that the nuclear submarine had become a white elephant in the swimming pool—a quixotic relic from a bygone era.

As we floated around the eastern Pacific, the rest of our deployment was surprisingly dull. We didn't see the famed Galápagos Islands, we didn't catch any terrorists, and we didn't bump into any Russian or Chinese or axis of evil submarines (does the axis of evil even have any?). On one particularly droll afternoon, I walked into the control room to relieve the watch.

"Anything interesting happen?"

"Well, we got some interesting pictures," Jake chuckled, pointing to the computer screen where our periscope's digital images were displayed.

"It looks like a fisherman taking a shit over the side."

"Yeah. Pretty funny, isn't it?"

Jake and I looked at the pictures in contemplative silence for a moment. My colleague crossed his arms and grinned, admiring his latest and greatest work.

"How far away is he . . . two thousand yards?"

"Twenty-four hundred."

"Nice focus."

Our ship soon pulled into Lima for a port call, where the Peruvian cabinet made a brief visit. Our crew enjoyed the best ceviche in the world while the cabinet officials enjoyed frozen cookies and bad coffee in our wardroom. Sadly, it was the last diplomatic courtesy of their careers. A week after we left port, the Peruvian prime minister resigned in protest over their president's decision to appoint his friend as the foreign secretary. The Peruvian Constitution required that the entire cabinet be replaced after the head of government's resignation, so the newly appointed minister held his nepotistic post for exactly eight minutes. Years later, I had the opportunity to ask President Alejandro Toledo to explain his version of what happened, to which he hilariously replied, "I had four prime ministers. I can't even remember which one you're talking about."

Our voyage turned homeward bound, and I had the honor of conning the ship through the Panama Canal. Just as in La Maddalena, I had a spectacular view from the bridge over one of the most amazing stretches of water on the planet. Unlike La Maddalena, though, our crew actually knew what we were doing this time. We took a professional pilot aboard and hoisted the Panamanian flag alongside Old Glory. While I held the microphone and gave the orders, the captain hovered over my shoulder, watching my every move.

"Come left."

"Come right."

"A little more to the right."

"Too much!"

"Okay, more!"

I immediately parroted the captain's orders through the microphone and occasionally gave an order fast enough to beat him to it, prompting some wry looks before he ordered something else. I could tell the captain was on edge and did my best to calm him as the ship inched forward. Regardless, the skipper continued to direct a hundred infinitesimal changes. I simply smiled, enjoying the scenery and the whole bizarre experience. For every twenty orders the captain gave, the salty, gray-haired pilot said something vague and nautical-sounding, like "Take'r in easy." I had no idea what the hell that meant, but it was clear that the pilot was more relaxed about it than Frank was. We sailed through Gatun Lake and toward the locks. At the entrance, a tiny rowboat with two Panamanian peasants towed a large steel cable out into the waterway. The cable looked impossibly heavy for such a tiny rowboat to be carrying.

Frank let out a cry of disbelief. "You gotta be shitting me!"

For all the power and sophistication of our submarine, our fate was now in the hands of two peasants in a pathetic wooden rowboat. We attached the cable to our sub and cut the engines while I marveled at mankind's unwillingness to relinquish control. It didn't matter whether it was driving a submarine or stocking the Peruvian cabinet or signing away the canal and letting the Panamanian people chart their own course. Mankind is always hesitant to collaborate when the alternative is the illusion of being in control. For the next several hours, a tiny locomotive towed the steel cable, and our ship glided through the locks. With the water draining beneath us, we sank into the basin as the sun cast our mysterious shadow upon the concrete walls. The massive stone doors of the final locks opened before us, the sun rode low in the sky, the pilot debarked, and the captain went below. It was just me and the lookout now.

"That was fun . . . but I'm glad it's over," Lewis confided. "Care for a smoke, sir?"

Of course I did.

Lewis took two delicious-looking Cubans from his breast pocket. I offered tremendous thanks, pulled out some matches, and lit up. A cool sense of resignation washed over me as the sky turned pink, then orange, then purple behind the darkening hills of the Panamanian coast. For the next twenty minutes, Lewis and I sat on the bridge in peace as the final rays of light glimmered on the Atlantic. The land behind

The shadow of the USS *Hartford* in the locks of the Panama Canal. Standing atop the sail are Captain Frank, the pilot, the machine gunner, and me (I'm driving). *Photograph by William Coulter.*

us sank into the edge of the world and our ship was once more alone, a silent hunter of ghosts in the vast unknown.

"Was this your last time driving?" Lewis asked. I nodded slowly, taking a long draw. We'd been aboard the ship for a few years together.

Lewis paused for a moment, then asked, "You think you'll miss it?"

"Not a snowball's chance in hell."

Lewis smiled with years of unspoken understanding. After the poocanos and paperwork and botched burials at sea and thousands of grueling hours away from home chasing terrorists and bashing at windmills, what else needed to be said? The two of us took our last drags, let out a good laugh, and tossed the cigar butts overboard.

"Come on, sir! Let's *take'r down easy . . .*"

"*Yarghhhhhh!*"

6

Surfacing

On our submerged transit home to Connecticut, I stood at the center of the control room, guiding our ship from the Panama Canal through the Caribbean. We came to periscope depth to check e-mail over our satellite uplink. In anticipation of our arrival, headquarters dictated six prescreened statements that we were permitted to tell the press about our mission. My watch team laughed at how staged and disingenuous it appeared, at least until the XO pulled me aside to reprimand me for allowing criticism from the men. Aside from that, the weather forecast was the most exciting thing in our official message traffic. A tropical storm had passed overhead a day before, but I didn't think anything of it; as long as the storm wasn't endangering my ship, it didn't bother me one bit. Even if a hurricane passed directly over our submarine, it wouldn't have affected us much—all we would have to do would be to dive a few hundred feet deeper and the raging storm above would subside into a gentle, deep-ocean wave.

As we steered the *Hartford* into her berth, trumpets blasted and drums banged, heralding our triumphant return with the pomp of John Philip Sousa. A sailor's wife, five days overdue for giving birth, was instead giving an interview to the local TV news. Her husband had won the "first kiss" honors and was the first sailor off the ship. As soon as the gangplank lowered, the young husband saluted the flag and leapt onto the pier in his immaculate white uniform. The crowd cheered . . . all eyes were upon them . . . they embraced . . . they kissed . . . the ecstasy was overwhelming! Alas, the ecstasy was perhaps *too* overwhelming for her—and she started to give birth.

"My fucking water just broke," she shouted in a panic as the television cameras zoomed in, capturing her every move and word.

"Could you say that again, but a bit *nicer*?" the reporter urged, pressing the microphone close. The mother-to-be covered her mouth with her hand, remembering the camera in embarrassment.

"Oh, my God! My water just broke," she chirped daintily before waddling off to a car and a police escort that immediately drove her to the hospital. The second version of her statement made the nightly news. But despite her mothering drama and the high of our navy family reunion, it was another television broadcast that caught my attention that evening. The weather report that I had casually brushed off as inconsequential a few days earlier was no laughing matter—we had driven home right behind Hurricane Katrina.

As the images of bodies and flooded streets flashed across the screen, I wondered how the hell we hadn't known about it sooner. Was the hull of my submarine so impermeable that Katrina had destroyed New Orleans and we couldn't hear a thing until three days later? There were times aboard the sub when I missed the big news stories, like the crash of the Concorde, but this was different; it was too big for us not to have known. We knew almost immediately when Baghdad fell and when Saddam had been captured. But how big did the *human* tragedy have to be before the news made its way down the rose-colored periscope?

I was baffled by the isolation of my ship, but that soon paled before my absolute bewilderment over the lack of response to the tragedy. How could the most powerful nation on earth be so isolated from its own people's suffering? It seemed nightmarishly improbable that days could pass before a serious effort was mustered to help the victims within our own borders. A civilian friend asked me if my submarine would be helping out with the Katrina relief efforts. The question seemed absurd—my billion-dollar nuclear-powered warship was powerless to help. It was built to fight the Cold War, not to deliver medicines and supplies or rescue refugees behind the walls of a flooded city. There would be no heroic voyage into New Orleans for this *Hartford*. Silently, I damned the torpedoes for their conspicuous uselessness in to our modern plight.

Since the end of the Cold War, the submarine force had been flailing to find a mission. In the absence of a clearly defined strategic role that only subs could perform, the force was literally and figuratively driving blind. The fiscal bureaucratic mêlée for defense dollars continued, and proving the relevance of each new $2 billion submarine became our leadership's focus, regardless of whether or not nuclear subs were still needed in the Global War on Terrorism. For the roughly seventy fast-attack nuclear submarines already in existence, the hunter-killer mission against Soviet nuclear weapons platforms had long since faded, and the likelihood of total war, even with rising world powers like China, had evaporated as well. This inconvenient reality didn't stop the admiralty from inventing new "core competencies" and administrative requirements as fast as they could dictate an e-mail to their secretaries. Under this strategic context, proving our worth on paper had become more important than the substance of our missions. In the absence of a problem, it became a formidable administrative challenge to prove that a problem has been solved. I thanked the spirit of Rickover that we hadn't been tasked with driving our ship to the moon—the crew just couldn't have survived that much paperwork.

A week later, I transferred off the submarine and fell in love with a beautiful French neuroscientist who was visiting

Yale. At least for me, things were looking up. With one year left on my navy contract, I received new orders to the blissful nirvana of shore duty, where I taught officers how to drive submarines using sonar. It was a highly technical field, but I discovered a metaphysical side of teaching that brought me great pleasure. Teaching students how to perceive the world with their ears and not their eyes had the surprising effect of improving my perception with both. On a fundamental level, we examined the process of how we perceive the world and react to our surroundings. Through this examination, my students learned the limits of physical perception and even the limits of our minds upon processing what we observe. Every presumption was questioned as we sounded the depths of our abilities to see and analyze the world around us. In this regard I felt more like a philosophy professor than a technical instructor.

I took a vacation to France to visit my beloved neuroscientist. Alas, she preferred the lab mice in Strasbourg to me, since they were actually born in France and could discern the differences between Brie and *fromage de chèvre* (her experiments proved this conclusively). Stymied by love, I wandered the streets of Strasbourg, where, amazingly, I discovered something even better. In the center of the city, between the cathedral and the town square, stands a large bronze statue of several people holding books, scrolls, and other instruments of art, science, and knowledge. Around the base of the statue, the names of various writers, philosophers, and mathematicians from centuries past are inscribed. The names are those of giants like Descartes, Renoir, Sartre, Curie, Fourier, Newton, Shakespeare . . . every one a genius—someone who had changed the world! As I read the small chiseled names, it occurred to me that the names had been added after the statue was built; *it was a work in progress!* Encircling the monument, I realized with a sense of amazement that fully half of the space was left blank for more names to be added! A sense of awe gripped me as the weight of that empty space set in, for in that blank space lay faith in the capacity of mankind— the most powerfully humanistic statement I had ever seen. A tear came to my eye as I stared at the beautiful emptiness of those bronze panels, wondering whose name would come next and what extraordinary thing that person would have accomplished.

Then, just as quickly as this audacious faith in mankind had gripped me, the emptiness of another monument seized hold and dragged me down. My spine tensed, the hair on my neck stood on end, and I imagined myself standing once more at attention in the central rotunda of the Naval Academy. On the large memorial to our fallen alumni, several new names had appeared since my graduation, yet the vastness of the empty space seemed unchanged. On that massive wall with movable plastic lettering, the emptiness had become the most salient feature. I realized with a sense of horror that my life had been a pursuit of that emptiness. Until that point, I had struggled to control the things that would prevent the names of my classmates from appearing in that unbearable space. My faith in those white plastic names had dignified my pursuit! But at that instant, I realized that my quest had been hollow because of what lay within the emptiness of that godforsaken wall. Instead of faith in the capacity of mankind, that emptiness chanted in an austere, commanding tone the insidiously pessimistic dogma *War will never end . . . War will never end! WAR WILL NEVER END!!!*

"SHUT UP!!!" I shouted in anger at the cold, blackened wall. My voice echoed in the hall as though I were standing alone within a canyon. Suddenly tears were streaming down my face, my fists were clenched, and I howled, "I will not follow you anymore! You can't have my life!"

I sobbed, exasperated and purged. The albatross that hung from my neck broke loose and fell into the sea. I knew what sort of monument I wanted my name to be inscribed upon, and that knowledge carried me forward with a newfound sense of hope.

My faith in the navy had been shattered. No longer did I believe that we could save the world from my hollow little boat. And no longer could I believe that the awesome force of the U.S. military was even relevant to keeping America safe and protecting our freedoms. Surely there remains a need for defense, but the greatest problems that lie before the world are not problems that can be solved by military force. And despite the fact that our amazing little ship could sustain its environment and mission independent of oil, my country at large was unable to achieve such a feat, a failure that brought great consequences.

The war in Iraq raged on. In the same way that the impoverished citizens of New Orleans found themselves caught up in looting and violence, so were the destitute of Baghdad caught up in a quagmire of fear and hatred. Everyday citizens were driven to acts of desperation and extremism by the injustices and iniquities around them. And above the Iraqi people's heads, there hung like a Damoclean sword the all-important question of oil.

I hated the idea that the United States invaded Iraq to guarantee access to oil, but this was the reality of an age-old dilemma. The American Dream of prosperity depends on a steady stream of oil to fuel the massive engines of economic growth. The rhetoric of statesmen had changed in the course of a century, but the chilling echo of history was all too clear. *"I do not care under which system we keep the oil, but I am quite clear that it is all-important for us that this oil should be available."* And while the Bush administration worked to help Iraq liberalize its economy and make Iraqi oil available for sale on the world market, I couldn't help but feel that nothing much had changed over the course of the century. At the dawning of the third millennium, the most powerful country in the world still managed an unsustainable energy policy with violence.

It was almost time for me to leave the military. I had been accepted to Yale's business school, and I couldn't wait to start working on solving the human problems that loomed before my generation. At work, a salty Cold Warrior in my chain of command asked me to teach the topic of submarine minefield avoidance. It seemed absolutely absurd to think that a 7,000-ton ship could thread the needle through a submerged minefield, but such was the navy's tireless pursuit of control. We had glossed over the reckless words of Farragut by elevating them to the status of official doctrine. Damn the torpedoes indeed! At that moment, I knew that I would never regret my decision to leave.

But while I stepped into the escape trunk to eject from the world of submarines, my colleagues were leaving unexpectedly for a different reason altogether. Week after week, new sets of orders arrived on our captain's desk. Week after week, the captain submitted my colleagues' names to a random morbid lottery. Every so often, one of our colleagues would draw the shortest straw and be whisked off to training at some army base before being sent to the wars in Iraq and Afghanistan. The blissful nirvana of shore duty had quickly morphed into a ready source of fresh, warm bodies, fodder for a quiet interservice draft.

The army was strapped for personnel, but the generals in the Pentagon refused (or weren't permitted) to announce their manning problem until after the November elections. The major press releases came three days after the Democrats took control of Congress. But ironically for me, the army wasn't the only organization to face recruiting problems. Yale's business school was faced with a manning problem of its own. The school's new curriculum, highly lauded by international reviews, had been almost too successful. With all the international press, the number of candidates who actually accepted Yale's offers of admission spiked unexpectedly by 60 percent over the previous year, leaving the school completely overbooked for its small class. *If only the army could be so lucky!* To rectify the problem, the dean changed his long-standing policy and allowed incoming students to defer enrollment. Before I finished reading the dean's e-mail, I knew what it meant for me. My friends needed me. My country needed me. And even if the Iraq war was driven by my country's thirst for oil, there was still the chance that I could do something good to help the Iraqi people. My decision was made; I was going to Iraq. It would take more than submarine minefield avoidance skills to make it back from this one.

7

Fish Out of Water

Jumping on a hand grenade is not an act of bureaucracy. When you do it, everything stops while passersby cringe, peeking out of the corners of their eyes with a sense of morbid curiosity to see what will happen. Whether the grenade goes off or not doesn't really matter—the mere decision to take one for the team is enough to buy some serious karma. There are many variations on this theme, each worthy of recognition. For example, when our ship pulled in to foreign ports, the married officers would flirt casually with the ugly girls so that their single buddies could flirt unhindered with the hotties. It was a devious and superficial tactic, but effective. The married men who jumped on the grenades usually earned themselves a beer or two, compliments of the bachelors who scored phone numbers and good-night kisses or perhaps better.

When I volunteered to go to Iraq, it was the equivalent of jumping on the grenade. Everyone stopped to look. Everyone cringed a bit—*I'm glad it's not me!* Then the karma arrived. The bureaucracy around me simply vanished. No longer did I need to wait in line after taking a number at the health clinic. When I walked into the room, somehow people knew what had happened, and they treated me like a human instead of a number. Women smiled, kids waved, an enlisted administrator looked through my stack of orders and signed an entire block of signatures.

"There you go, sir. The last thing you need to worry about is this paperwork."

Across the submarine base, crowds parted as I breezed to the head of every line. All eyes gazed upon me with a bizarre sense of reverence. *Am I already dead? Is this heaven after a life cut short by an overdose of administrivia?* Needless to say, I enjoyed the special treatment as I walked from building to building, collecting the myriad checks-in-boxes that would certify my readiness for war. The two-page resignation letter I had submitted nine months earlier was still being processed by the Bureau of Naval Personnel, but my paperwork for Iraq passed through the chain of command, as Patton would say, like crap through a goose.

Before I left for training, there were numerous PowerPoint lectures on gun safety, the Geneva Conventions, and the army's core values. Online multiple-choice quizzes verified that we had completed each and every slide show. My predeployment medical exam was supposed to screen me for problems that could prevent me from serving in Iraq, but it was evident that the doctor wasn't looking very hard. The physician spent most of the exam trying to get my unresponsive knee to twitch by striking it incessantly with a small rubber mallet.

"It's not really important," the doctor said with a smirk, giving it a few more whacks. "Just wanted to see if I could get it to work."

Soon thereafter, I joined naval augmentees from around the country at Fort Jackson for basic army training. I had gone through basic at the Naval Academy, but apparently the survival skills they taught me—like how to inflate my pants into a life preserver—were no longer necessary. We soaked up more PowerPoints on our final destinations, the "down-range countries." Our group also received three laminated pamphlets filled with cartoons of war experiences, complete with captions in transliterated Arabic. These "cultural survival

Sailors-turned-soldiers meander about during our army boot camp at Fort Jackson, South Carolina, the army base where individual augmentees trained.

guides" included dozens of key phrases for relating to the Iraqi population, like *Stop or I'll shoot* and *Where are your bombs?* A medical pamphlet included cartoons of brown-skinned people with various conditions ranging from spider bites to blood streaming from severed limbs. One cartoon showed a woman with a catheter inserted into her vagina, which was difficult enough for me to understand in English, let alone to explain in pidgin Arabic. A veterinary pamphlet showed how to diagnose a cow's malaise through bovine facial expressions and visual examination of its poop. I folded up the pamphlets, gulped, and took a swig from my canteen, my head spinning like a gyroscope turned on end. Nothing was making any sense. I wanted to answer my country's call to duty, but *what the hell was it calling me to do?*

The drill instructors herded us like cattle to the clinic for a slew of vaccinations. Mine included smallpox, anthrax, and a host of other diseases that stand no chance against the modern navy. If it weren't for STDs—the sailor's Achilles' heel—we would have been biologically invincible.

For a boot camp, our training regimen had a lot of downtime. Occasionally we'd find ourselves chitchatting before a briefing or bashing the French while cleaning our guns. I still had a soft spot for the French on account of my beloved neuroscientist, so I recused myself from that popular pastime. Saddam was a hot topic—his trial was under way in Baghdad. Despite President Bush's statement that there was no connection between Saddam Hussein and the terrorist attacks of 2001, the majority of the officers among us still blamed him.

"Saddam had nothing to do with 9/11," I remarked. My comment was met with silent stares and a few looks of distaste—*Whose side are you on?*

When our plane touched down in Kuwait, a commander in the seat behind me let out a gleeful shout. The entire cabin turned to look in surprise.

"What the hell are you so excited about?"

"We're in the war zone, man!"

Silence. A few puzzled looks.

"No more taxes this year!"

Sheeesh, a few men grumbled. *Is he serious?* A few others shook their heads. The commander knew that his job would never leave the Green Zone, but the rest of us wouldn't be so lucky. The onlookers turned away, scowling, preoccupied with things more important than counting their new tax breaks.

Our group spent a week in Kuwait, allowing our bodies to adjust to the formidable Middle Eastern heat. It was the hottest part of summer, peaking at around 130 degrees at midday. We slept in semipermanent tents with concrete floors and air conditioners the size of pickup trucks. An overzealous navy chief turned the thermostat down all the way. That night, when we returned to the tent, the temperature inside was shockingly cold; it felt like a refrigerator.

"Jesus Christ! I'm gonna freeze my balls off in here," one of the men grumbled. I turned the thermostat up to 65, noting that tax dollars were paying the electric bill.

Our final training exercise took us deep into the desert, fifteen kilometers from the Iraqi border. The exercise was basic—we were learning to walk and shoot at the same time. No gum was allowed, on the presumption that three things at once would short-circuit our brains and get someone killed. The training lasted all day, so we camped out in the desert. A single large tent provided the only shelter for our group of fifty. Men and women of all ranks crammed in to sleep within arm's reach of each other, packed like sunburnt sardines. That night, the weather outside was more pleasant than the concrete floor, so I slept in the sand under the open sky. My inflatable mattress and sleeping bag made a pathetic campsite, but the evening was still and shelter was not necessary. A few other men had planned to camp outside, but a rumor of camel spiders and scorpions and scarab beetles changed their minds. *Lions and tigers and bears, oh my!* I broke out an MRE for dinner—#4, Country Captain Chicken with mashed potatoes, peanut butter, and crackers. *Maybe God will find me out here all by myself,* I mused while pondering the mysteries of the universe. And there were important mysteries to ponder, like what to do with those strange miniature bottles of Tabasco sauce that appeared in every field ration.

I rested my head on my dusty duffel bag, and the emptiness of the desert drew me in. Like the ocean, the desert is formless and shifting; the difference is a matter of time. Sand flows with a sense of memory, lingering before it takes its new shape; water is quick to adjust, less fearful of change. Neither the ocean nor the desert has a well-defined present—only a state of motion. With my life changing in the course of days, I felt more like water than sand. The sun fell behind the flat, empty horizon, and our camp lit up with blinding electric lights. The sound of diesel engines droned on, cranking kilo-watts of power into the oversized air conditioners and high-powered halogen lamps above our camp. The exhaust from the diesels wafted over the campsite, leaving me drunk with fumes. Drifting between delirium and dreamland, I was carried away by the sound of those engines. The gentle summer-time swells of the Atlantic rolled back into my heart, and I longed to be at sea. Slipping into unconsciousness, I dove once more into waters off a strange and alien shore. My head pressed into the pillow of my six-foot-by-two-foot-by-eighteen-inch rack, the monotonic lullaby of machinery humming in the distance.

In the Green Zone of Baghdad, I joined an ad hoc unit of recalled reservists who directed the Iraq war's civil-military operations. Our directorate worked in the strategic headquarters toward the mission of bridging the divides between diplomacy, development, and military force. Generally speaking, our job was to win the hearts and minds of the Iraqi people. My new colleagues hailed from Australia, the UK, Macedonia, the USA, Georgia, and South Korea. Of the twenty people in our unit, the majority were senior officers, a few were close to my rank, and a handful were enlisted army personnel who coordinated security. For such a small team, our mission was extremely broad, ranging from coordinating elections to humanitarian aid. Each of these sectors was important in its own right, but the crown jewel of Iraqi reconstruction—energy—also happened to fall under our purview. Oil and electricity were foremost among our responsibilities, and we were the only unit that reported directly to the commanding general on energy every single day. Our unit was nestled within the ballroom of the Republican Palace, Saddam Hussein's former presidential seat, a space we shared with the U.S. Embassy. Unlike the military officers at Camp

Victory who pushed boots, our team pushed PowerPoint slides in some of the finest office space ever commandeered from a monomaniacal dictator. There were chandeliers the size of Volkswagens, gilded doors inscribed with Saddam's initials, and a café with sixty-foot ceilings, silk tapestries, and a full-service coffee bar.

It took me a while to grasp the concept of a military unit acting as a bridge between diplomacy and force. Until I arrived in that office, I had no idea that coalition militaries had such a high level of involvement with reconstructing Iraq. When President Bush spoke at my Academy graduation, he was quite clear that the military should be used to fight and win wars, not for nation-building.

This was my first time working in a strategic headquarters, which also took some adjustment. It was impressive to me that the coalition forces were making efforts to stimulate agriculture and form a crisis response center for Iraqis. *If we're taking care of these things, then everything must be under control.* One of my new colleagues was a lawyer and former New York state legislator who handled legal matters for detainees; another was a bovine veterinarian who actually helped Iraqi farmers. This veterinarian had never seen the army's shiny new cow-poop pamphlet, so I offered mine, earning her instant affection.

"This is fantastic," the veteran veterinarian exclaimed.

"Glad you like it, ma'am!"

My new boss was a navy captain one year shy of mandatory retirement, which made him (unofficially) the Old Man of the Desert. Upon meeting Wilbur Cross, I was comforted to see the familiar submariners' dolphins on his uniform pocket; another submarine officer would be easy to get along with, and we could at least speak the same language. Wearing gold dolphins on one's uniform is like wearing a résumé— I knew exactly what the training meant. However, Wilbur's dolphins looked the same as mine only because of the camouflage. In actuality, Wilbur had earned his *silver* fish three decades earlier as a young enlisted sailor in Rickover's fleet, but our camouflage uniforms made both dolphins look brown. While silver dolphins still connoted a high level of technical training in nuclear power, Wilbur's role had been that of an operator, not a supervisor, and certainly not someone who was being groomed to command a ship at sea.

While my own experience amounted to a meager six years on active duty and some master's-level studies in engineering management, my new boss, old enough to be my grandfather, had been an active-duty officer for only six months. Nevertheless, Captain Cross had worked a long career as an engineer, most recently in the field of wind turbines. He was also extremely nice, with a soft Minnesota accent and jovial manners that made him immediately likable. He wore his pistol concealed in a holster behind his back so as not to appear aggressive toward his civilian colleagues. I followed suit—after all, it was the most diplomatic way of packing heat.

Wilbur's boss, an army colonel named Peter Dawson, had served several years on active duty before becoming a certifiable oilman. Dawson was very well suited for his job, having managed battalions of troops and multimillion-dollar budgets in the oil industry. Above Colonel Dawson, yet another field-grade officer stood in my chain of command, Colonel James Mulder. Mulder introduced himself as a plumber and claimed that the only reason he'd volunteered for Iraq was that "the pay [was] better than fixing toilets."

Colonel Mulder was a grizzly bear in camouflage. At a distance he seemed nice enough, with big, soft cheeks and broad, hulking shoulders. But an astute observer could recognize that his wandering, indifferent gaze was actually a perpetual search for food. Mulder frequently lumbered into the office with his kill: arms full of potato chips and soap bars and socks sent from concerned mothers and church groups—

intended for soldiers in the field, not bearish colonels. Mulder bragged about having several sticks of deodorant and playing cards with Elvis on the back that he had recently found while foraging through the palace.

"You gotta see it! I got three more decks like these back in my hooch—and some cardboard funnels!"

"Oh, hey, you never know when you might need a good funnel," Wilbur interjected with enthusiasm. My eyes darted back and forth between the two senior officers, trying to catch their inside joke. There was no joke; they were genuinely excited about the funnels.

The leader of our directorate was the first Korean officer ever to command American troops in war. General Kim was an athletic, enthusiastic, and disciplined infantry officer who rejoiced in helping the Iraqi people as much as he rejoiced in promoting the Christian faith abroad (which was specifically against the rules). Though animated and well intentioned, Kim spent a great deal of time in Kurdistan, where the sole division of Korean troops in Iraq was stationed. The general's responsibilities over civil-military operations may have been nationwide, but his focus was clearly on the hearts and minds of the docile Kurdish north. General Kim frequently traveled with an entourage of Korean officers who numbered a fifth of our directorate. From what I could discern, Kim's plethora of aides handled limited functionary roles, ordering cakes from Halliburton on people's birthdays, playing Ping-Pong with the general after every lunch, and snapping thousands of photos like Asian tourists with guns.

Several other unlikely colleagues fleshed out our directorate, ranging from a Brooklyn police officer to a prosthetist named Joe. An army colonel dreamed aloud about the profits to be made by shepherding young Iraqis to the lucrative industry of American porn. The diversity of our team immediately struck me, but at the same time something seemed wrong. None of my colleagues had prior training or experience in civil-military operations, and none had ever worked at such a high level of a major organization. It wasn't what I expected from a special operations unit (which we were, technically). Instead of a well-trained team of specialists, we seemed more like a catchall for quirky multinational misfits who couldn't really help with combat operations. The internationals in our unit seemed a frail homage to the coalition of the willing—little more than lip service to multilateralism in a U.S.-dominated war effort. The sheer variety of flags and spoken languages was so dazzling that it took me a month to realize that none of us spoke Arabic and none of us were Iraqi.

Despite my reservations, it was clear that I had landed in the right place. My official job title was "liaison officer" to the electrical sector. My responsibilities included working between the military headquarters, the State Department, and the Iraqi Ministry of Electricity while reporting to the commanding general each day on the state of Iraq's energy situation. Rebuilding Iraq's oil and electrical sectors was a critical step for ending the insurgency and leading the Iraqi people toward success. Energy drives the engines of economies and empowers people to demand the freedoms that Americans cherish. Poll after poll showed that the single most important thing on the minds of Iraqi citizens was not suicide bombings or terrorism but having enough electricity and gas to live and work comfortably. I loved the idea of being a liaison officer in this sector—Hyman Rickover had also been a liaison officer while building the nuclear submarine force. It wouldn't hurt to follow in Rickover's footsteps. To top it all off, the spirit of John Paul Jones had won me over; I was already planning to become a diplomat at the State Department after Yale. Working with the Department of State would be the perfect way to learn what American diplomacy was all about! Compared to me, with surprisingly relevant training and interests, my colleagues appeared more like fish out of water than I did, but as Donald Rumsfeld declared, "You go to war with the army you've got, not the army you wish you had."

Rumsfeld was right. Besides, there was no time for wishful thinking. There was work to do on the most important thing that America could bring to Iraq—energy independence!

8

The Process We Do

The digitized image of my commanding general covered the television screen at the front of the Green Zone's strategic operations center. Every morning, the who's who of the willing few gathered before their computer monitors to brief the general on everything that had transpired the previous day. Most of the time, General Casey and his top aides sat in a boardroom at Camp Victory, while the rest of our secretive world joined them by teleconference. It didn't seem unusual that our commander was geographically separated from his own strategic headquarters in the Green Zone—it was simply how things were done. On that day the general looked tired, impatient, and detached as he slouched in his chair, fiddling with his pen. It was Casey's third year as commanding general of the Multi-National Force, and his tense, wrinkled brow showed it.

The operations centers where we sat each morning were mesmerizing vortexes of technological noise. Ours in the Green Zone housed two hundred fifty computers, arranged three to a seat on a stadium-style terrace. Seventeen big-screen televisions spread throughout the tremendous hall, silently flashing network television channels. A screen on the right played CNN while an identical screen on the left played Fox News. This peculiar arrangement made sense to me only when I turned my back on television altogether (which I did, with a sense of liberation). The twelve largest TVs, at the front, formed a massive array of video, ten meters wide. Dilapidated chandeliers illuminated the cavernous hall with energy-efficient lightbulbs, glowing like spiral-shaped candles with soft reddish light.

Most of the details of each day's Battle Update Assessment (BUA) are classified, but it's fair game to discuss the abomination of technology that facilitates the most sacred ritual of contemporary warfare. From the Pentagon to Saddam's palaces, technological nerve centers around the globe linked up every morning to conduct real-time Internet-based briefings on the state of the war. A dozen computer cameras and headsets with microphones allowed the experts from the most important functional areas to speak directly to the commanding general through an encrypted Internet chat room. Every morning I sat at one such workstation, delivering a highly scripted briefing on Iraq's energy sector.

"Good morning, sir. The national dispatch center's rotation schedule for Baghdad was two hours on, four hours off. Oil exports for the day were 1.8 million barrels from the south."

It was important to read the script confidently, Captain Cross told me. "Otherwise, the general might ask us questions." It was a new twist on an old game; if you don't have anything useful to say, then just say *something* boldly. My script continued as we flashed our slides, each filled to the brim with operational data about power plants, refineries, and the all-important oil exports. General Casey rarely asked questions, which seemed to validate Wilbur's theory. Casey was an infantryman; he'd never supervised a power plant as I had or an oil refinery as had Colonel Dawson.

Military historians may debate at length which innovation in technology has had the second greatest effect on modern warfare, but it is undisputed that the PowerPoint presentation takes the prize for first. Our sacred morning briefing was a PowerPoint presentation like no other. Averaging over sixty slides in length, with more data per slide than safety regula-

tions should allow, it was a daily headache of gargantuan pro-
portions, an addiction to information, a crack habit for data
that left most attendees drooling from the corners of their
mouths and twitching intermittently with the changing of
the slides. Some chose not to listen out of self-preservation.
While I read the script to the general, Captain Cross checked
his Yahoo account to look for pictures of his newborn grand-
son. I kept up with a few slides on politics and major operations, but for the most part, I couldn't stand the sheer volume
of monotonous crap. Statistics on every bombing and rocket
attack were reported and then compared to how the media
perceived the same event. A "golden nugget" slide attempted
in vain to highlight the untold success stories of Iraq. It was
almost as though the media were the enemy and setting the
record straight for posterity was the most important thing.
There was never any discussion of what the general wanted
his headquarters to do or any public display of how he felt
things were going. Every slide show concluded with the words
"commanding general's comments" on the screen, but in
front of his entire headquarters, General Casey rarely said
anything at all.

To me, the daily briefing was little more than a formality—a ritualistic litany to prove our faith in the war effort.
But a great many senior officers considered PowerPoint slides
to be their most important "deliverable." Wilbur told me
repeatedly that our primary role was to "report the facts" to
the general each day; everything else was secondary to the
slide show. If the energy sector had bad news to report and
the general didn't ask us any questions, then Cross considered
it mission accomplished. "I didn't think we'd make it out of
that one," he admitted when particularly bad news slipped
past General Casey's attention. It was clear to me that Casey
had only a limited understanding of energy. If our team didn't
highlight the problems and offer solutions, then we were simply passing the buck up the chain of command to someone

who didn't know what to do with the information; Wilbur seemed fine with that.

"Take it easy, Chris," the captain cooed in a soft, comforting tone. "If the general wants us to do something, he'll tell us."

I wasn't so confident about that.

After reading the morning scripts each day, Captain Cross and I sauntered back to our ballroom office, coffee cups and secret documents in hand, while my superiors showered me with congratulations.

"You did a wonderful job, Lieutenant!"

"You're the best reader we've got," Colonel Mulder said, beaming. I thought it was some sort of patronizing joke, but they were quite serious. Apparently my confident and virile young voice made my bosses look good in front of their bosses. Even General Kim lavished me with laudatory remarks, occasionally asking me to speak slower so he could keep up (his "Engrish" was a bit rocky). Here, as in the submarine force, a confident report cast the illusion that everything was under control; whether or not we actually had a plan didn't enter into the equation.

"You don't understand, Chris," Captain Cross explained. "This briefing is a vital part of our operations here."

"That may be, sir, but it's only a slide show; it's not going to win the war."

Fixing Iraq's energy problems wasn't going to win the war either. Nevertheless, it quickly became apparent to me that without some serious progress in Iraq's energy sector, there could be no stability. While many different things were required for victory, a systemic failure of Iraq's oil or electricity sectors would send the frail government into cardiac arrest.

The lifeblood of Iraq flowed out through the oil fields and

back through the veins of high-voltage power lines. With neither enough power plants nor enough fuel to operate the generators, the country was forced into rolling blackouts. Every
few hours, the power would flicker on, stay on for a short
while, then vanish. A small portion of Iraq's oil was kept in-
country to produce refined fuels for power plants, but even at
their best performance, the refineries couldn't have kept up
with Iraq's increasing demand. After the sanctions and the
damage from the first Gulf War, these refineries decayed into
jury-rigged industrial accidents waiting to happen (and accidents did happen). Theoretically, Iraq's nationalized electrical
grid was controlled by the Ministry of Electricity, which
switched the power on and off to each province across the
country and each *belladiyah* of Baghdad throughout the day.
In reality, Shi'ite militias had infiltrated the system, sending
power and fuel to their sectarian and political allies while
leaving their Kurdish and Sunni countrymen literally in the
dark. The only saving grace for Iraq's energy sector was that
Basra—the southern port at the confluence of the Tigris and
Euphrates—continued to pump enough oil to keep the government financially afloat.

An enormous amount of work needed to be done. From
the outset, the coalition knew it would take years for energy
supplies to equal demand—that Zen-like moment when the
invisible hand claps. Currently, Iraq was producing around
4,000 megawatts of power each day, but it needed twice that
much to meet the country's needs. Only a handful of homes
had electric meters installed, which made billing people for
their energy use a practical impossibility. With "free electricity," the Iraqi people used as much as they could, overloading
the system. Developing the oil sector was another long-term
problem, requiring at least fifteen years and tens of billions of
dollars to reach optimal production capacity. To me, understanding where the coalition fit into the long-term plan was a
key element of making headway and stabilizing the country.
There were a million questions on my mind.

"What are our big-picture goals for electricity?"

"We don't really have any that I know of," Wilbur replied.

"Why don't we have any?"

"Oh, wait . . . It's five thousand megawatts."

"Okay, sir . . . by when?"

"Ummm, I don't know that."

"Hmmm . . . Is there a strategic plan that I could read, sir?"

Colonel Mulder, who was squinting at an iPod movie held close to his face, started up and roared with laughter.

"*Plan?* We never had a *plan!*"

The phone rang. Wilbur jumped at the opportunity to answer, apparently relieved to dodge my questions. As my new boss chatted into the receiver, I grew incredulous that someone in Captain Cross's position had no knowledge of any overarching strategy. In the energy sector, Cross and Dawson were the top military officers in the coalition; if *they* didn't know the plan, then who did? My head spun as I flashed back to that horrible moment aboard the *Hartford* when I realized that my captain was lost at sea. As I watched Wilbur speaking into the phone, it struck me that he was wearing an "Airborne" patch on his left shoulder; the navy captain had never jumped out of an airplane in his life. The captain hung up, stared at his computer screen, and acted as though our brief conversation had never happened. His eyes peeked over his bifocals to see if I had gone away yet. I stood awkwardly by his desk, slowly coming to the realization that any more questions would only embarrass him. Besides, I had all that I needed to know: in the third year of the war, our team was starting from square one.

Our office was drowning in data. Every square inch of palatial wall space was splashed with maps and spreadsheets, every corner flooded with file cabinets and puddles of documents. There had to be a plan somewhere. I rolled up my sleeves and dove in. A thorough search revealed thousands of unused ballots from the 2005 elections, some Korean public

Bathroom graffiti in Saddam's presidential palace. One notable inscription reads, "Saddam had nothing to do with 911." The response: "Yeah, but he's still a dick."

relations pamphlets, a box of Bronze Stars, and a handful of cow-poop pamphlets under a fine layer of dust. It was going to be a long day.

Soon thereafter, my quest for a strategic plan tripped over the chains that shackled me to my desk. Every afternoon, a man I never met from the Ministry of Electricity would send me an e-mail message. It was my first contact with an actual Iraqi, which I found to be mildly thrilling (in a "MySpace friend meets foreign exchange student" sort of way). The message contained a spreadsheet in Arabic with operational logs from every power plant in the country. Every afternoon I took that spreadsheet, copied the numbers, and pasted them into an identical spreadsheet with English labels. This process took only a few minutes, but the spreadsheet was just the beginning. The real "product" that Captain Cross and I created for the war effort was the slide show for the daily briefing to the commanding general. The slide show took forever—everything had to look perfect, and every single word of the briefing had to be scripted the night before, right down to the deep, virile, and confident "Good morning, sir."

In my first days in Baghdad, I marveled that war could be so routine. Sometimes I would imagine that fixing all of Iraq could be as simple as preparing my daily report. *Copy "Western values." Paste into the column between "Tigris" and "Euphrates." Easy stuff.* But then, invariably, my fantasy world would have its own problems. I'd forget to save the file for "Iraq 2.0" or Windows would crash and some elitist francophone Mac user would blabber on about how America had gotten it all wrong from the beginning anyway . . . *C'est la vie* . . .

One night while I was preparing a slide for the morning briefing, some peculiar little symbols on the screen caught my attention—they looked like cartoon bombs.

"What do the bombs mean, sir?"

"I don't know," my captain replied, cocking his head. "I always wondered about that myself."

"Well, should I delete them, sir?"

"NO!" Cross shouted, his neck stiffening and his face lighting up with surprise. "All I know is moving them makes the general angry."

"I see," I said (but I didn't really see). *Why would the general get angry? Are the cartoon bombs some sort of sacrificial offering to his greatness? Does Casey keep a printed stash of PowerPoint slides with cartoon bombs in his desk drawer to count at night before bedtime?*

Wilbur, concerned about my confusion, felt the need to warn me further. "You wouldn't want to *anger* the general . . . would you, Chris?"

"Uhhhh . . . of course not, sir . . . but I don't underst—"

"Just leave the bombs alone, *Lieutenant*. It'll be all right."

Things were getting serious. Calling me "Lieutenant" instead of "Chris" was like my mom invoking my middle name.

"Yes, Captain," I replied, thoroughly confused. But at least our slide show was finished—we could go home for the night.

"See you tomorrow, Chris."

"Yes, sir. See you tomorrow."

When I got back to my trailer, my roommate—an air force officer—was up and reading a book. It was an unusual coincidence; his shift work as a security agent for the Iraqi vice president meant that we didn't usually see each other awake. Our total time in conversation had amounted to less than five minutes. He laughed about his job, noting that the VP didn't want to be seen in public with American security agents. I laughed about being an overpaid PowerPoint jockey.

"Oh, that's your voice on the slide show?"

I nodded in affirmation.

"I hear you every day. Sounds great!"

"Gee, thanks," I replied dryly.

"But I've got to admit, you guys are getting your asses kicked."

We were getting our asses kicked, but there was nothing I could do about it that night. I stretched out on the bed, closed my eyes, and wondered aloud . . .

"'Twas the night before Ramadan, and all through the hooch . . ."

My roommate chuckled, goading me on.

"Not a creature was stirring, not even the pooch . . ."

The moments passed. As we fell asleep, a low rumble shook the ground. It sounded like a car bomb. *Probably just over the Tigris.* I clenched my teeth, waiting for signs of what would happen. Seconds passed. *Maybe it's an isolated attack* . . . I relaxed with practiced resignation. A lot of people had probably just been killed, but it happened almost every day and it was starting to feel routine. The feeling of tightness in my throat and chest dissipated slowly . . . I closed my eyes and exhaled.

Bam!!! An explosion rang out—*definitely close!!* The trailer walls shook . . . *We're taking mortars!* I jumped out of bed in time to see a marine colonel running outside in his underwear, heading for a concrete bunker. My roommate bolted out the door, following suit. My heart raced. If the marine was running, we were in trouble. I reached instinctively for my pistol, then stared at it dumbfounded. *What the hell am I going do with this?* Reality set in and I hit the deck, pistol in hand, noting that my survival instincts weren't exactly the sharpest. I slipped on my shoes, tossed my body armor over my T-shirt, took a deep breath, and ran out the door, grabbing my helmet on the way. As I raced toward the palace, a brilliant flash in the sky lit up the Green Zone like fireworks. A second later the sound hit—it was immense, way too big to be a mortar. I scurried into the palace, where the Peruvian security guards anxiously shuffled me through the blast-proof doors. *Safe!!!*

Not knowing where else to go, I walked to my ballroom office. A lawyer in our directorate sat at his desk, typing away with two fingers as though nothing had happened. I sat down next to him, out of breath and shaking, pale white legs sticking out under my body armor, helmet strapped to my head.

"Rookie," he mumbled, cracking a tiny smile. When the attack began, Commander Giovanni Panetti had been walking outside. Unfazed by the explosions, he calmly returned to the office to prepare some legal briefs. He didn't even start to run.

"Why didn't you run for cover, sir?"

"If it's my time to go, it won't matter if I'm running or standing still. My way, I can at least keep my dignity."

I admired Giovanni's sangfroid, but found it a bit too fatalistic for my taste. I logged on to my computer and read through some old e-mails, passing the time until the loudspeakers sounded "All clear."

Fortunately nobody was killed, or even wounded that night. The loudest explosion turned out to be an ammunition dump, cooking off at the other end of the Green Zone. I could only imagine the joy that our insurgent assailant must have felt when he saw the results of his one-in-a-million shot. While the initial boom was far more impressive than a single mortar round, a lengthy fireworks display followed the massive blast. For the next hour, one explosion after another lit up the sky with flashes of brilliance and plumes of black smoke. As I realized the source of the continuing booms, I went outside to marvel at the explosive chain reaction.

Walking back to my hooch from the relative safety of the palace, I noticed for the first time the chimneylike flare stack of an oil refinery burning brightly against the hazy nighttime sky. In Western countries, refineries light their flare stacks only in emergencies, to burn off excess natural gas. In Iraq, the flames of refineries' flare stacks are perpetually visible, burning fiercely like religious beacons. Experts estimate that thousands of megawatts of electrical power could be generated from the gas that Iraqi refineries burn in this way every day.

The morning briefing went off without a hitch. Casey seemed oblivious to our report. General Kim lavished me with compliments for my talented reading of the five-sentence script. I thanked Kim politely, but my mind was elsewhere—I wanted to find that strategic energy plan. Unfortunately, my quest was once again interrupted, this time by an act of Congress. In response to the recent killings of several innocent Iraqi citizens, Congress mandated that all the "boots on ground" undergo ethics training. At the city of Haditha, several American marines had cracked under pressure, shooting Iraqi civilians and evoking an international outcry. The Civil-Military Operations Directorate—responsible for the hearts-and-minds part of the war—filed into a small briefing room. The Korean entourage arrived last— Lieutenant Kim, Major Kim, Colonel Kim, and the leader, General Kim himself.

"Here comes the Kim Collection," someone muttered.

"Yeah," his neighbor chimed in. "If we got a Captain Kim, we'd have a complete set."

General Kim walked to the front of the room and began to speak with great pith and moment. Though Kim's delivery was mechanical, his vocabulary was quite good and he spoke almost entirely in metaphors. And so it came to pass that the congressionally mandated ethics training began with wild Korean geese flying together in formation and the challenges of soaring against the wind. There were frogs and squirrels and chickens and beavers that followed along, too. For a fleeting moment, one could almost hear the sound of a bamboo flute. The audience remained stoic, listening patiently to Kim's awkward Mesopotamian transplant of a sylvan allegory. When the tranquil woodland creatures had danced under the moonlight long enough, the grizzly bear lumbered forth.

"The difference between the CEO of General Motors and the military officer," Colonel Mulder growled, "is that one manages people and equipment while the other manages violence."

The flare stack of the Daura oil refinery burned constantly. Industrial countries use "associated" natural gas for fuel, but Iraq lacks the infrastructure to capture this precious by-product of crude oil production.

The real training had begun. The Haditha killings inspired a lot of controversy in our ranks. Opinions ranged from the moral high ground of "not firing until fired upon" to "going from safe to semi" whenever an Iraqi gave a dirty look (the prosthetist wasn't taking any chances). We talked about rules of engagement, international laws of armed conflict, and the split-second decisions that soldiers face every day in war. The lawyer, Giovanni, brought up the Geneva Conventions, claiming that our troops were confused about how to treat prisoners. He argued that Guantánamo Bay and secret prisons condoned by the president seemed to throw the conventions of law out the window, creating a no-holds-barred atmosphere.

"Should we be surprised that Abu Ghraib happens when we tell Private Timmy that the Geneva Conventions are just 'guidelines'?"

"Whose side are you on?" somebody grumbled.

Panetti became angry, shouting, "I'm on *the law's* side, and that means doing the right thing—even when nobody's forcing us."

The prosthetist shook his head. With that, our ethics training quickly adjourned. Congress checked its box for "upgrading" the military and filed a lengthy report to prove so to posterity.

Giovanni was a reservist commander who had managed a private law firm before being recalled to active duty. He was a devout Catholic, socially conservative, and opposed to the war on the basis of Saint Augustine's "just war" doctrine. Commander Panetti's recall to active duty forced his aging father to come out of retirement to look after his son's law practice. Within a few months, the stress on his diabetic dad landed him in the hospital with an amputated leg. The law practice closed immediately, and years of Giovanni's life's work vanished as he sat beside me in that ballroom office, helpless.

Despite Giovanni's personal struggle, his "Panetti Plan" to

win the war was a constant joke within our unit. Legalistic and Hitleresque, the Panetti Plan called for invoking the wrongful-death compensation policy that had been accepted by the Iraqi government. This policy called for a payment of $2,500 to the estates of Iraqis who had been killed as "collateral damage." Culling the entire population of 26 million Iraqis at $2,500 each would cost the U.S. government only $65 billion, Giovanni argued—far less than the hundreds of billions that we were presently spending.

"Kill 'em all—let Allah sort 'em out," the lawyer said, laughing, hunched over his keyboard, hunting and pecking with his forefingers. "Besides," he continued, "with all the oil concessions, we'd have the bill paid in a year."

But while Giovanni joked about the macroeconomics of Wergild, he was actually an ethical and reverent man. On 9/11 a base-wide loudspeaker announced a moment of mournful silence. Commander Panetti stood rigidly at attention in front of his desk. I followed his lead and stood, but simply bowed my head, remembering. The old-timers, including Captain Cross and Colonel Mulder, remained seated, chatting away through the moment of silence, working on their PowerPoint presentations. Mulder even cracked a joke; Panetti winced. As a New Yorker, Giovanni stood with the absolute reverence of someone who would never forget his principles. But he had other ways of showing respect toward his fellow man that were much deeper than mere ceremony, like sticking his neck out to protect Iraqi human rights.

The detainee review boards, where Commander Panetti worked, were used to determine the legal status of captured Iraqi prisoners. The boards were nicknamed "catch and release boards" by the field-grade officers who participated. In reality, most of the detainees were not released but were held indefinitely. Giovanni, who reviewed thousands of cases, confided that most of the detainees had simply been rounded up from the area around a house where weapons were found, then held under loose accusations. He further explained that the published doctrine for determining a detainee's status required several checks and balances that were completely ignored. By agreement between the U.S. and Iraqi governments, each detainee review board was required to have Iraqis in at least 50 percent of the seats. During Panetti's months on the board, every panel consisted entirely of American military officers. There were requirements to have one expert in human rights and one expert in the Iraqi government. These requirements were also ignored. According to Giovanni, the only requirement of agreed and published doctrine that was actually met for these detainees was the requirement to have a representative expert on military intelligence reports—a senior American or Iraqi military officer (an American officer always filled this spot). Giovanni described how the process had recently been "streamlined" to handle higher caseloads with fewer board members.

"We aren't even *allowed* to take notes anymore," he revealed, much to my surprise. "And each detainee's case has been limited to a single-page form in an effort to 'save paper.'"

The attorneys who prepared the cases were each expected to file 170 cases per week.

"Most officers are ready to stamp a guilty verdict before they ask a single question. There's no evidence and no representation," the commander lamented. "It's not due process, but it's the process we do."

9

The E-Team

Every war has its heroes—even the mythical ones. The Trojan War had Achilles, who crept from the belly of a wooden horse to unleash his sword upon Troy. Emperor Charlemagne rode his personal elephant into battle, trampling the terrified Danes. T. E. Lawrence crossed the sands of Arabia on camelback, sabotaging the Hejaz railroad and cutting off the Ottoman Turks from their supplies. Sturdy Teddy Roosevelt crested the top of San Juan Hill upon his gallant steed, leading the Rough Riders to victory in the Spanish-American War. Without a quadruped to call their own, even the mathematicians of Project Ultra became heroes, decoding the secrets of the German Enigma machine on the blackboard battlefields of the Second World War. Of course, the Iraq war had its share of heroes, too, but as I sat in front of my computers, pondering what color scheme Ghengis Khan would have preferred for his morning slide show, it occurred to me that the heroes of my war worked somewhere else.

"Whatchya thinkin' about, Chris?" Wilbur chirped in soft Minnesotan, pushing his bifocals back onto his nose as he approached my desk.

"Nothing, sir," I lied. *Mauve and teal are decidedly out.*

"Good! There are some people I'd like you to meet today."

"Really, sir? Who?" I was eager to meet more people in the headquarters. After all, I was a liaison officer, which meant, theoretically, that I was supposed to work between different organizations. Up until then, I hadn't met anyone outside of our own office. It was my second week in Baghdad, and life was about to get interesting.

Captain Cross took me to the opposite end of Saddam's Republican Palace to the Iraq Reconstruction Management Office. The space was nicer than our civil affairs unit's ballroom, but only because it hadn't been subdivided with plywood sheets to fit in more desks. The office was on the top floor, housed a reasonably well-stocked liquor cabinet, and boasted a lovely view of the pool where the State Department's young female interns could be seen sunbathing. The occupants were all men, except for an Iraqi translator in her fifties (the first translator I met). The men who worked in the Iraq Reconstruction Management Office were consultants, hired by the State Department to advise the Iraqi government on the technical aspects of reconstruction.

As the electrical liaisons, Wilbur and I worked directly with these consultants. The leader, Ian, was an economist in his seventies who had worked on development projects in Africa. Two others were former nuclear submariners who had become successful engineers. Most were operational engineers who had built power plants, supervised electrical grids, and prospected for oil in their youth, decades and decades earlier. As far as America and the coalition forces were concerned, the responsibility for rebuilding Iraq's energy sector lay between these consultants and my civil affairs unit. There were contractors and army engineers who carried out the operational side of things, but when it came to strategy, we were the bottom line. Together, our small team of economists, engineers, and I—the English major—formed the E-Team. I was twenty-six years old. Without me, the E-Team's average age was sixty-two.

Wilbur spent a great deal of time with these consultants. "I'm actually trying to get a contract with them when I retire," he explained. The high-paying State Department job was so appealing that Captain Cross actually printed separate business cards for himself with the consultancy's logo, which he gave exclusively to our non-military associates. By pretending to have his dream job, Wilbur hoped to make his aspirations a reality. In the civilian world he was a retirement-age engineer who designed wind turbines and staunchly denied global warming. "I just don't think that mankind can make that much of a difference in the world," he rationalized.

Landing a job with the State Department consultants would quadruple Captain Cross's annual military salary to $450,000. In civilian life, Wilbur's career was basically over; a high-paying contract in Iraq was his best shot at hatching a golden nest egg.

A few days after meeting the E-Team, Wilbur approached me hurriedly when the morning briefing was over. He was wearing full body armor and breathing fast. "Chris, a spot just opened up in our convoy—do you want to go out today?"

Of course I did. My complete ignorance of where the hell "out" was didn't really matter. Anything was better than making PowerPoint slides in the ballroom office or prospecting for a strategic plan that probably didn't exist.

"Yes, sir!" I stood up in excitement. "Where are we going?"

"No time to talk! Get your gear and meet me at the Humvees in fifteen minutes."

My heart was thumping. I grabbed my bullets and armor and ran out the door for my first trip into no-man's-land. The mission was a meeting at the Ministry of Electricity, though the details remained sketchy. I got the impression that I would be in "watch and learn mode" for a while, so it didn't bother me that I didn't know what was supposed to happen. Cross and I traveled in a well-armed convoy guarded by six Humvees, sporting 50-caliber machine guns. A shiny black SUV sat in the middle—supposedly for the "high value" passengers. To my surprise, Ian climbed into the backseat of a Humvee, and the captain motioned me into the shiny black Suburban. I was instantly incredulous.

"Do I really have to ride in *that*?" I asked, pointing to the brilliant, freshly washed late-model Chevy.

"Why? What's wrong with it?"

"Well, sir . . . it's the only one that screams *Shoot me*."

Wilbur grinned wryly. "Don't worry about that, Chris—they're all pretty good targets."

I locked and loaded, then hopped into the backseat of the Suburban.

"Buckle up, Chris. It might get bumpy." The familiar voice rang out from the front seat. Instead of a soldier behind the wheel, it was Joe—the naval commander and prosthetist who sat near me in our office. Without enough soldiers to support our missions, an officer who held the same rank as my submarine's captain was forced down a dozen pay grades into the job of security guard—equipped with nothing but an American driver's license, an itchy trigger finger, and inside knowledge of how to file Medicare claims for wooden legs.

"You know where you're going, sir?"

"Away from the bad guys." The prosthetist grinned; he wasn't taking any chances. "Buckle up, Chris," he repeated. The seat belt fit awkwardly over my body armor. Cross climbed in the front seat. The prosthetist picked up his radio and signaled, *Ready to roll*. Wilbur turned, pointed to the foam earplugs he'd just inserted, and shouted, "Just in case an IED goes off." I followed suit, plugging in my foamies and drowning out the world with synthetic silence.

The convoy rolled out, Humvees in the lead and the shiny black target in the middle. The prosthetist hit the gas pedal, and we surged forward with impressive oomph for a heavy vehicle with rocketproof shielding. As we passed through security checkpoints, the world transformed before us. No longer were there patches of green grass with sprinklers and girls in swimsuits lounging by the pool. Outside the opulent embassy, the war zone engulfed us like an urban jungle. It was the first time I had left the embassy compound in the light of day. Palaces in which Saddam had once housed his political party lay all around us in a state of ruin. Broken columns and gaping blast craters made every structure look as though it was about to collapse. A few Iraqi security guards slouched by rusted gates, each shabby soldier carrying a dirty AK-47 and looking malnourished. Our convoy drove for half a mile, passing palace after palace and run-down apartments that were once part of a lively and popular neighborhood, at least for Saddam's politicos.

Ahead on the road, a large tank with a heavy-caliber machine gun loomed before us—the last American bastion before the vast unknown of the Red Zone. Ominous guard towers stood overhead as we passed through the gates, barrels of rifles pointing downward through desert camouflage netting. The base perimeter was a shambles, at least on the outside walls where Baghdad truly began. The concrete walls were cracked and broken, the barbed wire haphazard and bent. Large barriers that resembled steel cages full of sandbags were broken open, spilling their sand across the dilapidated highway. The convoy zigzagged between concrete barriers, jolting me back and forth in my seat, shaking and stirring the adrenaline in my blood. This was it—my first time in a real war zone, but not at all what I expected. Instead of the *Rambo*-esque scenes that Hollywood lionized throughout my childhood, we were packed like sardines in a rocketproof Chevy, encased from head to toe in body armor with every orifice covered or plugged with some sort of protective device. I felt simultaneously invincible, menacing, and absolutely ineffectual. With earplugs inserted, I could barely hear the massive engine as we raced to keep up with the Humvees, which lumbered like angry bulldogs through the sprawling metropolis. The streets were littered with garbage and concertina wire. Several improvised explosive devices (IEDs) had blown up large chunks of concrete on both sides of the roadway. Abandoned cars lay strewn about like scavenged carcasses of herd animals, killed by an unexpected drought.

Iraqi traffic stood still as we careened along the litter-strewn roads. Dilapidated cars ground to a halt, engines occasionally stalling with the sudden stop. Drivers shook their fists. Lanes had no meaning for us, and we frequently drove on the wrong side of the street, "to trick the roadside bombers." Drivers of the oncoming cars were terrified, sometimes spinning off the road in last-ditch efforts to prevent a head-on collision with our tanklike hulks. Every passerby on the sidewalk turned to behold the fearsome train of vehicles that automatically assumed the right-of-way. The multilingual signs on our bumpers were quite clear—"Stay back fifty meters or you will be shot." Every café patron and every child kicking a football barefoot by the concertina wire stopped to glare at our commanding, transient presence. From the sheltered innards of my opulent-looking coach, I felt every single stare. Occasionally an adolescent flashed a thumbs-up or a toddler waved in awe, but the adults all cast the same looks: resentment, jealousy, anger. Half a dozen beggar widows, shrouded from head to toe in black, shook their fists at us in angst, as though our convoy embodied everything that was wrong with their world. Maybe it did—maybe we had killed their husbands. As we drove away, the women sat on the street once more, their meager possessions beside them in boxes with Exxon logos.

The E-Team arrived at the Ministry of Electricity—a small, shabby building surrounded by concrete blast walls and razor wire. The guards were not Iraqi Army, but something even less organized. As politics played out, many of the large ministries preferred to keep their own security details rather than relying upon the Iraqi Army or the Ministry of Interior's politicized national police. Sectarian rivalries made the central government's control over each ministry a dubious question. At the time, I hadn't yet realized that many of the guards at the Ministry of Electricity were part of Moqtada al-Sadr's Shi'ite militia, the infamous Madhi Army. The prosthetist pulled to a stop by the building's entrance, hopped out, and swept the area for anything suspicious. *All clear.*

Captain Cross and I climbed out and headed toward the front door.

The prosthetist put his hand firmly on my shoulder, locked eyes with me, and ordered in a calm, fatherly tone, "Be courteous, be diplomatic, and always have a plan to kill everyone in the room."

We passed through a flimsy metal detector that made not a peep about our arsenal and armor. A handful of Iraqi security guards sat in the foyer, smoking cigarettes and shaking our hands as we entered.

"*Ahlan wa sahlan!*" Hello and welcome!

Cross motioned for me to follow, and we split off from the group and went down a dimly lit corridor. Dozens of posters of Moqtada al-Sadr lined the walls, as though the radical Shi'ite cleric was about to perform a concert in the park. Around a few corners and up a few broken marble staircases, Wilbur and I arrived at our destination. The captain knocked on a thin glass door, then walked in immediately.

Two Iraqi men in business suits stood up and greeted us. "Hallo, sir! Welcome, sir! Mr. Haitham is coming!"

The men in suits whisked us into an office, and a veiled woman entered, carrying a steaming pot of tea. The men in suits left for a moment, only to return with a small dish of candies. The veiled woman poured the tea into our tiny shot glasses, each rimmed with imitation gold and weighed down with hefty spoonfuls of sugar.

"*Shukran jazeelan.* Thank you very much," I said quietly.

She bowed her head and left without speaking a word.

"You get the sugar whether you like it or not," Wilbur whispered. "If you don't like it sweet, then don't stir it up."

As we finished the last syrupy sips of our tea, an Iraqi man in a somewhat nicer business suit entered the room. Cross stood up and I followed his lead. The man was Haitham Yaseen—a politician and technocrat who coordinated the flow of power from the generation sites to the cities. Haitham was the only person in Iraq who could properly manage the transmission network. He was an important official, made even more so by the circumstances of our war.

The high-voltage power lines carried electricity from power plants scattered around the country into the cities. Normally, these lines permitted Iraq to operate on a stable, synchronized grid of electricity, but in the summer of 2006 things were anything but normal. Two months earlier, a group of Al Qaeda extremists had coordinated an attack on the transmission lines, demolishing several transmission towers across the country and cutting the flow of power from the outlying provinces to Baghdad. The blow was crippling. At the same time that General Casey's much-talked-about Baghdad Security Plan was getting under way, the extremists shut off the lights on the six million people that Casey was hoping to protect. Needless to say, that kind of security won neither hearts nor minds. When the lines were cut, the electrical power that typically flowed into Baghdad remained out in the countryside, flooding the rural provinces with more power than they had ever seen under Saddam's rule. Tribal leaders seized the opportunity to thank Al Qaeda for bringing them electricity, while doing their best to prevent the restoration of the grid to normal functionality. Looters made off with tens of kilometers of high-grade aluminum cable from the transmission lines, selling the cable for scrap metal and burying the possibility of a quick repair.

Technically speaking, Haitham had his work cut out for him, but technicalities were the least of his problems. Haitham lit a cigarette and passed a small piece of paper over to Cross. It was a handwritten note—a death threat from Al Qaeda against Haitham and his family. It was the third threat he had received in a month.

"My job has become *difficult*, Wilbur," he explained with resignation and coolness, taking a draw on his cigarette. Haitham was around fifty, though the heaviness of his work weighed greatly upon his health. He was unnaturally thin and practically swimming in his clean, undersized suit.

"I'm sorry to hear that, Mr. Haitham."

Captain Cross slowly waltzed through a diplomatic litany of pleasantries. "How is your family doing?" *Blah blah blah* . . . "Iraqis like to talk about their families," Wilbur had explained to me privately. *Oh, you mean just like real people?*

Wilbur pulled out a box of pistol bullets and slid them across the desk.

"Thank you, sir. These are difficult for me to find."

Haitham gently hefted the box, like a child holding something precious. A few distant gunshots could be heard outside, but the conversation continued without pause.

Cross rattled off a series of questions about the downed power lines, scribbling notes on a small schematic that he unfolded from his notebook. It quickly became apparent that Wilbur was collecting the data for our PowerPoint slide, one painstaking question at a time. Haitham knew most of the answers to Wilbur's questions, but occasionally he picked up one of the four telephones on his desk to call his workers in the field directly. He seemed very polite about my captain's questions, but there was something more urgent that he wanted to talk about.

"Captain, we need your help."

"What is it, Mr. Haitham?"

"Our workers were attacked yesterday. Four more of them were kidnapped."

"That's terrible," I blurted out.

Wilbur remained motionless, unflinching.

Haitham begged. "We need security, Captain. My men are not soldiers."

Cross shifted in his seat uncomfortably. "I'll see what I can do."

He looked at his watch. "Excuse us, Mr. Haitham. The minister will be arriving soon."

Haitham nodded his head in agreement. "Yes, we must be going now."

The captain and I walked into the hallway lined with

Sadr-style wallpaper and broken chandeliers. I was over-whelmed with curiosity.

"What was that all about, Captain?"

"It's simple—they want troops, we don't have any."

"Sir, are you saying that we can't send *anyone* to help?"

"We could ask, but it's not going to happen, Chris."

"Why not?"

"The corps doesn't have enough troops."

"What about the kidnappings, Captain?"

"Chris, I'm not going to tell you to get used to it, but . . ."

An awkward pause finished Wilbur's thought.

"Come on, Chris. We've got another meeting to attend."

Captain Cross and I walked briskly down the corridor to the broken marble staircase, where Iraqi guards eyed us with a mixture of suspicion and envy (our guns and equipment were nicer). The minister of electricity was arriving shortly for a meeting with the E-Team. The minister's office looked like a modern boardroom, complete with a long table, micro-phones at each seat, and a large flat-screen television on the wall. Several men in suits brought trays of tea for the Ameri-can guests to sip during the meeting. Three other Iraqis in nicer suits were discussing details of power plants with Ian, the economist. The minister had not yet arrived. I took a seat as far from the head of the table as possible, showing deference to the much more senior officials present. When the minister arrived, both Americans and Iraqis stood to greet him.

"For this week, I am the minister of both electricity and oil," Dr. Karim Hassan Waheed declared proudly to the group in an authoritative, accented voice. The man wasn't joking—the minister of oil was out of town and Dr. Karim really was standing in.

"For this week only, my power plants will have enough fuel!"

The E-Team chuckled as the tensions of diplomatic for-mality broke. The minister smiled and took his seat at the head of the table. Dr. Karim's quip about getting enough fuel held a ring of truth. Widespread fuel shortages had shut down power plants across the country. Also, mismatches between the required fuel types and the fuels that were available in Iraq had caused even more power plants to shut down or, worse yet, to burn the wrong type of fuel in desperation, shortening the life of the equipment that could keep the lights from flickering out.

The meeting began with Ian, the E-Team's leader, updating the Iraqis on a difficult project. Earlier that year, the United States Agency for International Development had installed a state-of-the-art natural gas power plant near Kirkuk. This massive gas turbine, dubbed the Mother of All Generators, was commissioned in February with amazing fanfare from the *Washington Post* and the *New York Times*. Under Paul Bremer, the previous USAID director, James Stephenson, spent considerable time and effort getting the generator from the Mediterranean to its final destination. All the king's men lauded the investment of $240 million of American money—the natural gas turbine was a clean-burning, progressive step toward Iraqi energy independence under American leadership. Ironically, all the king's horses knew that three months after the Iraqi operators assumed control of the pristine turbine, it was nearly destroyed by improper operation on the unstable national grid.

The minister of electricity was furious about the damage to his country's largest and newest generator, and he requested that the E-Team go to inspect the facility. As Dr. Karim spoke, the air conditioner in the office went silent and the lights went out. It was my first blackout in Iraq (the Green Zone had its own American generators). I glanced at Captain Cross, who met my pleading gaze with his own look of resignation. *Get used to it, kid* . . . The cabinet minister—one of the most powerful men in Iraq—was so accustomed to the lights going out that he finished his sentence without skipping a beat. This was Dr. Karim's life in Baghdad. He was a

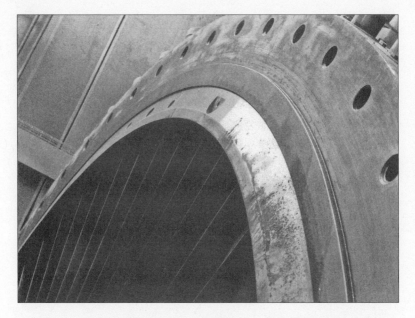

The exposed internal blades of a $240 million state-of-the-art
gas turbine—the single largest generator in Iraq. This brand-
new turbine was nearly destroyed by the unstable conditions
of Iraq's failing power grid and by desperate operators who
pushed the massive machine beyond its limits.

multicultural, bilingual diplomat with a Western Ph.D.,
stuck in a thoroughly modern office with state-of-the-art tele-
conferencing, microphones galore, a plasma-screen television—and not a single watt of power.

Dr. Karim earned his Ph.D. in mechanical engineering in
the United Kingdom. His vocabulary in English was impressive, even by native-speaker standards. The cabinet minister
chose his words meticulously and frequently finished the sentences of the less articulate Americans on the E-Team. He
made a point of being grammatically correct, asserting,
"*These* data *are* conclusive" and referring technical questions
to his "director*s* general." But he also spoke quite frequently
in Arabic (presumably also with a high level of grammar),
leaving our small team (with a high level of salary) not only
literally but figuratively in the dark. Whether Dr. Karim

spoke to his Iraqi colleagues in Arabic because their English was lacking or because he wanted to conceal his words from the foreigners I will never know. But the Arabic conversations were frequent and lasted for several minutes before the non-Arabs were once again invited to parley. Occasionally in the middle of a bout of Arabic, the minister would turn to Ian and demand his opinion, knowing full well that our fearless leader hadn't understood a single word.

"I think it's a great idea," Ian would reply, chuckling and lighting a cigarette. To Ian, it seemed, "Arab talk" was a good excuse for an in-place smoke break. During another long exchange between the minister and his directors general, Captain Cross leaned over toward me and whispered, "Sheesh! How do you think *they* would feel if we started talking to each other in Spanish?"

I laughed at the novel suggestion. "*¿Quiere hablar en español?*"

Flustered, Wilbur mumbled in a wavy Minnesotan warble, "Oh, uhhhh, I don't actually, uhhhh, speak Spanish either."

What a ship of fools we are! But whatever the language of our discourse, the conversation was punctuated with the full stop of a nearby explosion. The thin office windows rattled in their rickety frames. The minister started up and motioned for his men to follow him into the hallway, where the walls were thicker. I looked out the window apprehensively, searching for signs of the blast.

Wilbur cautioned me in a worried, fatherly tone. "I wouldn't stand too close to the window if I were you."

The captain had a point—if another blast went off, the flying glass could tear me to shreds. I felt suddenly childish for wanting to behold the destruction.

The prosthetist entered, still clad in his full body armor, motioning me close.

Easy there, Joe. I don't need a wooden leg yet.

"It was a truck bomb," Joe whispered, pressing his finger

to his radio earpiece to listen to the reports from around the city. Joe's eyes were wide open and nervous, but his voice remained calm and controlled.

"It wasn't that close . . . several blocks away . . . but we still need to get out of here. Pack up and meet me at the convoy in five minutes. I'll go grab the others."

"Yes, sir."

I grabbed my helmet and notebook, then reached behind my back instinctively to check for my concealed pistol. *Still there.* For some strange reason, the gun gave me comfort.

The E-Team rendezvoused in the parking lot, where our ad hoc security detail waited. The prosthetist nodded as I approached, apparently relieved that I didn't have to kill everyone in the room that morning. Ian flashed a thumbs-up as he donned his helmet and hopped into a Humvee, disappearing behind its thick rocketproof glass.

With that, our mission was over. The E-Team saddled up, plugged ourselves with protective devices, and rode back to the Green Zone. The trip was a blur. The angry faces that had glared at our convoy as we stopped lunch-hour traffic were replaced with desperation and panic in the aftermath of the bombing. The radio chattered away with reports of snipers on a downtown rooftop, while the butterflies in my stomach evolved into small, flightless birds. Some gunshots fired a few hundred yards away.

I was appalled by the breadth of our problems. Kidnappings, decimated infrastructure, failed projects, looting, death threats from terrorists, and the shocking absence of American soldiers to save the day were the tip of the iceberg, and this iceberg wasn't about to melt. After what seemed like hours, our convoy crossed through the security checkpoints, and our shiny black steeds pulled into the "stables." While the E-Team was nothing like the Rough Riders that Roosevelt had led, it was becoming clear that the year ahead would prove to be anything but just another desk job.

10

Ramadan Soirée

The celebration of Ramadan begins with an observation of the moon. This lunar month of religious fasting is not started automatically on a specific calendar date or predicted by the calculation of astronomers but pronounced upon the moon's actual physical sighting. Almanacs be damned; only the clerics know when the moon will be just right for this religious holiday to commence. The Muslim clergy's insistence upon actual observance of the moon may seem strange to a non-Muslim, but it's really no stranger than an American waiting for a groundhog to see its shadow. Besides, from a scientific standpoint, a visual sighting of the moon's phase is a lot easier to verify than a subjective assessment of whether or not some furry little beast actually sees any particular thing at all. And unlike Ramadan, the presumptuousness of the Pennsylvanian tradition begs the literary question of whether there ought to be a groundhoggian equivalent of the word "lunatic." Furthermore, while tens of thousands of multilingual moon-spotting clerics exist, the difference is exacerbated by the global shortage of qualified linguists who can actually speak to groundhogs.

I like Ramadan. I like Groundhog Day. In all seriousness, I even like Santa Claus, Buddha, Jesus, and the Easter Bunny. I would happily have them all over for Iraqi chai if given the chance. Of course, outsiders would logically regard such hospitality as outrageous. And honestly, I don't really believe in all of these gods and customs and things, but that's not outrageous—one can't logically believe in all of them. Quite simply, the world would be much less interesting to me without the possibilities afforded by six-armed, scimitar-wielding goddesses, red-nosed anthropomorphic reindeer, and Punxsutawney Phil's penchant for divination. For that reason alone, I'm willing to hang my criticisms on the door and let the spiteful outsiders hurl stones at Ramadan while the Easter Bunny and I enjoy our pot of tea.

In my earliest days of submarine life, my own observation of the moon nearly got me killed. No, Jerry Falwell didn't issue a fatwa against me for seating Jesus next to Muhammad at a Ramadan soirée. Reality is much more banal.

It was midnight on the North Atlantic in spring. As our ship sailed in darkness through a thick ocean fog, I scoured the horizon for signs of light. There were fishermen afoot (well, afloat, actually)—Narragansett Bay, miles and miles from shore, was the best place to trawl the ocean's waters. On a clearer night in this locale, we had seen dozens of trawlers at once, their running lights piercing the dark like fireflies on the water. But on this night the fog was so thick that we couldn't make out our own stern light, less than three hundred feet from the periscope. The radar screen looked like pea soup from a high school cafeteria; the little green blips could have been anything. Crab pots? Merchants? Waves? Maybe the blips were just fishermen, asleep under a blanket of mist on a warm night at sea. It was a tense drive, but not because of our own safety—we were trying not to hit and sink another vessel with our thick steel hull. American submarines are painted black for stealth, and most of their mass lies below the surface, invisible. Even if another vessel could see our puny running lights, it was unlikely to recognize what we were or the inherent danger of our hulking presence. The tension in the control room was high as we threaded our way through the radar soup bowl in complete blindness.

I strained my eyes to find something, anything, in the darkness. A pure white light began to break through the fog. My heart raced! If it was close enough for me to see it, then it was close enough to collide with us at any second! I fell back on my training, announcing the contact's presence to the control team.

"Initial observation, victor seven, number two scope."

The party fell silent, in rapt attention of my every word.

"Bearing, mark!" The fire control technician entered the contact into the tracking computer.

The senior officer in control, Rick, urgently demanded, "What is it? We don't have anything on radar in that sector!"

"I don't know, sir! I can only see a light!!"

My eye was jumping out of its socket to see better. The tension in control mounted and the light began to take shape. A lump formed in my throat. Fifteen people waited in suspense as my single eyeball acted as the ship's only sensor that could tell if we were about to have a collision. I wanted to laugh.

"Mr. Brownfield, how far away is the contact?" Rick demanded.

"It's pretty far away, sir."

"Dammit, Brownfield! *How* far is it?"

"It's the moon, sir."

The control team breathed a sigh of relief.

"I don't think we're gonna hit it."

The crew chuckled, and I fought to keep my composure, perhaps a little too amused by my own joke. With my eye glued to the scope in a spiraling search for contacts, I couldn't see that Rick didn't share my humor. He was fuming. As a former Naval Academy football player, Rick once held the school's bench-press record for hefting over 450 pounds. When he was angry, he looked like a bull about to charge. As I circled the horizon in my visual search, the now infamous white light shone before me once more.

"Yup, it's the moon, all right," I quipped in a lighthearted tone. The crew chuckled again. Steam started pouring from Rick's nostrils and ears.

I lingered for a few seconds, unaware of my impending doom while getting a better look and chiming, "Oh, hey! It's a waxing gibbous!"

The crew broke into laughter, but Rick nearly exploded. His powerful arm grabbed me by the shoulder and yanked me away from the scope as he growled through clenched teeth, "Mr. Brownfield! Your continued presence is neither required nor desired!"

"Aye, aye, sir," I yelped sheepishly, turning tail and fleeing the control room. On my way out, the quartermaster flipped furiously through his nautical almanac—he was looking up the moon's phase.

"I'll be damned," he declared, raising aloft his little orange book of nautical wisdom, index finger pointing triumphantly to the page. "It *is* a waxing gibbous!"

In Baghdad, three years later, the morning slide show commenced precisely on schedule. General Casey, unusually attentive, had an important question to ask the headquarters' most important staff member.

"When does Ramadan start? Doesn't it have something to do with the *moon*?"

The Strategic Weather Woman froze like a deer in headlights. It was uncomfortably silent. The weatherheads were rarely ever asked any questions by the general, let alone questions about the moon. *Who the hell knew that kind of stuff, anyway?* On most occasions, she simply read her script and the slide show advanced without comment.

"In the north, the weather will consist of dust and dusty winds. In the south, the weather will consist of dust and dusty winds. *Next slide, please.* In the west, the weather will be mostly sunny, with bouts of dust . . . and dusty winds."

We typically endured the litany without complaint, but today was different.

"What I want to know," the general repeated, "is if we know when Ramadan starts. Is it Saturday or Sunday?"

Reduced to a stammering child by his digital awesomeness, she blurted out a desperate guess. "Uhhh . . . Saturday, sir!"

Casey glared. It was an important question. His theory was that murders and executions would decline once Ramadan began. If correct, then such a theory could prove how far America had come in learning the all-important nuances of Iraqi culture; victory would be within our grasp. It felt like generalizing about American values by counting Christmas suicides, but there was no stopping Casey when it came to statistics. One day, some glorious number would descend from the heavens, appear before him in that glimmering slide show, and the entire war would make perfect sense.

The first weekend of Ramadan, I lunched by Saddam's pool, nibbling gleefully on the greasiest of Halliburton's fare. Lieutenant Kim, the youngest of the Kim Collection, joined me with a plate full of octopus jerky and a sidelong look of diplomatic disgust.

"How can you eat that stuff?" He laughed, motioning to my buffalo chicken wings soaking in a puddle of artificial Ranch dressing. His Korean cabbage smelled like bile.

"That's funny. I was gonna ask you the same thing."

Kim smiled and took a seat. Culinary preferences aside, we had a lot to talk about. Kim was ecstatic about Ban Ki-moon's nomination to succeed Kofi Annan at the helm of the United Nations. It was an unexpected nomination, not only because South Korea had never before held such a high international post but also because the previous favorite for the job had been killed by a suicide bomber in Iraq. Sergio Vieira de Mello was perhaps the most qualified candidate, but after his death, a Korean nominee would likely prove beneficial to both our countries' interests. After all, the Koreans were one of the greatest of America's allies in the coalition, second in troop counts only to the Brits.

"Speaking of interesting nominations . . ." I changed course. "What do you think about the ambassador here?"

Zalmay Khalilzad had been the U.S. ambassador for quite some time, having left his post in his motherland, Afghanistan, to take the reins in Iraq. Kim shrugged his shoulders, indifferent.

"Well," I declared, "I think the man's a rock star."

Kim laughed—not what I was expecting.

I became defensive. "No, really . . . the guy's a rock star. Uh, at least as far as politicians are concerned." I had to qualify my first statement, segregating the political rock stars from rock stars who are actually considered by the general public to be cool. But our ambassador *was* a rock star . . . sort of. Wherever Khalilzad went, an entourage of powerful people floated alongside under an impenetrable shield of security guards bristling with guns and ammo. Compared to the military security guards, the ruggedly stylish Blackwater men looked like bouncers from the trendiest gun club in town. Foreign Service officers rounded out Zalmay's posse, dressed to the nines like it was a D.C. country club instead of Baghdad. The diplomats were young, good-looking, and bedecked with Ivy League résumés. Needless to say, I was a bit jealous.

"Think about it, Kim . . . this ambassador's been the go-to guy for the administration in both Afghanistan and Iraq. Who else could handle that kind of responsibility—and speak the native languages?"

"You got me."

As an Afghan-born, Arabic-speaking Ph.D., Khalilzad was an ideal candidate for understanding how this part of the world functioned. The fact that Condoleezza Rice and President George W. Bush couldn't pronounce his name correctly was only a mild detraction from his diplomatic stardom. But despite his ain't-from-Texas accent, Khalilzad used his unique abilities to attain great political power, earning the coveted title Ambassador Extraordinary and Plenipotentiary of the United States of America to Afghanistan.

"I'd really love to meet the guy," I remarked, nibbling on a deep-fried jalapeño popper with delectable cream cheese filling.

Kim smirked incredulously. "What for? His autograph?"

A Blackwater security agent at the table next to us interrupted. "You really wanna meet the ambassador?"

Kim and I froze, greatly interested, and I nodded.

"That can be arranged; I'm on his security detail."

"Cool! Thanks!"

The Blackwater agent and I exchanged business cards, and a big smile crept onto my face. Kim's eyebrows raised in surprise.

"Expect an e-mail from his assistant," the agent told me.

"Yeah. Uhhh . . . we can have his people contact my people." The agent smirked, then left the table shaking his head and muttering, "Rock star."

"Lucky you," Kim laughed, taking his last bite of cabbage. "By the way, Chris—who exactly are *your people*?"

"Just you wait, Kim. Someday I'll have *people* to do my bidding."

"In the meantime," Kim chided, rolling his eyes, crossing his arms, and kicking back in his chair, "why don't you get me some coffee?"

Time became a quagmire. Captain Cross and I continued our work, piecing together the daily slide show from data we squeezed out of the ministry. Assembling a complete list of problems with Iraq's electrical sector was like drinking water from a fire hose. The E-Team returned several more times to the Red Zone, but the missions quickly became routine. Wilbur wanted nothing more than to find the facts for the daily report; anything beyond that was someone else's job.

Every week more electrical towers were toppled, more equipment was looted, and more threats were made against Haitham and his family. A critical power line had been cut, blacking out half a million people for several weeks. The repairmen refused to fix the line, for fear of retaliation against their families. A ransom note demanded $10,000 for the safe return of four Iraqi workers who had recently disappeared.

"Where am I supposed to find so much money?" Haitham worried aloud, exasperated by his futile sense of responsibility. The ransom went unpaid.

Nothing had improved since my arrival in Baghdad two months earlier. The workers lacked security, the Iraqi Army was on another planet, the national police were corrupted by sectarian politics, and the Americans didn't have enough troops to help.

"What about the army's engineers?" I asked the captain, baffled by our inability to bring resources to bear on the problem. But the Army Corps of Engineers had changed a lot since previous wars. No longer did our soldiers perform any of the construction work themselves—they simply outsourced every job to high-paid civilian contractors. They had become, in effect, a middleman for defense contracting. In late 2006 the Corps' purse strings were drawn tight; its $8 billion budget was spent. Ironically, even if the army engineers could have done the job, they wouldn't have been able to do it as fast as the Iraqis. When it came to rebuilding sabotaged towers and pipelines, the Iraqis had become the fastest in the world.

One afternoon in the palace, two of our officers shared the same birthday. General Kim ordered a cake to commemorate the occasion. After an off-key rendition of "Happy Birthday," one of the colonels leaned over to blow out the candles.

The general shouted, "No!"

The directorate froze, startled as if someone had pulled a gun.

"You make wish first," the general explained softly, his lips pursed in a thin mechanical smile.

The office breathed a sigh of relief as the two colonels, both in their late fifties, made their silent birthday wishes.

The general confirmed the situation. "Have you made wish?"

The colonels nodded. "Yes, sir."

"Now, blow out candle," Kim directed. The colonels executed the order, then looked up again, waiting for the next step in the procedure. Kim stood silent. One of the birthday boys started cutting the cake.

"No!" the general shouted once more. Again the crowd stiffened.

"You must cut cake to-ge-ther," General Kim ordained.

Afraid of causing an international incident, the two colonels each put one hand upon the knife and ever so slowly sliced the first piece of birthday cake, peeking up at the general to see if they were doing it right.

Incidentally, there was also a wedding anniversary to celebrate. General Kim presented the sojourner spouse with wooden statuettes of two kissing ducks symbolizing love. The female duck had a tiny pink ribbon tied around her beak to keep it shut; none of us had the courage to ask why, and apparently, neither did the duck.

When Ambassador Khalilzad's people called, it proved to be worth the wait. The ambassador's assistant found out that I was bound for Yale and leaning toward the Foreign Service. Apparently she decided to seize the opportunity to recruit me. And what better way for the State Department to recruit than to show me firsthand what American diplomacy was all about? The invitation was to an Iftar feast at the house of Dr. Ahmed Chalabi. *Cool,* I thought. *What's an Iftar? Who's Ahmed Chalabi?*

These were important questions, but the invitation also mentioned something that seemed at the time a much more pressing concern. There was a dress code: no camouflage allowed. Unfortunately, my entire wardrobe of civilian clothing amounted to a single T-shirt with a comical juxtaposition of Che Guevara and Bart Simpson. If I was going to ride with the rock stars, I needed to find a way to dress like one.

Fortunately, Giovanni happened to have a suit that fit me perfectly. It was a green tweed, lawyerly-looking getup, but it would do the trick. *Besides,* I thought, *I'm not trying to pick up chicks.* Even so, the washed-out black polyester tie he loaned me was flat-out unacceptable, even in Baghdad's fashion circles. Beyond the trailer park of fast-food restaurants with McDonald's, Burger King, and Pizza "Hat" sat the *haji* shop, where I purchased a knockoff Ralph Lauren tie. *Ready to rock!*

Ahmed Chalabi was an Iraqi-born Gentile with degrees from MIT and American University of Beirut—an intellectual and a politically connected heavyweight whose far-reaching family ties led to the top of Arab society. Ahmed's uncle was a senior OPEC official; his cousin was a former oil minister of Iraq. While Ahmed was exiled in London, he received nearly $80 million from the U.S. State Department to support his Iraqi National Congress—an opposition group against Saddam Hussein. By that night in 2006, most accounts placed overall responsibility on Chalabi for feeding Colin Powell and the U.S. intelligence community bogus reports of weapons of mass destruction. While the secret informant, "Curveball," didn't actually work for Chalabi, the two are believed to have collaborated in convincing America to go to war. Ambassador Peter Galbraith, a longtime friend of Ahmed, wrote that Chalabi had indeed lied to encourage the invasion. Nevertheless, Galbraith explained, it was understandable for Chalabi to lie—he was an Iraqi exile who wanted to get rid of Saddam and return home.

The United States had lofty plans for Chalabi. After the invasion, he was appointed to the positions of transitional president, deputy prime minister, and chairman of the energy committee (a failed effort to consolidate Iraq's oil and electricity under a unified energy ministry). When full-time Iraqis rejected Chalabi's appointments, Paul Bremer saw to it that the good doctor was gainfully employed as a hatchet man. De-Ba'athification—the political purging of Saddam's Ba'ath Party from the Iraqi government—would soon be regarded as one of the most critical mistakes of the war. The Ba'ath Party was much more than just a collection of Saddam's cronies; it was a comprehensive professional organization to which most doctors, lawyers, and ministerial officials in Iraq belonged as a matter of necessity. In this regard, Chalabi's return from London on the coattails of Americans to cut off the head of Iraqi professional society made him one of the most hated men in the country. In the 2005 elections, Chalabi's Iraqi National Congress failed to win a single seat in Parliament. Nevertheless, I was personally thrilled by the opportunity to meet both the chargé d'affaires extraordinaire and the infamous doctor at the same time. Besides, it would be fun to hang up the camouflage and play diplomat for a day.

On the night of the feast, I knotted my designer-impostor tie in a perfect double Windsor, donned my borrowed tweed suit, strapped on my Kevlar helmet, and headed to the rendezvous point. For the first time in two months I left my trusty pistol behind; killing everyone in the room was not on the evening's agenda. In the palace rotunda, a small group of Foreign Service officers waited, lounging on an ornate couch. Several of the diplomats were attractive young women, dressed in summery blouses and slacks (skirts were verboten during Ramadan). I immediately regretted settling for the lawyerly tweed suit. It would have been nice to make a better first impression with the desert princesses—the first women of childbearing age I had spoken to in months. The ambassador's assistant greeted me with a warm smile and introduced me to the others. It was time to go. The men took off their jackets and strapped on their armor. The women followed suit, slipping into something a little less comfortable.

Blackwater drove the ambassador's convoy, and they drove like professional maniacs. Instead of using tanklike Humvees, the Blackwater agents chauffeured their high-value targets exclusively in shiny American SUVs. The drivers swerved back and forth across the highways, quickly passing each other, then slowing to be passed with random precision. It was a life-and-death shell game for the would-be assassins and roadside bombers.

Dr. Chalabi's compound resembled an American military base—from the outside, it was nothing but concrete and razor wire. A handful of henchmen stood watch over an iron gate and waved us through a narrow passageway. Inside, the property seemed remarkably normal—there was a yard and a large diesel generator. The house looked well built, with a pleasant veranda under a canopy of date palms. On that warm September evening at twilight, Chalabi's home could well have passed for a desert island getaway—an oasis from the chaos.

The home was clean and comfortable compared to the shabby governmental offices of the ministries. It wasn't extravagant by American standards, but it was certainly nicer than the homes of Iraqis who had never faced the indignity of exile to posh London apartments. The spacious house boasted Western furniture like sofas and lamps and coffee tables, whereas many Iraqis of Baghdad simply sat on the floor under uncovered lightbulbs. A tray of fresh dates sat on the coffee table. The scrumptious little bites were a stark contrast to the shriveled imported dates that Halliburton served (regulations prevented the serving of local food for fear of poisoning). A man in a Western business suit invited us to break the Ramadan fast by partaking of the delicious-looking morsels. We refused the first offering out of customary politeness, then gratefully accepted the second. The dates were perfect, with a firm, moist texture and the sweet but subtle complexity of a fruit that spends its entire life concentrating in the desert sun. The beet may be the most intense of vegetables, but only the date has wisdom.

From the doorway a flash of motion caught my eye. The ambassador had arrived. A flood of Iraqi henchmen in cheap suits surrounded Khalilzad to lavish him with formalities. Strangely, we had traveled together in the same convoy, but this was my first glimpse of the rock star up close. My spine tingled in his presence—I straightened my posture and smiled like a fawning sycophant. A second later, the lord of the manor entered in an expensive Western suit and tie. Chalabi grasped the ambassador's hand and beckoned us to begin the feast. The table held a spread of Middle Eastern cuisine the likes of which I had never seen. Platters of grilled lamb, curried chicken, whole roasted peppers, freshly baked flatbreads, and spinach salad with onions covered the entire dining room table. The diplomats and I filled our plates and drifted out to the veranda. From the moment we sat down to eat, manservants attended to our every desire, offering up freshly squeezed apricot juice, cups of intensely soured yoghurt, and bowls of spinach soup. I accepted all in a foolish quest to sample the whole smorgasbord.

Ahmed and Zalmay chatted for a moment, recounting their years at university in both Beirut and Chicago. By strange coincidence, both men had either studied at or taught at both universities during their lives. But the small talk didn't last long—Chalabi hadn't arranged this Ramadan soirée to reminisce about the past, and Khalilzad seemed to understand.

"So, you want to rejoin the political process?" Zalmay questioned in a nasal, high-pitched voice.

My ears perked up like those of a puppy whose master had come home.

"Yes, yes, of course," Chalabi answered with enthusiasm.

Though he had lived in England from his early childhood, Chalabi spoke with a pronounced Arabic accent that many considered to be feigned; he knew the role he was expected to play. Despite his dubious past, I couldn't believe what I was hearing—the man had lost handily in the 2005 elections, but my State Department was there in force to reopen the door that the people of Iraq had democratically closed in Chalabi's face. The doctor wanted power and the ambassador seemed to be offering it.

A servant interrupted my concentration with a platter full of spiced-beef cutlets. I had already finished my first plate and whispered a polite no. Unfortunately, I think he heard *na'am*, which means "yes" in Arabic. Anyway, I got the beef cutlets, which were oh so succulent and tasty. My stomach started to stretch. When I was growing up in Michigan, my mother taught me to eat the food that I had taken. In Arabia, however, the host traditionally shows his wealth and generosity by intentionally giving his guests more food than they can possibly eat. This generosity is legendary, to the point that a poor Arabian man will feed a Bedouin traveler before he feeds his own family, even if the children starve. Needless to say, I was completely ignorant of this bicultural contradiction. I raced to empty my plate; they raced to show their hospitality by filling it up again. My expanding stomach and all of Arab tradition were at loggerheads. It felt like a trap—delicious, but still a trap. The platter of curried chicken came back for round two. I couldn't resist; I literally didn't know how. And when the food was already on my plate, I couldn't leave it there— that would have been rude. Allah be praised, both the ambassador and Dr. Chalabi ate lightly that evening, and the dinner ended just as my stomach was about to explode. The entourage filed into the house, and I in my little green suit waddled behind them.

The conversation continued in Chalabi's living room. The lack of electricity was the biggest complaint. Chalabi lamented the sorry state of the transmission lines, wondering aloud how much longer the people of Baghdad could take it. The great city of Baghdad had been cosmopolitan in the fifties and sixties, but now it seemed more like the Middle Ages. Chalabi complained of his government's inability to spend its $7 billion federal surplus—a major bureaucratic roadblock. While Ambassador Paul Bremer made frequent use of his unchallenged executive power by disbanding the Iraqi Army, he did not install an effective temporary system for distributing Iraq's oil revenues to its provinces and cabinet ministries. On the contrary, he imposed an American system of federal procurement that instantly transformed Baghdad into a complicated computer-age bureaucracy with six hours of electricity per day.

When Iraq's officials were able to spend their government's money, they were often accused and convicted of corruption. Chalabi didn't lose any sleep over such accusations; he simply wanted power.

"Give me control of one American regiment—no questions asked—and Iraq will be restored to order in a month."

A twinkle of lust flashed across Ahmed's eyes. I could only imagine what kind of strongman he wanted to become . . . but did he really think that winning the war could be as simple as lording it over Iraq with the iron fists of ten thousand American soldiers unchecked by the ethics of war? On that note, Khalilzad stood and beckoned Chalabi to join him in private while the rest of the diplomats waited. Two more servants paraded silver trays of baklava and gold-rimmed demitasses of Turkish coffee. A third followed with thin slices of perfectly ripened honeydew.

"This is *awesome*," I gushed to the young woman sitting next to me on Chalabi's plush couch as I sniffed my honeydew in delight. The lovely young diplomat smiled, apparently quite pleased herself. With the night's business out of the way, I couldn't help but notice that she was extremely attractive—even compared to the other desert princesses. I turned on my "suave mode" and went to work. *Might as well try to get her phone number* . . .

"What's your name?"

"Jessica."

"Good to meet you." I smiled, doing my best to show more than casual interest without being too obvious (after all, it was kind of a weird place to flirt).

Another diplomat with a shaved head and a politician's smile interrupted my subtle overture. "What do you think they're talking about back there?" he asked, referring to the ambassador and our host.

"No idea," Jessica said with a shrug.

In my estimation, Khalilzad was probably helping Chalabi to proofread his résumé.

"You need more action verbs, Ahmed," the ambassador explained in my imaginary dialogue. "Don't say that Iraq 'benefited' from your leadership. Say that you 'restored' Iraq to glory! And where's that bullet about your presidential experience?"

"I thought I'd leave it out."

"Don't be ridiculous! Write this down: 'Served as president of the Republic of Iraq for one term.' "

"But it was only a month . . ."

"Everybody embellishes a little."

On the ride home from the feast, I sat next to Jessica in the van. Normally, there would have been plenty of space, but our cumbersome body armor made it necessary to pack together like sardines. Her leg rubbed against me with every bump and swerve.

"So, do you go by Jess or Jessica?"

"Jess is fine, but for some strange reason everybody calls me Jessica Rabbit."

"I believe you," I responded with an ear-to-ear grin. Apparently Jess was too young to know of the cartoon sexpot, and I was too old to believe my luck.

Another Foreign Service officer jumped into the conversation. "Hey, what does Chalabi do in Iraq now, anyway?"

Another diplomat answered, "Nothing important. I don't understand why we even bothered to go there."

Some of the junior diplomats hadn't caught the drift of the meeting. The senior Foreign Service officers remained silent. I quipped lightheartedly, "Yeah, but it was the best baklava I've ever had." The diplomats chuckled; as odious as the man may have been, Ahmed Chalabi's baklava was beyond reproach. Our Blackwater convoy raced back and forth across the road, and Jessica leaned into me again and again. I could not have contained my excitement had it not been for my hefty Kevlar groin protector.

We gazed out the window as I wondered what the hell had just happened. I had expected to learn firsthand what American diplomacy was all about, but this was a whole different animal. The stars were bright, and as always, the arid sky was cloudless. Our bulletproof car crested an overpass, revealing the flat and sprawling city below. In the midnight light of the Ramadan moon, only one thing was clear to me: across Baghdad the power was out.

11

Black Gold

The environmental movement in America destroyed my family's perfectly good name. It's not that they caught us dumping chemicals into rivers or pouring crude oil down the backs of sea otters while giggling with delight and counting our profits. No, it was a lexical matter. According to contemporary dictionaries, a "brownfield" is a former industrial or commercial site where future use is affected by real or perceived environmental contamination. In other words, it's an industrial wasteland. While I grew up in Michigan, it was perpetually embarrassing to read the headlines of the *Detroit Free Press*:

MAYOR OF DETROIT VOWS TO
RID THE CITY OF BROWNFIELDS

BROWNFIELDS A PERENNIAL PROBLEM
FOR DEVELOPMENT

$1.2 MILLION ALLOCATED TO
CLEAN UP THE BROWNFIELDS

When I first arrived aboard my submarine, a fellow officer exclaimed upon meeting me, "Holy shit! I did my thesis on brownfields!"

Fascinating, I thought. *It must have been a brilliant read.*

But unlike my family, the top oilman in the coalition didn't need the collateral damage of progressive environmental lingo to tarnish his name; John T. Wellman managed to accomplish that feat all by himself.

"Why the hell are we spending ten million dollars on ID cards?" Wellman barked at the men who sat around a 1970s Arab art deco table in the palace-cum-embassy. John was a large man to begin with, but his imposing figure was made even more so by his expensive suit, his shirt with embroidered initials on French cuffs, an impressive Rolex, and a college class ring the size of a baseball. John was the spitting image of the modern Texas Oilman—bigger than life and tough as nails.

"John, it's not just IDs," Kurt answered politely but firmly. "That money will purchase biometrics, ID cards, and a central database for the Iraqi government to track and vet its employees."

Kurt was the State Department's hired gun for implementing a program to secure Iraq's infrastructure. As a former police chief who regularly competed at karaoke, Kurt was by no means academic, but by all means social and pragmatic. At the time, Iraqis who befriended the right officials were double-dipping from the treasury, drawing salaries from multiple ministries at once. Militiamen from Sadr's Madhi Army had infiltrated the ministries, using their inside knowledge to wreak havoc on the government's repair and reconstruction efforts. This infiltration was partly to blame for the downed power lines that kept electricity from flowing into Baghdad. Kurt's plan for biometrics and ID cards would virtually eliminate the possibility of infiltration and double-dipping. That morning, our meeting was the final discussion before settling on the infrastructure security budget—$276 million. Kurt's plan was well organized, and the meeting would have lasted less than half an hour except for the incessant protests of one particular man.

" . . . Then why the hell are we spending $50 million on a goddam fence?" Wellman continued like a broken record. Combativeness was John's default position, and admitting ignorance would have caused a fatal implosion of his Texas-sized ego. Kurt drew a deep breath. Colonel Dawson, who abstained from sitting at the same table out of deference to Wellman, simply rolled his eyes. *Here we go again . . .*

The fence that Wellman complained about was the reason I was there. Over the past few weeks, I had spent my off time doing research on technologies that could help to secure the pipelines and electrical towers. I looked for motion sensors, video surveillance, automated weapons, and land mines with exploding dye packs (to catch and interrogate the bad guys instead of just killing them). The work was a wild brain-storming effort that elicited a few chuckles from the others by virtue of the overly important title I gave it: the Asymmetrical Strategic Defense Initiative. The week after sharing the work with the State Department consultants, they mocked me by singing the *Star Wars* theme song whenever I entered the room.

"Didn't you know that Reagan already used that name?" they chided, alluding to the "Star Wars" missile defense sys-tem (officially the Strategic Defense Initiative).

"Guess that was before my time," I apologized sheepishly while feeling extremely dumb.

My work drew upon the research of an MIT professor who studied engineering for social control—basically con-trolling criminal behavior through better system design. I rec-ommended burying and fortifying pipelines, putting them out of sight or making them resistant to the frequent attacks. The law-enforcement aspects of my work resonated with the police chief in Kurt, and he invited me to join the final dis-cussion on his quarter-billion-dollar budget.

The consensus among Kurt and the military officers was that building a security fence around the pipelines near Bagh-dad would improve the energy position of the capital city by protecting its fuel supplies. A security fence was the worst way to secure a stretch of oil pipeline—except for all the others.

Frankly, we were desperate to try anything. The attacks on pipelines and electrical towers around Baghdad had reached the tipping point. On some summer days, if there had been any less energy, the water treatment plants would have had to shut down, and that city of six million would have gone dry. Without running water, the citizens would have been forced to drink from the polluted rivers—a potentially deadly alternative to the irrepressible desert heat. Fortunately, the attacks on energy infrastructure were focused in a small geographic area. Building security zones around the area would force the attackers away from the city and out of their comfort zones to areas where they could be more easily stopped or caught. Kurt called for guard towers, snipers, and razor wire along these critical miles of infrastructure, but he also wanted to equip and train the Iraqis who were tasked with guarding the oil pipelines. Under Saddam, tens of thousands of soldiers guarded the pipelines with rigid discipline, but Paul Bremer had put a stop to that order by disbanding the Iraqi Army. In 2006 the guards who "secured" the pipelines were the Arab equivalents of redheaded stepchildren: ignored, underequipped, undertrained, and even underfed.

To everyone but John Wellman, it was essential to build up more physical security and provide a stable situation to rebuild the energy sector. John, however, dismissed the military's efforts to work with him, repeatedly claiming, "Security is not my problem."

Colonel Dawson had another opinion, which he stated only when Wellman was nowhere to be seen. "Dammit! Security is everybody's problem!"

Colonel Dawson had a special relationship with Wellman. It was clear that Dawson's blend of oil industry knowledge and military expertise made him a threat to Wellman's authority. For that reason, Wellman apparently did everything in his power to prevent Dawson from having influence. John withheld information about important events, refused to invite Dawson to meetings, and complained very publicly when a pipeline was blown to smithereens. At one point Wellman seemed so threatened that he demanded that Pete remove himself from the "big boy" table of high-paid State Department consultants. The colonel acquiesced, choosing to face personal humiliation rather than being cast out of the loop without accomplishing his mission. But the relationship between the State Department and the military was strained for bigger reasons than territorial pissing. There was the matter of intentions.

"I can't fathom why Wellman is putting all of State's money into well makeovers," Dawson declared bluntly one morning.

"What do you mean, Colonel?"

"Wellman spent his entire budget on upgrading the oil wells! All he seems to care about is getting Iraq ready for business!"

"What about the insurgency, Colonel? The oil's useless if Iraq can't get it to market."

Peter shook his head in desperation, agreeing with me. "It just doesn't make any sense to be 'priming the pump' when the pipelines can't last a week without getting blown up!"

But well makeovers were only the technical side of pump priming. To the diplomats in Khalilzad's entourage, Wellman was a mere technocrat, a useful tool for greasing the skids toward the real prize—liberalization. Getting Iraq's hydrocarbon law through parliament was State's number one objective. If Iraq was able to open the doors to the major-league oil companies, then billions of dollars in capital would pour into the country, stimulate the economy, and placate the malcontents. Of course, a liberalized Iraq would also provide a steady stream of oil to help stabilize the world market. OPEC would be weakened, Iraq would prosper, oil would remain cheap, and America's energy habits would not have to change.

The confrontation with Wellman and the lofty objectives

of State weighed upon Colonel Dawson day in and day out. As he reeled from the repeated blows of the insurgency, the State Department fought tooth and nail to open the doors to international business. The story was nothing new; when America had rescued Kuwait from the clutches of Saddam Hussein fifteen years earlier, the Kuwaiti government promised, in extremis, to open its oil fields to foreign investment. But when the war was over and Saddam had been ousted, the political will for liberalization never materialized in Kuwait's parliament. To this day, Kuwait's oil remains nationalized.

Despite the colorful history and bureaucratic dynamics, I was encouraged by the meeting with Kurt. Iraq needed the security measures that we were planning. Iraq needed to guard the pipelines and electrical towers. Iraq needed to crack down on corruption. But inexplicably, none of the measures that Kurt planned actually came to pass. Shortly after our meeting, the entire collection of contracts and plans that Kurt had meticulously crafted vanished into thin air. The paper contracts disappeared, Kurt's computer crashed, and the network backups were mysteriously deleted. In the next appropriations bill passed by Congress, a significant portion of Kurt's infrastructure security budget was cut.

"I didn't spend the money fast enough," he explained to me in abject confusion. "I just don't understand what happened . . . Someone pulled the rug out from under me!"

But while someone in the headquarters was pulling the rug out from under Kurt, Giovanni the attorney was pulling back the curtain on the detention system. One afternoon, Giovanni arrived in the ballroom with a hangdog look upon his face. He sat next to me, red-faced and silent, staring straight down at his keyboard.

Wilbur looked up with grandfatherly concern. "What's up? You look distressed."

"I am distressed, sir," the commander replied mechanically. "I was just fired."

"Fired? *Jeesh*, what happened?" Wilbur asked, dropping the papers on his desk and peering over his bifocals.

"Apparently I asked too many questions."

As a seasoned attorney and legislator, Giovani had complained to his chain of command about the way detentions were being carried out. According to him, the legal process was still stacked against the Iraqis, many of whom Giovani insisted were innocent and denied any sort of legal process to prove it. Specifically, Commander Panetti complained because the boards still didn't include the required Iraqi officials, and none of the board members who reviewed cases even spoke Arabic.

"The bottom line is I pulled back the curtain, and they asked me to leave," he explained with resignation.

"How do you feel about that, sir?"

"Well, at least now I don't have to go to confession just for doing my job."

My patience was wearing thin with our Iraqi counterparts. It had been months since the crippling attacks had left Baghdad without power, and there wasn't a shred of progress. Time after time, the high-paid E-Team loaded up and drove to the Ministry of Electricity to discuss Iraq's problems. Time after time, the situation went from bad to worse. It felt more like a therapy session to console the Iraqi officials than anything else; we had nothing to give but moral support.

As Captain Cross and I sat across from Haitham, he replied meekly to every question we asked.

No repairs yet . . . no workers . . . more death threats . . . blah blah blah blah blah . . .

What the hell is the matter with these people? I found myself wondering in disgust. *Why can't they fix the goddam power lines?* As Haitham continued to list the myriad excuses, I grew increasingly agitated. Cross sat motionless, absorbing Haitham's comments unflinchingly. Gunfire rattled off in the distance. I thought of the recent mortar attacks, and a sense of urgency gripped me. I'm risking my life to be here, and *what are the Iraqis doing? Nothing?!* Haitham continued like a pathetic child, whining about why he couldn't handle his responsibility.

I'm going to kill him, I fumed in silent fury. *I could kill him . . . right here and now.* The coldly rational part of my mind took over . . . I wanted to pull out my gun, put the black steel barrel to Haitham's pathetic little head with his shabby salt-and-pepper mustache, and order him to *fix the fucking power lines!!!* My blood was boiling. There had to be a solution. We needed a goddam plan!!! *If this bastard can't handle the responsibility, then I'll find someone who will.*

Haitham coughed deeply, startling me from my violent fulminations. His body was gaunt and enervated, and shook terribly with his cough. It was the last week of Ramadan, and Haitham had been fasting until sundown for the entire month, breaking the regimen only for an occasional cigarette. Under the stress of his work, he had lost a great deal of weight. His cheeks were sunken and bony; his eyes looked soft, hollow and pleading. The man was broken by the weight of his struggle, and I felt suddenly ashamed.

"We'll do our best to get some security for the repair teams." Wilbur comforted Haitham but saw no visible reaction.

"Of course you will, Captain," Haitham whispered, clearly unmoved by the hollow offer.

"Uhhh . . . and we'll try to get you a place in the Green Zone . . . for your own safety," Cross added, probably improvising out of pity, searching for some small way to help. Anything would be better than promising troops that would never materialize. Haitham's eyes raised in a meager display of hope.

"Thank you, sir. That would be most gracious of you."

Wilbur nodded and gulped, looking pensive and apologetic behind his drooping spectacles. The captain motioned to me. *Time to go.* Haitham sat still, looking like death while his cigarette ash grew long and curled. The captain and I bade him farewell, saddled up, and rode back to the sheltered comfort of the Green Zone.

A group of field-grade officers assembled in the embassy for an important meeting. I followed Colonel Dawson and Captain Cross to take notes. The pipelines around Baghdad were in pieces, the electrical towers were toppled, and the broken metal was being stolen and sold for scrap. A bright and perceptive colonel from the Strategic Operations Center led the meeting.

"Gentlemen, the city is on its knees. We need to start thinking outside the box," Colonel Ripley urged the inveterate audience.

"Ha! No need to worry about that, sir," a young voice interrupted. The crowd of colonels paused, focusing upon the sergeant sitting in the corner who dared to laugh out loud.

"Explain yourself, Sergeant," Colonel Ripley demanded.

"You want us to think *outside the box*? With all due respect, sir, 'the box' has already been looted."

A few officers chuckled. Most remained silent; the young sergeant was dead serious. Whereas most men in the room worked in the headquarters, the sergeant spent most of his time in the field, reporting in on the status of infrastructure projects. There was dirt ground into the young man's body armor and somber wrinkles worn into his face.

He continued with a strange aura of wisdom and authority. "Sir, none of us have worked inside the box since we got here. What we need is a plan to pull ourselves together!"

A long pause lent weight to the young man's words.

Ripley nodded, "You're right, Sergeant. Let's get on with it, then." The meeting continued, though somewhat awkwardly.

When oil and electricity came up on the agenda, Colonel Dawson and Captain Cross landed in the spotlight. Ripley spoke slowly and with great emphasis, pointing to my two bosses. "Would you mind explaining to me what you're doing to solve this problem?"

The question was loaded with accusation. Everybody in the room listened to the daily briefings and knew damn well that no progress had been made. Captain Cross felt the need to explain his work in wavering Minnesotan.

"Well, Colonel, uh, I go to the Ministry of Electricity, I find out about the damage and report back to the general every—"

Ripley waved his hand dismissively at Cross to shut him up. "I can get a *private* to collect data for PowerPoint slides," he shot back acidly. "What are you doing to solve the problem, *Captain?*"

Wilbur was taken aback, clearly embarrassed by the accusation that the quality of his efforts fell below his pay grade.

Colonel Dawson stepped in, levelheaded and logical. "I've been looking for the reason that things are failing," he said, "and I think I've found it. The Iraqi Army has enough troops, but they aren't cooperating with the ministries. The way I see it, we need to convince the ministries to trust the Iraqi Army enough to cooperate on their security operations. We need to knock their heads together and make them act as a team."

Wilbur sat back in his chair, apparently relieved to be off the hook. Pete had been formulating a plan for a while, but this was the first anyone had heard of it. While the ministries maintained their own security forces, they were ill-equipped to handle the dangerous jobs of securing critical pipelines and electrical towers. At best, they were basic security guards, not soldiers. Despite this inadequacy, the ministries felt territorial about ceding responsibility and the army was happy to let the energy ministries handle "their" own problems.

Dawson continued to explain his plan. "I'm working to bring together officials from the Ministry of Oil and the army. If we can get these guys from around the country to sit down together, then I think we can hash out a better way to coordinate security. Saddam deliberately divided the ministries to prevent them from becoming too powerful, so most of these officials are new to the concept of national coordination. Most of them have never even met face-to-face."

Colonel Ripley shook his head in approval. "Sounds good to me. When can you make it happen, Pete?"

"Give me two weeks. I'll need that much time to prepare the briefings in Arabic and to bring the right provincial leaders to the city."

"Get on it, Colonel. We needed it months ago."

"I know, Colonel," Pete replied humbly.

On the way out of the meeting, one of the E-Team consultants, Thomas Perkins, pulled me aside. In the seventies Thomas had been a nuclear-trained electrician aboard submarines before beginning his successful career in the civilian power industry. In Iraq, he advised the Ministry of Electricity on technical matters for operating its power plants. Perkins was smart, polite, and eager to expand the scope of his responsibilities. The two of us got along splendidly.

"That was a brutal meeting," he began. I nodded. It was humiliating to see my boss put on the spot like that.

"I'm sorry that you've got to work in that office," Tom continued. "Cross is in way over his head."

"I'm glad someone else noticed," I whispered, looking around to make sure no one was within earshot.

"There are too many problems that nobody's even trying to fix," Perkins lamented as we walked toward his office. "Somebody's got to take charge of these things!"

I couldn't have agreed more. We were both submariners—we'd both learned about Rickover. And while some people, like Wilbur, had never learned to seek responsibility, others, like Tom, had grown up well beyond the point of simply taking orders and writing down numbers in the hourly logs. Thomas typically avoided talking about his navy experience

"Tom," an ex-submariner, worked his way up the ranks of the civilian electrical industry before joining the State Department as a consultant.

around the other military folks; he had been enlisted, and most of his present colleagues had been commissioned officers.

"To them, I'll always be enlisted," he confided, looking somewhat resentful. "I'll just never measure up in their minds if I tell them that I was only a blue-shirt."

I'll never know why Tom told me that, but I do know that he felt personally responsible for doing something good on behalf of America, and he was more than good enough to get the job done. For that reason, I was more than willing to follow his lead, whatever color shirt he was wearing.

"Look, Tom . . . with this job as a liaison . . . it's not enough to be a go-between. We've got to identify ways to solve the problems and connect the right people."

Thomas smiled. "That's exactly the attitude I'm looking for."

"What do you mean?"

"Chris, I've got something that might interest you, but I don't want you to tell Wilbur about it—at least not yet."

"What is it, Tom?"

"I've got a special project with your name written all over it."

12

Learning to Fly

In the barren mountains above Aqaba lay the infamous Wärt-siläs of Iraq. Though not as large as Godzilla, these monsters weighed almost a million pounds each. The Wärtsiläs numbered twenty, and they rested in a deserted mountain pass, watching the seasons change, waiting for the right time to move. A century earlier, through the very same mountains, Lawrence of Arabia led a band of warriors to a surprise attack on Aqaba. The city was a strategic port for the Ottoman Turks, who defended it from the British and French navies with formidable seaward-pointing guns. The nearly impassable desert surrounding Aqaba and the disorganized Arab enemies left the Turks unsuspecting of a landward attack. But when Lawrence emerged from the sands of the unforgiving Nefud, he unified an army of tribesmen and hit Aqaba like a stroke of lightning. In 2006 the coalition forces had a new reason to take Aqaba, but this time around, something Finnish, not Turkish, was the problem. Even stranger was the fact that we developed a plan to attack our foe in Aqaba not by sea, not by land, but by *air*. The Wärtsiläs didn't stand a chance.

A Wärtsilä is a diesel engine from Finland designed to drive oceangoing ships. However, each of these massive engines could also be configured to produce twenty megawatts of electrical power—enough for tens of thousands of families and businesses. In 2004 the first minister of electricity of the new Iraqi government (an Iraqi American citizen) purchased twenty of these diesel engines in a $500 million deal. The same minister, Dr. Al Samara'i, soon became embroiled in charges of corruption that led to a conviction in Iraqi courts, an appeal, and his escape into the Green Zone from a detention of dubious legality. Dr. Al Samara'i's involvement in the alleged corruption was never clearly revealed, but the broader political context was more obvious; the returned exiles like Dr. Al Samara'i were easy political targets. The conviction did, however, have broader consequences in the Iraqi government. In 2006 the Iraqi Council of Representatives passed the Iraqi Nationality Act, preventing foreign citizens from serving in government positions of "sovereign or high security." From that point on, if anyone was to profit from corruption in Iraq, that person would at least be a full-fledged Iraqi citizen, not a dual citizen or an American transplant.

The engines were supposed to be transported by sea to Jordan, then by land to Samarra, an ancient holy city north of Baghdad. Needless to say, there were complications. When the insurgency erupted between the Sunnis of Saddam's old regime and the Shi'a of the newly elected majority, the transportation route—straight through the infamous Sunni triangle—quickly became bogged down in the quagmire. Two years later, the engines had yet to move from their dusty rest stop in Jordan. Though the Wärtsiläs could boost Iraq's total power production by only about 7 percent, they were strategically important because of *where* they would help. Samarra had been hit hard, physically and spiritually, when the city's Golden Mosque was bombed in February 2006. In retaliation, insurgents near Samarra attacked some critical power lines that serviced Baghdad, cutting off the capital from the north. If the coalition could succeed in bringing reliable power to the people of Samarra, then it could take a major step toward closing that wound. To top it all off, the engines could burn heavy fuel oil—the refinery waste that was filling up the storage tanks in the capital and creating an enormous logistical problem. For all these reasons, it became my duty to transport these beastly diesels far from their seaside mountain view in Jordan and deep into the heart of Iraq.

"Wärtsilä versus Ramadi—I know it sounds like some sort of bad monster movie, but that's our mission," Thomas explained to me and George. The three of us composed the team that would tackle the challenge. Colonel George Goodman was an air force pilot who worked from the Strategic Operations Center to improve infrastructure security.

Perkins and Goodman had been working on the Wärtsilä project for several weeks when they asked me to help. The bulk of their work involved analyzing a ground transportation route. The plan was massive, requiring precise seasonal timing to avoid the rains, reinforcement of several bridges, removal of interfering power lines, and an enormous convoy of specialized flatbed trailers that could distribute the weight without crushing the soft asphalt roads. And of course, there was the matter of security. By George's calculations, it would take an entire battalion to guard the convoy as it crept a thousand clicks across the western provinces at the steady pace of a well-bred camel.

"There's no fucking way that this is going to work," Goodman grumbled on more than one occasion. "One sniper round in the wrong place and these engines are ruined—and look at the stupid things! They're the size of a goddam barn! You'd have to be an idiot to miss them!"

Overall, George was right. The prospects of a successful transport were slim, and we couldn't ignore the danger that would be imposed upon the soldiers and workers in the convoy. A lot of people would likely be killed if the mission went forward. But when Thomas approached me, the ground transport was not the topic of discussion.

"Chris, I've heard there's a plane that the Russians made to carry oversized cargoes. It might be possible to *fly* these things into Iraq. I want you to look into that option."

Despite my first impression—that "Flying Wärtsiläs"

sounded more like a circus act than a serious mission—I was intrigued and agreed to help without a second thought.

"There's one more thing, Chris . . ."

"What's that?"

"The other options don't look good. This is my last shot—if you don't find anything out, I'm dropping the project."

"I understand, Tom. Thanks for telling me."

"No problem. Now get to work!"

"Yes, sir!" I cocked a mock salute and scampered down the corridor to my ballroom office.

They say that a camel *looks* like it was designed by a committee. However, the Antonov AN-225 Myria is a plane that actually *was* designed by a committee—a Cold War Soviet Russo-Ukrainian central planning committee, to be precise. The AN-225 is as close as a plane can get to a camel with wings. It is ungainly, round and thick, with huge sloping wings that appear to droop under the weight of its six enormous jet engines. Designed to carry the Russian space shuttle on its back for spectacular sky launches, the one-of-a-kind Myria is the largest airplane in the world that can actually carry cargo. There would have been two such airplanes, but the collapse of the Soviet Union left little room for such governmental behemoths in the capitalistic competition of commercial aviation fleets, so the second plane was canceled. For most customers, the smaller AN-125s, C-130s, and 747s were more than adequate. Needless to say, the Ukrainians who now owned the plane had never met a customer like me.

"What, precisely, are you trying to do again?" a gentleman with a British accent inquired incredulously on the other end of the phone. The gentleman was an official for the British company that operated the AN-225 for the Ukrainian owners. I repeated that I wanted to rent his plane to fly some marine diesel engines into Iraq. There was an awkward pause.

"I see," the gentleman stated, still sounding a bit puzzled.

"If we can get it to work, it might be possible to charter up to twenty flights," I explained. Suddenly the gentleman became much less puzzled.

"Right. I'll send you the specifications right away!"

"Thank you, sir!"

The plane's technical specs arrived by e-mail, and they were extremely impressive. Loaded up and with a full tank of fuel, the Myria weighs over 1.2 million pounds, making it the single heaviest thing ever to take off and land again on its own propulsion. As amazing as this may be, the weight limit still fell shy of what we needed to heft the Wärtsiläs, and the cargo hold was too small by at least a meter in height. It looked like a quick, fatal blow to the project. I reported back to Perkins that the biggest plane in the world couldn't even come close to the task.

"At least we tried, Chris . . . At least we tried."

I went back to work for Captain Cross, cranking out PowerPoint slides, briefing the commanding general, and sipping coffee in front of my computers while slowly going insane. There were no trips planned to the Ministry of Electricity that week, so time seemed to drag on forever.

There's got to be a way to move those engines. We're just not approaching this the right way.

If any of us had learned a bit of history before coming to Iraq, we could have realized that Arab ingenuity had overcome such problems before. But in our present state of ignorance, we simply had to think a bit harder. In 1953 King Faisal of Saudi Arabia was faced with a similar problem of logistics. Faisal's kingdom was the home of Islam's holiest city, Medina, but there was no modern roadway to facilitate the flow of worshippers on their pilgrimage. Until the major oil discoveries started to pay off, the kingdom's revenues depended upon the number of people making the pilgrimage, and the lack of modern roads was starting to limit the king's budget. Logically, Faisal saw it as his patriotic and religious duty to build a road connecting the Hijaz region to the Saudi interior before he died, but this proved to be a momentous challenge. The task of building a modern road across Saudi Arabia's mountains and deserts was rife with technical showstoppers. None of the major international construction firms would bid on the project—to them, it was infeasible. But none of the major companies could have predicted the genius of Osama bin Laden's father.

Mohammed bin Laden was a classic success story of capitalism and ingenuity. Born a tribesman in rural Saudi Arabia, Mohammed landed a job as a laborer with the Arabian American Oil Company, Aramco. Mohammed's work ethic and intelligence got him a management position, which helped to open the doors for his own construction business. Within a few decades, Mohammed became a billionaire and owned some of the largest construction companies in the world. When all the other international companies balked at Faisal's road proposal, Mohammed bin Laden took the contract, and even promised a completion date for the job. In a stroke of genius, he disassembled the heavy machinery needed to build the roads, loaded the parts on the backs of camels, and set out into the sands. With this strange Bedouin crew, Mohammed bin Laden forged the path that no other man could—and he built the road to Medina.

"I've got it!" I shouted, then raced down the palace halls to Tom's office.

"Tom! Tom! Listen to this!"

"Jesus, Chris! What's gotten into you?"

"Mohammed bin Laden!!!"

"What?"

"Never mind . . . Listen to this—we take the Wärtsiläs apart and ship the parts separately! It'll be twice as many flights, but the pieces might be small enough to fit!"

Perkins furrowed his brow in concentration, lost in

thought as he shuffled through the papers on his desk. "Yeah . . . I was thinking about that, too." He pulled out a schematic for the Wärtsiläs and looked closer to see how the engines were assembled.

"I think we might be onto something. I'll call the manufacturer in Helsinki and see what they can do!"

A few days passed while the engineers in Finland analyzed the possibility of taking the machines apart and shipping them in pieces. When the call came back, the results sounded good. The engineers could travel to Jordan, remove the engine heads, and leave the steel body at 190 tonnes and just under four meters high—a perfect fit for the saddlebags of our flying Ukrainian camel!

"Are you ready to set a world record?" George asked Tom when I told them the news.

"What do you mean?"

"The way I see it, this is either gonna be the single biggest piece of cargo ever flown or the biggest plane crash in history."

Perkins laughed. "Do I get a vote in the matter?"

"Just cross your fingers and go buy us some expensive plane tickets," George said with a chuckle. "I've got some pilot stuff to figure out."

The three of us made a great team. While I dealt with the businessmen in England, trying to sort out the logistics for the forty potential flights and the new ground route, Perkins dealt with the engineers and Colonel Goodman sorted out the technical details with the airports. Fortunately, Aqaba's international airport was a few kilometers away from the Wärtsiläs, and a military airfield at Balad was twenty kilometers from the installation site at Samarra. All told, the engines would travel less than thirty kilometers over land to reach their final destination! The total cost of the whole operation was less than $50 million—a meager 10 percent more than the budgeted cost at the project's inception three years earlier.

"Compared to the ground route, this airlift is a slam

dunk," George remarked. It was the most elegant solution, particularly because it could be done without tying up a battalion of soldiers for several months or risking civilian lives.

Over the next month, Goodman, Perkins, and I worked out the details during our off hours (we still had our day jobs to perform). By that point, the morning slide show had become so routine that I could brief the commanding general in my sleep. Whenever I'd try to slip a recommendation into the briefing or hint at the need for a certain plan, Captain Cross halted my intentions like the old detective on *Dragnet*.

"Just the facts, Chris . . . just the facts. The general will tell us what to do if he wants something."

Bullshit, I thought. *The general hasn't said a thing to us except to ask what our technobabble reports actually mean in English!*

The coalition would make no progress under Cross, so I decided to focus on my side project of flying those engines to their new home; the people of Samarra needed us. Thomas, George, and I sweated over anything that could potentially kill the airlift: engine dimensions, component weights, runway limits, aircraft turning radii, crane availability, air-traffic patterns, and the equipment required to reassemble the engines. We even asked a navy master chief—another nuclear submariner—to call the Norfolk Naval Shipyard and scrounge up some marine diesel mechanics.

The shipyard was ecstatic about helping. "If it supports our troops in Iraq, we'll make it happen!"

"Hooyah!" I shouted upon hearing the news. "It makes me feel like singing 'Anchors Aweigh'!"

One evening, Captain Cross surprised me by peeking over my shoulder after returning with some coffee. Pictures of the engines and our detailed plans were displayed on my computer screen in plain view. *Caught!!!*

"Whatchya workin' on, Chris?"

I hadn't planned on telling the captain about the Wärtsilä

project, but he caught me off guard, I was tired, and I didn't see the point of keeping the project secret any longer.

"I'm helping Perkins and Goodman with the Wärtsiläs, sir."

The captain was not amused.

I tried to explain. "It's only during my off time, sir. It doesn't get in the way of the briefings!"

Cross was unmoved. "I, uh, heard some talk about this project before. You know, Chris, we don't, uhhh . . . want our office to get too close to this plan."

"What do you mean by that, sir?"

"Well, uh . . . it might *fail*."

My heart sank. It was a classic case of social Darwinism in the office jungle. In that single moment, Wilbur managed to capture the essence of all that was wrong with our team. We were losing the war; if we didn't try something different, if we didn't take some risks, then it was game over for the coalition. But Wilbur wanted to play it safe, probably because a high-profile failure would jeopardize his prospects for an E-Team consulting job when his mandatory navy retirement came up five months later.

Perkins was livid. "I can't believe Cross said that! Whose team is he on?"

"He's trying to get hired by your office," I reminded him.

"Not if I can help it."

Against my captain's wishes, I continued to work on the project. I couldn't just sit there with practically nothing to do while Perkins and Goodman needed my help! I kept a low profile, but continued the work at strange hours and from the Strategic Operations Center.

Thomas approached me a few days later with a look of bewilderment. "Remember what you told me about Captain Cross's job prospects?"

"Yeah, what happened?"

"Ian just offered him the job."

"Great. I guess that means you're stuck with him."

"Suits me—at least we'll have someone who's good at making PowerPoints."

I grinned and went back to work.

The plan was coming together extremely well. In less than a month, our team of three had worked practically every major detail of the operation. The level of excitement was building as we started to prepare briefings for the higher-ups in the chain of command.

Then came the fatal phone call—it was the British gentleman whose company operated the plane. "We've got a problem, sir. There's an important safety precaution that we haven't accounted for. We must have a backup airport within range of the destination, in case there is a problem in Iraq. At the present distance, there won't be enough fuel for us to reach the backup airports in Kuwait or Jordan. In short, we can't accept the job."

My stomach knotted into a tight little ball.

"Thank you, sir," I replied meekly, then hung up the phone.

Thomas was crestfallen. "Dammit, we were so close!"

"Can we cut the weight down any further?" I asked.

Thomas shook his head. The Finnish engineers strongly discouraged further disassembly of the engines, which could damage the sensitive internal parts.

"Well . . . I guess that's a wrap, isn't it, Tom?"

"Yeah, Chris. Thanks for your help."

"I'm taking a break, Tom. See you later."

It was the beginning of November, and the weather in Baghdad was gorgeous. As I walked outside toward my hooch, a strange and ethereal popping sound enveloped the city. Saddam Hussein had just been convicted of crimes against humanity, and the news of the conviction started an extraordinary rain. When the word hit the streets, the city erupted in a hailstorm of gunfire aimed at no particular person (except the man who was already condemned to death).

The sound resembled popcorn on the horizon, as though the entire metropolis had been transformed into a theater where the moviegoers and concessionaires walked about the streets, enjoying the show-trial. The international zone sounded its alarm for incoming shells, but there were no explosions, just thousands of guns firing off simultaneously in every direction. Instead of rushing for cover, I found myself drawn inextricably outside to listen, at least until the *tink, tink* of bullets on rooftops brought me to my senses. The following day, General Casey described the hailstorm as "celebratory violence," eliciting grins from the headquarters in a welcome reprieve from the humorless droning of data.

When the celebratory violence ended, the real violence began once more. The mortar attacks on the Green Zone came more frequently—almost every day. The timing was quite predictable, since the insurgents needed to blend in with the city's population if they wanted to escape. There were never attacks after dark—the curfews made the empty streets too open to hide. The first mortar attacks came after prayer, the second after lunch, the third after teatime, and the last ones typically came at dusk. It was really quite orderly, considering the nature of the beast. One night, after a few loud shells exploded near the palace, my cell phone rang—I didn't recognize the number.

"Hello, Chris?" It was a woman's voice. "It's Jessica. Remember me?"

"Jessica Rabbit? Of course I remember you!" After we met at Ahmed Chalabi's house, Jessica and I had bumped into each other in the café a couple of times. I was flirtatious, but I didn't think she'd ever call; she was way too good-looking for a nerd like me.

"Is everything okay?"

Jessica responded in distress. "Those last attacks were right outside my hooch. I'm so afraid. . . . will you come to see me?"

"Of course I will. I'll be right there."

Ten minutes later I arrived at the trailer park where the

diplomats kept separate quarters. Jessica cracked open the door and her face appeared, smiling. "Is that you, Chris?"

I could see through the dim light that she was wearing nothing but skimpy shorts and a T-shirt.

"Yeah, it's me."

Jess beckoned me inside, where I was immediately impressed by her accommodations. Junior diplomats started out with four times as much space as the senior military folks. Not only that, but her place was decorated like a desert-island getaway.

"Nice Lebensraum," I said.

"It better be nice—those plastic palm trees were hard to find," she said with a smirk. "How did you know I spoke German?"

"Lucky guess." After all, I knew that Jessica was fluent in at least five languages (and rumor had it she was good with knives, too).

"You could have just planted a *real* palm tree," I joked.

"Yeah, the climate's probably perfect for it."

I glanced around the hooch and couldn't help but notice that the neatly turned-down bed had red satin sheets. Some scented candles burned nearby, creating an unusually soft ambience for a place that had just been attacked by insurgents.

"You certainly know how to make yourself comfortable."

"I only sleep on satin," she cooed, pointing to her shimmering red sheets—probably the only ones like them in Baghdad.

"Awwww, you diplomats have it so rough . . ."

"*They're* not that rough . . . Why don't you come try them?"

Jessica pointed again to the red satin sheets. I was expecting to calm her fears after the attack, but this was a full frontal assault, and my defenses were down.

I coughed, startled. "Uhhh . . . So . . . where, exactly, did the mortar hit?" I asked, a bit puzzled, trying to change the

The entrance to a trailer park in the U.S. Embassy compound. Sadly, the reminder "No Drinking While Armed" was necessary. A Blackwater mercenary got drunk and shot an Iraqi security guard to death on Christmas Eve 2006.

subject. From the outside I hadn't seen anything in the area, and the security guards usually cordoned off blast sites until they were deemed safe.

"Right over there." She motioned out the back window, leaning in a slow, exaggerated way that accentuated her tight, shapely legs.

"Well, I didn't see anything out there when I looked five minutes ago."

"Maybe you weren't looking *hard* enough . . ." she whispered, sliding her fingers slowly up my arm and gripping my shoulder.

I gulped.

" . . . or maybe you were looking in the wrong place."

She started unbuttoning my camouflage blouse.

"Jessica, are you trying to seduce me?"

"Chris, you're a fucking genius."

Admittedly, I was a bit slow, but there was also the matter

of the moral dilemma; any idiot could have figured out that her story about the mortar was a complete fabrication. *Hmmm . . . she tricked me so that I would come over and sleep with her. How do I feel about that?* Exactly two seconds later, I found it in my heart to forgive her, and the rest of the evening went just fine.

13

Flying Solo

In the chow hall of Saddam's Republican Palace, a man sat eating breakfast alone. The man's clothes were quite typical for a bureaucrat in his sixties in Baghdad—they were casual, neat, perhaps a bit sporty, if not quite rugged. It was unusual for this man to be eating breakfast in solitude, but not because of what he was eating or when he was eating. The man was surrounded by tables full of soldiers and contractors—the same crowd who arrived every morning for breakfast before work. A casual observer may have thought that the man wanted to be alone, like many of the brooding administrators of the International Zone who plug in to their iPods for Arabic lessons over a bowl of oatmeal. A private in the army may have thought it unusual for this man to be alone because soldiers traveled under the buddy system. A cynic might have predicted that the man was uncontrollably flatulent and deserved to be alone. But no matter what people thought, it was extraordinary for this man to be eating by himself in a crowded facility full of Americans because this particular man was Senator John Kerry.

Two weeks earlier, Kerry had inflamed American soldiers by remarking that leaders without a proper education will end up getting America stuck in places like Iraq. What started out as an insult aimed at President Bush's knowledge of Middle Eastern history quickly morphed into a condemnation of every soldier who has ever volunteered to serve. By the time the right-wing media rehashed the senator's words to their own liking, Senator Kerry had allegedly declared every soldier serving in Iraq to be uneducated cannon fodder, deserving of life in the bloody trenches. In response, a group of indignant (but not very well-informed) soldiers held up a banner begging, "Halp us jon carry. Weer stuk heer in Irak." The image quickly attained worldwide fame, and the senator's name took a nosedive into the quagmire of bad public relations. Later that day, a colleague reported seeing a man who fit Kerry's description shooting billiards by himself next to the empty palace pool; he came close enough to snap a picture, then left without saying hello.

But Senator Kerry wasn't the only member of Congress to get the cold shoulder from the strategic headquarters. Every time a congressman who "voted against the war" arrived in Iraq, an overeager colonel from the public relations office was quick to inform the entire headquarters by e-mail, "I just want everyone to know that Congressman X doesn't support the troops."

Needless to say, Congressmen X would be much more likely to have "technical difficulties" with his itinerary. But even if the helicopter flights and briefings weren't canceled at the last minute, Congressmen X would meet with an audience informed solely by the armed forces television network before dodging bullets from soldiers who were loaded up with lopsided invective.

Conservative pundit Bill O'Reilly arrived one day to distribute free autographed copies of his latest book, *Culture Warrior*. I glanced at the tome, surprised to learn that people who hadn't supported the war were actually the lowest form of life on the planet (one step down from viruses). O'Reilly's chapter titled "Hating America" began with a famous quote that O'Reilly attributes to the "secular progressive" leaders of the Black Panther Party: " 'Whenever any form of government becomes destructive . . . it is the right of the people to alter or to abolish it.' "

While it is true that the Black Panthers were radical secular progressives, it is comical that O'Reilly attributes this "America-hating" quote to them, when these words were first penned in the Declaration of Independence by our Founding Fathers (another group that was radical and progressive for its time). But given O'Reilly's grasp of American history, it's not surprising that the best place for him to promote his new book was the very same place where Senator Kerry warned about uneducated politicos getting themselves stuck.

Despite the recurring spectacle of *Mr. Smith Goes to Baghdad*, there was another reason for me to have politics on the brain: the ambassador had granted me an audience.

"Make your money, then go for a political appointment," Dr. Khalilzad advised me in his high, nasal voice. My conversation with the chargé d'affaires extraordinaire lasted fifteen minutes, but it boiled down to those two points: making money and having political connections. I mentioned that I'd be going to Yale; Khalilzad mentioned that his son would be starting law school at Stanford.

Wow, that was chummy.

"If you ever need anything, feel free to give me a call," Zalmay offered, extending his business card and shaking my hand. I took the crisp, sturdy card, wondering what sort of favor I could possibly ask of the man (and how I might be expected to repay it). Khalilzad repeated his advice about politics and money as I straightened my camouflage uniform and left, somewhat baffled. A strange and uneasy feeling swelled in my stomach. The top American official in Iraq had just sold out every career diplomat who served under his charge. It was like a general telling a young cadet, "Don't bother with the army, son. Just make some friends in Washington."

"How did it go?" Wilbur asked when I returned to the office.

"Fine, Captain. Everything went fine."

"Weren't you, uhhh, thinkin' about doin' the Foreign Service, Chris?"

"Yes, Captain, I certainly *was . . .*"

Jessica Rabbit took a vacation to D.C., so I took the opportunity to make a special request. I wanted two of the fuzziest, fluffiest, most adorable teddy bears that America had to offer. Sadly, the bears were not for me; I wanted to give them to two Iraqi kids in the hospital. When Jess returned, I took the cuddly little fluffballs in hand and set out for the Baghdad ER in full body armor. I must have looked ridiculous, carrying the bears in one hand and a rifle in the other. Some burly Blackwater guards passed me on the way, eyeing me and the bears suspiciously.

"Don't be jealous," I admonished them. The barrel-chested ogres burst into laughter.

At the hospital, two Iraqi children were in intensive care and unable to see any visitors. The doctors agreed to give one of the bears to a nine-year-old girl. The parents of a seven-year-old boy accepted the other as a gift on behalf of their son. It was better, I thought, for the gift to come from the parents than from me. The father thanked me with a hug. I thanked Jessica with something too private to print.

The senior members of the E-Team flew to Jordan with the minister of electricity for a one-week conference. Captain Cross decided to represent the coalition militaries, though he confided that his hotel view overlooking the Dead Sea was more exciting to him than the conference itself. The goal was to solicit international investment for Iraqi power plants. I was skeptical of what the conference could accomplish, since the basis for the meeting was the ministry's ten-year blueprint for development—the closest thing we had to a strategic plan. The blueprint was a silly document that simply presumed the

A typical vantage point from a Black Hawk helicopter. The E-Team frequently flew around Iraq to inspect energy infrastructure and facilities.

existence of physical security and eager investors. Worse still, the plan was purely electrical. There was no mention of how the power plants would be fueled. Without an integrated approach to developing Iraq's energy that also included oil and security, energy independence would remain on the drawing board.

While my captain lounged in his seaside hotel room, I was more than happy to take the reins. I was sick for the tenth year in a row from the mandatory flu vaccine, but held good spirits when Wilbur left the country. This was my opportunity to set a plan in motion.

The previous week Colonel Dawson had invited several Iraqi oil and defense officials from around the country to Baghdad. By putting oilmen, military officers, and bureaucrats in the same room together, Dawson forced them to discuss the process of coordinating security for repairs. It was the first time that many of the officials had met face-to-face. In the old regime, there was no such thing as a flat organization where people were expected to cooperate across functional lines. Power was deliberately divided to keep the ministries from challenging the will of Saddam.

At the meeting, an Iraqi general delivered a presentation in Arabic with English subtitles. Another general started to argue with him. The atmosphere grew tense as their voices raised louder and louder. Colonel Dawson's British assistant intervened in a splendid act of diplomacy, defusing the argument and refocusing the meeting. In the end, the gathering was a big success—the members found the dialogue so beneficial that they stayed and talked for an hour after the meeting adjourned. The next week, the very same officials coordinated a flawless repair effort on an oil pipeline—the first such act of high-level coordination between Baghdad and the provincial leaders. The standard had been set: collaboration was now a source of strength.

I spent the next few days preparing a briefing for the Ministry of Electricity. Though Captain Cross and I had made some mediocre efforts to get coalition forces to rendezvous with Iraqi repair teams, miscommunications between the soldiers, the headquarters, and the ministry left the repair teams vulnerable to attack. Several Iraqi workers were killed on account of our poorly coordinated security effort. I was determined not to repeat that mistake.

George and I decided to press for a meeting of electrical officials like Colonel Dawson had done with oil. Unfortunately, the city was forced into lockdown in the aftermath of Saddam's ill-handled execution. When the cell phone video footage of the angry-mob event leaked out, the streets erupted in violent protests, and all routine missions, including ministerial trips, were canceled. When the dust settled, George and I had one shot left to improve the security situation before the others came back from Jordan. Otherwise, it would be up to the *Dragnet* detective to push things forward, which meant that it wouldn't happen.

When the E-Team loaded up, strapped on armor, and set

out for the ministry, there was a newcomer in our midst. Martha Benning was a reservist navy commander trained as a construction engineer. She was the only person on the E-Team who had no previous experience in energy, and it showed. Her responsibilities normally included plugging holes in spreadsheets, but with Ian in Jordan, she was the only one left to represent the State Department. I was the only person on the E-Team who Commander Benning outranked, and she made sure to let that show, too.

Our meeting at the ministry that day was a disaster. At the last minute, Joe the prosthetist ordered everyone to travel in pairs on account of some recent kidnappings of British diplomats. I tried to pair up with George so that we could take care of business, but Martha grabbed me first. Despite my protests, she insisted that I accompany her—nobody else would.

"I suppose I can go with you, ma'am, but we need to be quick. I've got important business today."

"Don't be pushy, Lieutenant."

"It's important, ma'am."

"Everything is important."

We'll see about that.

Commander Benning dragged me in to see Fuwadh, the Aramaic-speaking Christian who worked as Haitham's deputy (Haitham was in Jordan with the minister). Fuwadh didn't know anything useful that day, and he was completely overwhelmed with his colleagues gone. This didn't stop Martha from bumbling through a list of questions about power lines that Fuwadh obviously couldn't answer. To make matters worse, she confused him terribly by making some comments about "pigs in a blanket" and "eggs in a basket," two idioms that Fuwadh hadn't picked up in his short time speaking English. The poor man simply smiled, baffled by the strange and dirty woman before him who apparently let pigs share the bed.

I interrupted the conversation, whispering to the commander, "Ma'am, this is going nowhere—and we don't need these data anyway. . . . Can we move on?"

"Don't give me attitude, Lieutenant."

"Ma'am, this isn't about you. Fuwadh can't help us, and besides, what you're looking for isn't important—nobody's going to die if the general's PowerPoint slide isn't up to date."

"We're staying right here, Lieutenant. My boss told me to get the data, and that's what I'm gonna do. End of discussion."

When Martha had finally checked off her list of routine questions—any of which could have been answered over a phone call or e-mail—I raced away to find George.

"What took you so long, Chris? I thought you forgot!"

"I was stuck with Martha."

George shook his head. "She's a fucking idiot."

I winced painfully in agreement with that assessment. "Where's the general?"

"He's waiting for us."

George and I quickly made our way to meet the general who commanded the ministry's security forces. If George and I could convince the general to meet with the Iraqi Army and the coalition, then we could make headway toward improving security, just as Colonel Dawson had done. The discussion with the general went excruciatingly slowly; his interpreter couldn't understand us, and as always, the E-Team had no interpreter of its own.

Minutes into the conversation, our security team entered the office. "Sir, we've got to go."

"Five more minutes—I need five minutes!"

"Sorry, sir. Time's up."

Shit!!!

George and I thanked the general for his time and excused ourselves. I was livid. Martha's bumbling quest for data had completely blocked our chances of improving the security situation that week. Another few Iraqi workers might die because of the delay, and needless to say, the power lines would not get fixed. We inserted our earplugs, hopped into the Humvees, and drove home in silence.

Captain Cross was still in Jordan for a few more days, and there was a chance that I could make it back to the ministry to meet with the general of the security forces. I wrote to Commander Benning, explaining that if she planned on going back, we needed to coordinate an agenda that met both of our objectives.

Martha was put off by my insistence and completely ignored the content of my message. "Lieutenant, I don't like your tone. Look at how disrespectful this letter is—you don't even sign it with 'Very Respectfully'! What has gotten into you?"

Benning was technically correct. Junior naval officers are required to close with "Very Respectfully" as a term of endearment on all written correspondence to their superiors. I had merely written "Respectfully yours."

"Ma'am, people are dying. Can we focus on the problem at hand instead of my letter-formatting skills?" I replied, committing the cardinal sin of e-mail (never hit "send" in anger). I should have spoken to her face-to-face; instead, my snide e-mail response only escalated the problem.

"That's enough, Lieutenant! I've never met a junior officer so insubordinate."

My next appeal was to the E-Team at large, most of whom were still in Jordan. I explained the situation and asked for support, but got no responses except from George and Tom, who laughed about me grabbing the bull by the horns.

"I'm glad you're pushing this forward—nobody else seems to get that it's even a problem," Tom remarked.

When Wilbur returned, he was "extremely worried" about my insubordination. "Chris, you could damage our relationship with the State Department!"

The office where Martha worked was the same office

where Wilbur was expecting to take a $450,000 one-year con-
tract.

"I think you're trying to make me look bad," Wilbur
declared in a worried, wavering voice.

I was dumbfounded. "Sir, this is not about you. This is
about solving the security problem and fixing the power lines
so some Iraqis can have electricity."

"Well, I think you're trying to torpedo me, and I don't
think I can trust you anymore, Lieutenant."

On our next trip to the ministry, Wilbur was nervous and
skittish around me. As always, there was no coordinated
agenda, no coherent plan. Cross even instructed me not to
speak; *eyes open, mouth shut.* I winced, remembering the last
time that someone had told me to assume that position.

The trip was unproductive. Cross and Benning mined
Haitham for the same data as always: *Which power lines are
down? Where are the fallen towers? Do you have GPS coordinates?* I sat in the corner, incredulous that we were wasting
Haitham's time with such pointless data mining. Nothing
had changed since the moment I had arrived seven months
earlier—Wilbur had learned absolutely nothing about how to
solve the problems, and Haitham seemed more and more desperate every time we showed up to collect our data. Still, my
captain bumbled along, unfocused and confused. Haitham
repeated himself with infinite patience. To clarify one point,
Wilbur started drawing a schematic of the power grid on a
napkin. I stared in disbelief as he became more and more
absorbed in his tiny little sketch; the real schematic was
posted on the wall behind us. After a few excruciating minutes, I could bear the idiocy no more.

"Captain, is this what you're looking for?" I pointed to an
electrical substation on the detailed wall chart.

Haitham smiled, thanking me with a relieved glance; the
napkin was becoming incomprehensible.

"Oh! Yes, that's the spot," Wilbur responded, pushing his

bifocals back onto his nose. He then looked down at his watch and shook his head. "Sheesh! It's time to go already! Sorry, Mr. Haitham!"

Wilbur, Martha, and I grabbed our gear and headed to Dr. Karim's boardroom. At the ministerial meeting, the E-Team listened in complete ignorance as the minister of electricity spoke to his directors general in Arabic. Cross looked nervous again—an officer from the Army Corps of Engineers was seated at the minister's table.

"You know, Chris, the engineers are trying to absorb our unit," Wilbur explained in a worried, hushed tone. The puzzle started falling into place. My captain was worried about losing his position in the bureaucracy. When the minister finished his discussion in Arabic, he turned to Ian and brusquely addressed the problem of the downed power lines.

"What can you do about this?"

Ian offered to hire private contractors to fix the toppled towers—at an exorbitant cost. The minister slowly grew angry while Ian condescendingly explained the benefits of privatizing the work that the Iraqi government had been unable to accomplish.

The minister snapped, "I don't need your damn contractors. I need security!"

An awkward silence filled the room, and Ian took a long draw on his cigarette. I stood up and walked over to Captain Cross, handing him the detailed security briefing I had prepared in English and Arabic—essentially the same plan that Colonel Dawson had prepared for the Oil Ministry. Wilbur took the brief from my hands, nodded okay, then sat motionless, seemingly paralyzed by fear, afraid to stick his neck out in front of the man who was about to become his new boss.

Ian waxed poetic about privatization, promising that a Western company could complete the repairs within two weeks of signing a contract. The minister looked incredulous, and for good reason: his workers were better than anyone else in the world at repairing blown-up towers. But whether Dr. Karim wanted Ian's contractors or not, he was going to get them, at the full cost of $25 million—exactly one hundred times the cost that his ministry typically paid for the same work. Security was not included in the contract.

At the Republican Palace, I could no longer conceal my frustration with Wilbur's lethargy.

"Captain, why didn't you speak up about the security plans? We have to take responsibility for this!"

The captain cut me off. "Lieutenant, we're here to report the facts, not to come up with fancy plans and wild ideas."

"Sir, look around! Nobody else is going to take responsibility! If we don't start coming up with some plans, then nobody will!"

"That's enough, Lieutenant!"

I lowered my head, dejected. Nothing I said seemed to communicate to the captain that we were responsible and that our situation required a sense of urgency. As I shook my head, I noticed on Wilbur's desk a picture of his son—an army helicopter pilot fresh out of college, posing in front of his bird with an American flag. I took my last shot at motivating the beleaguered captain.

"Dammit, sir! Don't you understand? If *we* don't finish the job here, then *your son* will have to come back for another tour of duty!"

The words struck a nerve—and I had pushed too hard. The poor old man shook his head nervously in denial, mumbling something incomprehensible. Captain Cross was in so far over his head that he couldn't come up with a plan to save his own life, let alone a plan to save someone else's. Apparently, the thought that his own failures could have consequences for his son was too much to bear.

It was horrible to recognize what had become of my captain. He was traumatized by the life-and-death responsibility of his work. Under that pressure, the gentle, kind, and caring grandfather reverted back to his earliest training in the navy, when he sat in Maneuvering as a reactor operator, watching his instrument panel and logging the parameters every hour on the hour. My work with Wilbur had come to an untimely end; once more, my captain had run his ship aground.

Colonel Mulder, however, was not one to be intimidated by fear of failure. And what's more, Mulder knew damn well that his unit was on the bureaucratic chopping block. The grizzly bear dragged me into the den. Cross and Dawson followed. A toy car that Mulder's girlfriend had sent as a Christmas gift sat in the middle of his desk next to his iPod. He brushed his toys aside and took the first swipe at me.

"I have never in my life met anyone like you, Brownfield."

Am I supposed to respond to that?

Mulder continued, "Captain Cross tells me that you're out of control, a loose cannon."

The captain looked down at the floor to avoid eye contact, nodding his head like a lapdog as the grizzly bear spoke. Colonel Dawson remained still, his hand upon his chin, simply listening.

"What the hell am I supposed to do with you, Brownfield?"

I started to respond—

Mulder cut me off, "Shut up! I don't want to hear your smart-ass ideas."

Well, that clarifies my options: eyes open, mouth shut.

"You've got a reputation around here, kid, and it's starting to become a problem to me."

I cocked my head in confusion. I did have a reputation, but as far as I knew, it wasn't a bad one.

The grizzly bear explained, looking somewhat annoyed that I didn't catch his drift. "You don't want to give the impression that you're overshadowing your superiors."

I was stunned.

"What are you talking about, sir?" I gasped, taken aback.

It had never once crossed my mind that my work was overshadowing anyone. The accusation that I was trying to outdo the people on our own team was ridiculous, offensive—after all, we were losing the war together.

"Sir, I don't think of it that way. We're all on the same team."

"Don't be stupid, kid," Mulder growled. "You come waltzing in here after crashing your submarine and expect your fancy ideas and dinner parties with the ambassador not to make a stir?"

I stiffened defensively. The submarine crash was never my fault, but this was no time for a discussion of history. It was lost upon my bosses that anyone on my ship could have prevented that crash if they had possessed the wherewithal to tell the captain that he was wrong. More importantly, the real problem was out in the open: my ideas were a threat to Mulder.

"Do you know how it makes me *look* when the general comes up to me, tells me about this crazy plan of yours, then asks me what plans *I'm* working on?"

You said it yourself, douche bag: "We never had a plan!"

"No, sir. I don't know how it makes you look."

"Well, you're making us look *bad*, and you need to knock it off right now," Mulder barked. "I want to know where your loyalties are, Brownfield. And if you want to keep this job, then you need to swear that you'll stay loyal to this office. A man can only have one master."

Loyalty oath? Master? Who the fuck is this guy? Big Brother?

"Sir, I can't swear an oath to your office."

Mulder grunted.

I continued, "The only oath I'll take is to support and defend the Constitution. If my work is threatening you in some way, then I request to transfer to another job."

Mulder's big, fluffy cheeks grew redder and redder. The second I requested to transfer, the bearish colonel slammed both fists down on his desk, shouting, "GOD DAMMIT!

You want a transfer? I'll transfer you—to *Abu Ghraib*, you little son of a bitch!"

After throwing me out of his office, Mulder set to work finding a way to get rid of me for good. I was fired, though none of them would actually say it. George quickly went to Colonel Ripley, his boss in the Strategic Operations Center, to ask if they could have me.

Mulder angrily denied the request. "There's no fucking way that you're going to work for them! You're staying right the fuck here," he snapped.

At that point I realized how much of a threat I had become. If Mulder allowed me to fall into the hands of his rivals at headquarters, then my knowledge of his ineptitude would be the nail in his coffin. I simply knew too much, and Mulder knew damn well that a loose cannon can sometimes hit the mark.

The whole time that Mulder fretted about where to transfer me, there were other political forces at work. The palace was alive with rumblings that a new general would be replacing Casey and would clean house before getting down to business. Colonel Mulder had just asked for a one-year extension on his deployment, an extension that would put him in charge of our directorate when the Koreans left the country.

"Who do you think really runs this command?" Mulder asked me in anger. "General Kim? Hah! While he's out there shaking hands and selling Jesus, I'm the one who's in control—*ME!!!*"

The problem for Mulder was that a lot of people at headquarters considered our civil-military operations unit to be functionally useless. I was one of them, and Mulder knew it. The new commanding general—someone named Petraeus—couldn't possibly fire the whole headquarters, so the race was on between Mulder and the others to separate the shit from Shinola.

Captain Cross approached me a few days later with Colonel Mulder's solution—there was a job opening in

Kuwait that needed to be filled within a week. It was a lame
assignment—receiving and distributing wheelchairs to Iraqi
amputees. Still, there were no other options. If I stayed in
Baghdad, I would be kept on a short leash and blackmailed
by Mulder. I accepted the job in Kuwait and started to pack
my bags. But that afternoon an unexpected phone call led me
to pack my bags for a different reason altogether. My grandfather was dying and had less than two weeks to live. If I had
been on a submarine, the headquarters would have informed
me of his death after I returned home from deployment, but
the army in the midst of war was strangely more humane.
Cross and Mulder immediately granted me emergency leave,
and I booked a ticket on the next flight out.

At the terminal there were others who were leaving Baghdad before their time was up. Two soldiers sat in the airport,
exhausted and broken. One was wearing an ill-fitting conva-
lescent uniform—his issued uniform had been torn to shreds
by an IED. The man walked with a bad limp, his left arm was
in a sling, his face was scabbed from shrapnel, and his handwritten name tag was stuck onto his chest with white medical
tape. The other soldier still wore the same uniform as he had
when his convoy was attacked; his shirt was darkened with
dried blood around his neck and shoulder. His nose was broken. I looked down at my own starched uniform and felt even
more keenly a sense of complete failure. All of my work so far
had amounted to nothing. Not a single person was any safer
or better off because of what I had contributed to the war
effort.

At home, my family was in the throes of change. My
grandfather began hospice care, and there was precious little
time remaining. My brother's wife gave birth just in time for
the newborn to meet his great-grandfather. I passed my hours
caring for my grandfather, feeding him, washing him, mas-
saging his shoulders with lotion so that he could continue to
feel his arms for a few more fleeting days. As my leave drew to
a close, we said our farewells and I packed my bags once

more, my body armor clinking on the floor of the bedroom where I had spent a happy childhood.

On the morning I left my family to return to Iraq, I received an unexpected message from Captain Cross. The e-mail was short, to the point, and full of nothing but the facts:

"Mr. Haitham has been kidnapped."

14

Non Sibi Sed Petraeus

The massive bronze doors of the Naval Academy's chapel are inscribed with the inspirational words *Non sibi sed patriae*—"Not for self but for country." These words reflect the deep and universal commitment to selfless service that soldiers around the world embrace. The day after I returned from emergency leave, my grandfather passed away. I regretted very much that I wasn't able to be with him to the end, but that's how the service works—you put your personal life on the back burner.

Captain Cross had packed my things into a cardboard box that waited for me when I arrived back in Baghdad. A naval commander I'd never met was sitting in my seat, working on the daily PowerPoint slides. The job in Kuwait had been filled, so I remained stuck in Iraq under Colonel Mulder's thumb.

"You're working in the Strategic Operations Center now," Wilbur explained to me softly, almost apologetically. "By the way, Chris, how is your grandfather doing?"

There was no further word about Haitham's disappearance, and he was soon presumed dead without so much as an investigation. Thomas Perkins was nearly killed on a mission to inspect a power plant when a mortar exploded a few meters away (the colonel standing next to him lost an eye in the blast).

When Jessica Rabbit heard that I had been fired, she

decided it would be best for us not to see each other romantically. "I don't want to date a loser."

Needless to say, my return had quite a pleasant landing.

Over the next few weeks, the insurgents in Baghdad launched a blistering series of mortar strikes on the Green Zone. On more than one occasion I awakened to the sound of explosions near my hooch—their aim was getting better. There is nothing quite so horrifying as hearing a close-by blast followed by another on the opposite side. I hit the floor and froze in disbelief. *I'm gonna be really pissed if I get killed today* . . . On my way home from the chow hall, an evening strike landed halfway between my trailer and the palace—directly on my hundred-meter route to work. A soldier that I'd seen playing Ping-Pong fifteen minutes earlier and a contractor for Halliburton were killed in the blasts. The solider died instantly; the contractor was less fortunate, moaning and bleeding to death slowly from the shrapnel she took in her stomach.

On General Casey's last morning as the commanding general of the Multi-National Force, his replacement, General David Petraeus, sat nearby, silently watching and listening. While Petraeus looked a bit jet-lagged, his appearance was otherwise immaculate and vigorous. Casey looked enervated and relatively old. The briefing progressed as always—mountains of data rained down upon our commander as he stoically tried to soak it all in. Casey asked a question about whether a slide depicting murders and executions showed a weekly average or a monthly average. It was the monthly average; he wanted the weekly average.

When the caboose of the PowerPoint train rolled down the tracks, the same words as always flashed before the headquarters: "Commanding General's Comments." The ragged general, unable to avoid talking to his headquarters this time, cleared his throat and spoke his farewell, surprising us all by reciting a few lines of poetry.

When you go home, tell them of us and say,
For their tomorrow, we gave our today.

I looked up the quote on the Internet for shits and googles. The words, written by John Maxwell Edmonds, are inscribed upon a memorial commemorating the four thousand British and Indian soldiers who died at the Battle of Kohima. This World War II battle marked the turning point in the Burma Campaign, where the Allied forces thwarted the Imperial Japanese conquest of the Asian subcontinent. A noted British historian later described Kohima as the "Thermopylae of England." But strangely, the connection between Kohima and the legendary Greek battle goes deeper. The words that Edmonds wrote and Casey spoke that morning are believed to have been inspired by the Epitaph of Simonides— a poem about Thermopylae. But while Edmonds romanticized the sacrifices of Allied troops, the words from the original Greek poem are much more compelling. After the legendary three hundred were slaughtered in their spectacular last stand at Thermopylae, the Epitaph of Simonides, inscribed in an austere stone memorial, impelled the reader to

Tell the Spartans, passers-by,
that here, obediently, we lie.

In short, the origins of Casey's parting words boiled down to a single ancient and horrifying thought: "Tell all your friends—we may be dead, but we did what we were told." I thought of General Casey's emaciated face on the videoconference screen, trying to inspire us with words of *non sibi sed patriae.* Instead, all I could think of was America's four thousand dead in my country's last stand for cheap oil. *Dulce et decorum est* would have been more appropriate, or better yet, how *light, sweet, and crude.* Needless to say, I was ready for the change of command.

. . .

"Praise the Lord! I just saved two homosexual souls," Mitchell declared as he sat down next to my new desk in the Strategic Operations Center. It was my first week working for Mitch Connelly—my new boss—and even though nothing had improved in the war effort, life was at least colorful.

"Ya wanna come to my Bible study tonight?" Mitchell offered with the vacuous ebullience of a telemarketer.

I nodded no and thanked the good chap for offering every week since I'd arrived in Iraq. Mitchell was a reservist lieutenant commander in his forties without a snowball's chance in Baghdad of getting another promotion. He volunteered for reactivation with hopes of polishing his résumé and boosting his retirement income. Connelly's jobs as a traveling used-textbook salesman and part-time evangelical minister weren't giving his family the lifestyle that he wanted them to have, so he took a gamble on Iraq. One hundred thousand dollars of tax-free pay would do wonders for their finances, and helping his family was worth any personal risk to Mitch. I respected him a great deal for that. However, the opportunity to "save a few souls along the way" hadn't escaped Mitch's attention, which tended to dampen our relationship.

"Man, it's gonna be great when you become a Christian," Mitch declared, loud enough for the whole office to hear.

I scowled, looking up from my Arabic spreadsheet. "What's wrong with me now?"

The smile faded as Mitch realized that I wasn't ready to accept Jesus. "Uhhh, nothing, Chris. You're great . . . *but* . . . man, it's gonna be something!"

The vacuous smile returned. "Did I tell you that I just saved two homosexual souls?"

I blinked, not surprised at all by the ridiculous claim.

"Yes, Mitch, you did," I replied dryly, copying and pasting the Arabic data into the English columns.

"It was beautiful! These two faggots—excuse me, homo-sexual men—decided to come to Jesus and *waa-laaa!* I converted them!!!"

"It's a miracle, Mitch."

I was ignoring him by then. He didn't want to talk to me anyway—he just wanted to use the phone on my desk to call home to his wife. I continued working as he whispered sweet nothings into the handset, three feet from where I sat.

"Hey, baby," he whispered in a deep, sultry voice. I shivered.

"Yeah, baby . . . The war's not going so well . . . We're just not killing enough of 'em."

Mitch's conversations couldn't go for five minutes without criticizing some group of people whom he didn't understand very well. It didn't matter if it was the "Muslim world" or "Catholic hocus-pocus" or AIDS victims or "homos" or liberals or liberal Muslim homos with AIDS who had converted from Catholicism. Mitch frequently complained that "the Arabs should have their own UN" and ended his sentences with "Praise the Lord."

Nevertheless, the gracious commander professed that all odious heathens had the option of renouncing their evil ways and coming to his particular version of Jesus. Mitch was Samuel Huntington on Prozac, with a loaded gun and a camouflage Bible. For a time, Mitch wanted to publish His own version of the Bible. He was convinced that U.S. copyright law required that 10 percent of the wording be altered for a legitimate claim to intellectual property. In this noble pursuit, He spent a great deal of time deliberating over which of His words could best improve the Holy Book. By serendipity, Mitch was also my neighbor in the trailer park. I frequently bumped into him after work, watching *Leave It to Beaver* and reading the *National Review* while listening to Frank Sinatra.

"Have you ever heard of Old Blue Eyes?" Mitch asked,

hoping to introduce a young whippersnapper to a whole new world of sonic delight.

"Yeah, Mitch. My aunt Sylvia listens to him all the time." His face lit up with enthusiasm. "She's sixty-five." The smile faded. I saw him holding the *National Review* in his hand, so I asked him why that magazine advertised so many wheelchairs, hearing aids, and low-dexterity phones with extra-large buttons.

"You know, Mitch, at your age, that socialized Medicare thing will pay for most of that stuff. You don't actually have to buy it."

The crestfallen commander turned around silently and moped into his hooch, longing for youth to the saccharine symphony of "My Way."

One day in the morning briefing, Palestine made the news on account of some protests against the Israeli government. Mitchell decided to play the hate monger.

"Those Palestinians are all a bunch of terrorists," he spat disgustedly. He didn't realize that a Palestinian translator, Rasheed, was sitting three desks behind us. Rasheed hadn't heard the comment.

"Hey, Rasheed!" I yelled, much louder than necessary.

"Yes, Chris?"

"Are you a *terrorist*?"

The others in the Strategic Operations Center took note, looking up from their work.

Rasheed laughed. "No, Chris. I'm pretty normal, I think. Why do you ask?"

"Never mind, Rasheed! Thanks," I shouted, flashing him a thumbs-up and a wink.

Connelly fumed in dead silence, furiously trying to concoct a reply. The office chuckled.

"See, Mitch? Rasheed's Palestinian, and he *says* he's not a terrorist."

Connelly looked ready to explode.

Another individual augmentee stands outside his hooch in our trailer park behind the Republican Palace. The trailers were surrounded by sandbags to protect us against the frequent mortar attacks.

"Wanna waterboard him? Maybe we can change his mind."

To say that my new job was boring would deny the utter profundity of the ennui it inspired. To my horror, I discovered that Connelly's team of four personnel was responsible for nothing more than taking the reports that Wilbur and I had written, rehashing the data into different slides, then sending new slides to the exact same recipients. By my calculation, our distribution list received the same data in four different formats every single day. On my first eight-hour shift, the job took me about two hours to perform. On my second eight-hour shift, it was down to one. By the third shift, I was so bored that I spent the whole time recoding the spreadsheet to fill itself in automatically. By the fourth shift, my entire job took no more than twelve minutes; I did the "work" of the next shift as an afterthought before taking a coffee break with seven hours to go.

"Chris, I know that you want to help, but you can't take our jobs away—we need to keep some work for the others to do."

"Mitch, we don't need the others to do *anything*. Send them somewhere else! Send them home! One person can handle this."

"Look, Chris," Mitchell countered firmly, showing a slight hint of impatience, "we've got our way of doing things. Let's not jeopardize the good deal we've got, okay?"

"Yes, sir," I replied dryly. I couldn't believe that Connelly was pulling rank on me, especially for this reason—he was defending a waste of resources simply because it made his own plans run smoothly. After all, eight-hour shifts with Sundays off left plenty of time for part-time preachin'.

Epiphanies, however, gestate in the womb of boredom. My epiphany was no immaculate conception, but it wasn't half bad either. As I sat at my desk in the Strategic Operations Center, trying not to drool, I found myself staring at a map of the Middle East. In my utter boredom, the map drew me in, and I imagined myself sailing my submarine from the Mediterranean through the Suez Canal. I imagined standing on the bridge, watching, waving at the oil tankers and freighters and warships that sailed along, overtaking us in the brown, tepid water. I imagined the skyline fading over the desert as we sailed through the Red Sea, past the Gulf of Aqaba and around the Arabian Peninsula—*Wait a minute! Past the Gulf of Aqaba and around the Arabian Peninsula—*

"Holy shit!" I shouted, startled back into reality. I grabbed the ruler off my desk and started to measure the map. Ha! My suspicion was confirmed. The Wärtsiläs were coming back to life!!!

"Thomas, listen to this!" I shouted into the phone. "We can't fly the Wärtsiläs from Jordan because the fuel would weigh too much, but what if we flew the engines from Kuwait?"

"But they're not *in* Kuwait, Chris."

"Yeah, yeah, I know . . . but we could *ship* them to Kuwait through the Gulf of Aqaba and around the Arabian Peninsula. It's a cheap sea transit, and Kuwait's airport is closer than Jordan."

"So you're saying we could cut the fuel requirement down?"

"Exactly!"

"You may be onto something! This baby still could fly!"

I called the Antonov operators in England to ask them to run the new numbers. The British gentleman was not amused—he'd already spent a great deal of time with our case, and there was nothing to show for it. I begged him to reevaluate the plan based on taking off from Kuwait and landing at the airfield near Samarra. A few days later the response came back from his engineers.

"We think it will work!"

"Thank you, sir!" I chimed into the phone.

Thomas quickly alerted the senior leaders of the E-Team that we had a workable solution. In two days' time, we were briefing the one-star generals. Colonel Mulder saw my solution as a last chance to make himself look good and begrudgingly followed along.

"You fuck this up, Brownfield, and I'll choke you," Mulder joked.

"Yes, sir," I replied, not knowing what else to say.

The one-stars loved the plan. In five days I briefed two different two-star generals, including the top general for strategic operations. In a week, I found myself sitting in front of the cabinet minister himself with the senior-most members of the E-Team and a two-star general backing me up while I briefed our plan to rescue the half-billion-dollar project.

Dr. Karim had been pushing the coalition to send him a letter denying the use of the Green Zone for an overland transit. A key point in driving the engines to Samarra was crossing the Tigris and the Euphrates rivers, and most of the bridges in Iraq were inadequate to hold the massive weight of the steel hulks. The 14th of July Bridge, named after the socialist revolution in Iraq, was a key to the minister's land transit. The problem was that the coalition forces assessed the 14th of July Bridge as inadequate to support the weight of the engines, not to mention that driving the Wärtsiläs through the streets of Baghdad would be an indefensible mess. If the coalition sent a letter denying the official use of the bridge, then Dr. Karim would have a scapegoat to blame for not delivering the engines. Otherwise, the minister would have to tell the people of Samarra that he had simply given up, which was not a good political option. Dr. Karim started to ask about the letter. Ian and the two-star took a deep breath. *Here we go again . . .*

But I expected the criticism and interrupted the minister. "Sir, when you hear what I've got to say, you'll leave the 14th of July to the French for Bastille Day."

The minister smirked and fell silent. I had his rapt attention. When I delivered the briefing, he was very impressed that we had found this option, believing that such a thing was previously impossible.

"I'm amazed that you figured this out."

But there remained one problem—the minister's scapegoat. The airlift option that Thomas, George, and I had developed would be entirely Iraqi-funded and entirely dependent on the Iraqis' ability to come through on a deadline with a lot of moving parts. That meant that Dr. Karim could be either a national hero or a fool responsible for the world's largest fireball if the plane got shot down. He wasn't willing to take that chance. As someone who was a likely candidate for an energy minister position or even higher, he was not going to take a political risk without something covering his six. He thanked me again for the extraordinary plan and respectfully declined the proposal. And so it came to pass that at the end of a long, dusty road, it was politics that finally killed the beasts.

. . .

Again, I found myself bored and with time to spare. The Kims took it upon themselves to teach me the Hangul alphabet, which I found much easier to understand than the Arabic script. I laughed aloud when I realized that the Koreans have the same letter for "L" and "R." *This explains why I keep getting invited to "runch"!* On my off time, I meandered toward an Iraqi shop full of brass trinkets, fake Cuban cigars, and Persian silk rugs. I was enticed there by a homemade poster advertising Iraqi art. "Celebrate Peace," the poster read. *Right*, I mumbled while jotting down the directions. *In which country?*

The directions on the poster led me to the back of a large Iraqi store where hookah pipes, fake Arabian swords, and knockoff Armani shirts packed the shelves. A round and mustached man sat on a wooden stool, barefoot, resting his feet upon a stack of Persian rugs; the room was covered wall to wall in exotic handmade carpets. Through a final door sat a man working on a canvas, paintbrush in one hand, palette in the other. The man was smartly dressed—designer-impostor specs, neatly fitting clothes, and a haircut stylish by Manhattan standards. The room was small and full of hundreds of oil paintings, stacked floor to ceiling. Large antique lightbulbs cast a warm glow over the space. Some replicas of Picassos and touristy sketches of stereotypical Arabs lay haphazardly about. Paintings of Christian religious symbols and a portrait of a soldier's family sat with photograph attached, waiting for Sergeant Smith to pick it up.

"Hi, what's your name?" I asked the artist.

"I'm Muslim. Actually, that's my name and my religion," he said with a gentle laugh.

We shook hands. "I'm Christopher. Good to meet you!"

Muslim smirked and quickly asked, "*Christopher* . . . does that make you Christian?"

"No, no, no . . . For me, it's just a name."

An abstract painting on the wall caught my attention. "This is great; who painted it?"

"Mohammed, my boss."

"I love it!"

"For you, sir, we have a special price," the salesman stated with practiced enthusiasm. I got the feeling that the special price was not so special. Still, I was puzzled about how an artist could set up shop in the middle of a war zone, and I wanted to know more.

"Muslim, how long have you been working here?"

"A few years."

"What did you do before this?"

"Al Jamiyah—the university."

"What did you study?"

"Art, of course!"

"And what about the other painters who did these works?"

"We were classmates!"

Amazing. Somehow, in the midst of the insurgency, a cohort of artists had managed to continue painting. It was a breath of fresh air—my first unlikely glimpse that life could go on despite the war. *I have to know more about these guys!*

"Who did you study? I see some Picassos here, but who else? Degas?"

"Yes."

"Rembrandt?"

"Yes."

"Van Gogh?"

"Of course!"

"Warhol?"

"Who?"

"Andy Warhol?"

"I don't know this person."

"What about Georgia O'Keeffe?"

"No."

"John Singer Sargent?"

"No."

"Jackson Pollock?"

Muslim shook his head no.

"What about Basquiat?"

"Never heard of him."

"Norman Rockwell?"

"Are you sure these people are artists?"

The puzzle was starting to take shape—Muslim had never heard of a single American painter.

"Did Saddam let you study American art?"

"No no no. *That* was forbidden."

"Would you like me to bring some books about American art?"

Muslim's eyes lit up with enthusiasm. "Yes, sir! Please!"

"Call me Chris."

"Yes, sir . . . sorry, sir!"

"*Maaku mushkila*—No problem." I laughed. "Now, let's talk about that painting I like!"

Suddenly the special price got a lot more special. Back at my hooch, I put in an online order for some decent books on American art and had them sent to my office. When the books arrived, I returned to the art shop and found Muslim working on an American soldier's wedding portrait. Upon seeing the encyclopedia-sized volumes full of big color images, Muslim smiled, delighted.

"I've never seen these artists before! Are these all American?"

"Yes."

"There are so many! Thank you so much!" Muslim threw his arms around me in a big, joyful hug. "Mohammed will be here soon—and he's bringing food from the city! Are you hungry?"

"I'd love to join you—and I can't wait to meet Mohammed!"

Sure enough, Mohammed arrived carrying a large plastic bag with takeout from a Red Zone restaurant. It was the first time I had eaten with regular Iraqis, and it was the best food I had eaten in months. Fresh tomatoes, cucumbers, pickled cauliflower, small-grain rice, and baked flatbread with delectable Iraqi chai graced our palates. Halliburton, with its deep-fried smorgasbord, had nothing on the local cuisine. Mohammed seemed friendly, though he was a bit suspicious of me at first. But when I genuinely complimented his works and showed him the books on American art, he warmed up a great deal, despite the enormous language barrier between us.

Though Muslim was very happy to be having lunch with Mohammed and me, Muslim was a bit nervous because the taxi driver who brought him to the edge of the Green Zone suspected that he was working with Americans—a dangerous piece of information.

"I'm not working with those dogs," Muslim insisted. "I'm trying to get paid for the damage that they did to my home," he lied.

In fact, all of the Iraqis in the Green Zone had to be careful not to reveal where they worked. A casual slip in front of the wrong people would mean the difference between living peacefully and being marked for death by local extremists. Even Muslim's wife didn't know where he worked. Typically, Muslim walked to work, changing his route every time and entering the base through different checkpoints. For artistic inspiration Muslim carried an American department store catalog, but he wrapped it in plain brown paper to conceal the English text—even a catalog in English could give the impression of collaborating with the occupiers.

As we enjoyed the meal, Muslim recounted his memories of 2003, describing in great detail the plunder of Baghdad's national museums. Hundreds of looters ran helter-skelter, hefting paintings and statues and ancient pottery. When Muslim tried to stop one, the looter pulled a pistol threateningly and made off with a priceless ancient vase. Since he knew a bit of English, Muslim ran till he found American soldiers who could help.

"That's not my job," one soldier responded calmly; he was guarding the Ministry of Oil.

As we sat in the art shop, sharing food and friendship, one of the large, ungainly lightbulbs above our heads burned out. Setting down his food, Muslim got up to replace it with a new bulb. As he took the old one out, I asked to see it. To my amazement, the ungainly antique-looking thing consumed a whopping three hundred watts!

"How common is this kind of lightbulb, Muslim?"

"They aren't the most popular, but I do see them a lot."

"Mind if I keep this?" I asked.

"Sure, but why do you want a burned-out lightbulb?"

"Trust me, I've got an idea . . ."

Mohammed and Muslim looked at me in bewilderment as I got up and left, pointing to the antique lightbulbs and counting them, one by one, on my way out the door.

15

The Precipitous Pullout

It started as a vice presidential quip about retreat from Iraq. A precipitous pullout, Dick Cheney declared with his jaw clenched in a bitter sneer, would be a defeat against all we stand for. After three hundred million Americans looked up the word "precipitous" in their dictionaries, the vice president's message of warrior angst had been transformed into lewd commentary.

"It sounds like a bad sexual encounter," I remarked to George.

"What, 'precipitous pullout'?"

"Yeah, 'precipitous pullout.' Quite—an unexpected ejaculation . . ."

George choked on his coffee.

" . . . in the oratorical sense."

Years before, the captain of the *Hartford* had warned the crew against acting "precipitously." One of our nuclear operators had violated a procedure, causing an electrical breaker to trip.

"We need to guard against precipitous operations," the skipper declared in a fatherly tone. We nodded our heads, *Yes, sir*. Then 139 of the *Hartford*'s 140 men looked up the word "precipitous." We were so happy with our newfound vocabulary that it became our word of choice for the next several weeks. Whether we used it correctly or not didn't really matter.

"How are you doing today?"

"Positively precipitous!"

"How's the weather up topside?"

"Lightly cloudy and precipitous."

"How's your girlfriend treating you?"

"She dumped me yesterday."

"Precipitously?"

"Indeed."

"Pity."

After a week, Captain Frank caught wind of something awry. "Why the hell does everyone keep saying 'precipitous'?"

We managed not to break, keeping straight faces and responding with practiced ignorance, "Beg your pardon, sir? Is something wrong?"

In Iraq, the precipitous pullout continued when Moqtada al-Sadr fled from Baghdad to Iran. While the radical descendant of the Prophet Muhammad insisted that he was simply visiting his Persian pen pals and finishing his Ph.D. in fundamentalism, the truth was obvious: he was afraid of Petraeus. By my assessment, Sadr wanted to skip town for a while to see if the much-talked-about "surge" would have any teeth. If not, then he could waltz back into Baghdad when the troop pullout began and maybe even pull off a coup. In the meantime, wintering at Uncle Ahmadinejad's house wouldn't cost Sadr any face.

Inside the Strategic Operations bubble, I tried not to drool as Fox News and CNN intermittently sucked the right and left brain cells from my skull. But all was not yet lost; the last and most exhilarating part of the precipitous pullout was about to begin.

On Petraeus's first morning slide show as commander, reports from around headquarters proceeded as if nothing had happened. I read the energy briefing that day and took the liberty of offering the new general my finest naval greeting.

"Welcome aboard, sir!"

Petraeus smiled. "Thank you! It's good to be back!"

This basic courtesy was, apparently, an important victory for Colonel Mulder's war effort—he was ecstatic that I "made him look good" with the new boss. I laughed inwardly at the colonel's shortsightedness. *I'll bet your ancestors worshiped weather events, you idiot.* On Petraeus's third morning briefing, a particularly inane "golden nugget" slide arrived, lauding the accomplishments of some Iraqi soldiers who had just graduated from a special training camp.

Petraeus wanted none of it. "Why does the graduation of twelve Iraqi soldiers from a two–week school warrant a golden nugget? Or even my attention, for that matter?"

The headquarters was silent. Inside, I was laughing hysterically.

"Let's not overstate the significance of what we're saying," Petraeus continued. "This kind of report undermines our credibility when we have *important* things to talk about."

Days later, Captain Cross was reading the energy report himself—something that he almost always delegated.

Petraeus interrupted the captain mid-sentence. "Gentlemen, you're only showing me data. Where is your analysis? Where is your plan to fix the problem?"

I could barely contain my delight. To say that it was emasculating for Wilbur to hear Petraeus voice my sentiments simply wouldn't do it justice. In three quick sentences, Petraeus managed to lift up Wilbur's skirt, point out that he had no underpants, then smack him on the hairy old ass to make him run.

"Uhhhh . . . next slide, please" was all poor Wilbur could muster.

"Yeah," Petraeus quipped dryly. "Next slide."

By the end of the first week, the good general had decided that my unit's performance was woefully inadequate. In a shocking break from his diplomatic demeanor, Petraeus turned to his deputy and declared before all, "We've got to do something about energy—there are a lot of guys in my headquarters who are doing nothing but making PowerPoint slides."

The general was referring to my three bosses, whose faces flushed with embarrassment. I felt bad for Colonel Dawson, whose solid, pragmatic efforts were hamstrung by his egomaniacal counterpart in State, but the others won no sympathy from me. Mulder stated the problem himself—*they never had a plan*. But in any case, the die was cast; the general had spoken. Soon thereafter, an order was written to disband the civil-military operations directorate. To my knowledge, it was the first time during the war that a strategic-level unit was disbanded before its mission was accomplished. As soon as General Kim departed for Korea, the remaining members of the geriatric special forces would be scattered to the desert winds. The precipitous pullout would be complete.

Of course, the mission of winning hearts and minds by providing essential services and caring for basic civil needs was not abandoned. When Petraeus arrived with a new strategy of counterinsurgency, winning hearts and minds became the central focus. Instead of delegating this critical mission to an ad hoc group of internationals, the entire army internalized the goal. From that point onward, every soldier was to embody the spirit of the civil affairs unit. Every soldier was to become an ambassador of dignity and respect while risking his or her life to protect the Iraqi people. In this overarching strategy, my unit had become obsolete.

In the Green Bean café, I took a cappuccino with a Naval Academy classmate who had just arrived in Baghdad.

"Man, General Petraeus really hates civil affairs right now," Colin remarked. I nodded in agreement, sipping my frothy caffeinated goodness.

"Where do you work, Chris?"

"Civil affairs."

Colin nearly shot coffee through his nostrils. "Sorry, man . . . I didn't know!"

"It's okay, Colin—those guys needed to be put out to pasture."

"Put out to pasture? Come on, Chris, let's call it what it is. Those guys have been *ethnically cleansed.*"

I couldn't hold back my smile.

"Here's to General Petraeus," I toasted, raising my coffee on high.

"I'll toast to that," Colin replied. "I'll definitely toast to that!"

As the Kim Collection prepared to depart for Seoul, constellations of Bronze Stars fell from the heavens to grace the heroes of our defunct unit. Mulder put himself in for a second Bronze Star; Wilbur got a big shiny medal with a citation so riddled with fiction that it could just as well have started with "Once upon a time . . ." Egos swelled as exploits were proclaimed before all. It didn't matter that most of the citations were based upon good intentions, not upon actual results. A few officers had performed admirably, like the colonel who established a crisis hotline similar to America's 911 emergency services. Another colonel—the one who aspired to bring the American porn industry to Iraq—had saved the life of an Iraqi politician during a suicide bombing, earning himself a Bronze Star, a Purple Heart, and a hefty solid-gold medal from the Iraqi Council of Representatives. These feats, however, were noble exceptions. For the most part, it was an orgy of self-congratulation among aging bureaucrats pretending to be soldiers.

"I'm putting myself in for an Arctic Service Ribbon," one newly arrived officer laughed.

I cocked my head, puzzled. "Why?"

"Because I'm about as close to the arctic circle as these colonels are to combat."

Following the masturbatory ceremony, General Kim

hosted a cookout to hail the newly arrived replacements and bid farewell to his multinational unit. The replacements found themselves in an awkward social limbo, mingling with their predecessors who had been collectively pink-slipped by Petraeus. The senior leadership of the outgoing unit lavished themselves with further accolades and letters of appreciation, documenting their extraordinary successes.

Lieutenant Commander Connelly, seizing the high spirits of the crowd, called our attention to Jesus. "Thank you, Lord, for the success of our unit. Thank you for the lives of those who were lost in this conflict of Good against Evil, and thank you, Lord, for our continued safe—"

"INCOMING!!!!" Giovanni screamed in terror. The all-too-familiar whistle of a speeding mortar shell streaked over our heads. I hit the deck with a thud while an explosion sounded nearby. Something wet and warm oozed across my arm. *Crap?!? Am I hit? Am I bleeding?* Not exactly—I'd just landed in the only mud puddle in Baghdad (Halliburton left the garden hose running while trying to grow grass by the pool). Another explosion sounded from a hundred yards away. I looked up and saw a Macedonian and some Americans who had just arrived in Baghdad that day. They were still standing up, confused and horrified. The "disciprined" Kims had long since hit the deck.

"Get down! Get down, you fools!!!"

The crowd scattered into the Republican Palace and the concrete bunkers. But like all the mortar attacks, it was over almost as fast as it began. Running was useless.

Back in the Strategic Operations Center, I sat, watching CNN report on the most recent attacks

Mitchell walked in, beaming with delight. "Chris, can you believe what just happened? I mean, there we were, praying for Jesus to protect us, and he answered us immediately! Praise the Lord!"

"You call that *protection*? I think you were just poking at Allah. Jesus had nothing to do with it."

Since nobody was hurt, I thought it fair to joke a bit, expecting Mitch to smile or come back with a witty reply, like our usual friendly parleys. But instead of smiling, Mitch lost control, growing red in the face and yelling, "It *was* a miracle, and I don't see why God can't get the credit."

Crap! I didn't mean to offend the guy.

"That's not what I meant, Mitch. It was just a joke." I tried to apologize.

"But that's what all you liberals think—" Mitch's face got redder as his tone got louder and more accusatory. "God is never the answer, just the reason for a lawsuit."

I felt like shit. *How the hell did I know that it wasn't a miracle? Maybe I would have been blown up without divine intervention. Or maybe my friends would have been blown up.* The fact is, I didn't know, and any rational person could never know as long as he lived. But I did know that it was at least the fiftieth mortar attack we had seen during our tour of duty. Mitch was going home in less than a week. I tried to defuse the tension so we wouldn't part company on such a bad note.

"I'm just glad that you're all right and no one was hurt. I'm sorry."

Mitch hung his head, clenching his teeth as though I had just punched him in the chin.

I continued to blabber an apology. "Just think, Mitch, by this time next week, you'll be home with your family . . ."

The forlorn commander nodded tersely in agreement, took a deep breath, then walked back to his hooch to pack his bags for the trip home.

During the next days in the Strategic Operations Center, seventeen big-screen televisions and two hundred fifty computers flickered before me, but I didn't notice and I didn't give a rat's ass about a single damn one. My twelve minutes' worth of daily shift work was over, which left me with seven hours and forty-eight minutes to contemplate the possibilities of

The Green Bean café, where "third-country nationals" from Sri Lanka and Bangladesh steamed some mean cappuccinos. The chandeliers are aglow with dozens of compact fluorescent lightbulbs.

lightbulbs. I was fixated on the enormous antique-looking Iraqi lightbulb that I held in my hand. I had never before seen anything like it. In America, the brightest commonly used incandescent bulbs are 100 watts each, and those suckers are intense. This thing looked like it came straight from Thomas Edison's laboratory—and it was 300 watts! To top it all off, the massive hunk of glass wasn't even very bright; it was more of a heater than anything.

George noticed me staring at the bulb on his way to his desk. "What's that ya got there, Chris? A vacuum tube?"

The shop where my Iraqi friends sold Persian rugs and paintings was lit by fifteen of the 300-watt monsters. The Strategic Operations Center, by contrast, was illuminated with state-of-the-art, energy-efficient lights that burned 11 watts each with the brightness of an "old" 60-watt bulb. Some quick bar-napkin math revealed that the tiny Iraqi shop used five times as much energy on lighting as the Strategic Operations Center (which was five times as large as the shop). In other words, the Iraqi shop was twenty-five times less energy efficient than the palace, where Halliburton had upgraded the bulbs.

The next obvious question was how many of those large power-sucking antiques were being used throughout the country—especially since the government was picking up the electric bill.

I broke down and logged on to my computer to crunch some serious numbers (having run out of room on my bar-napkin notes). After a few hours, I estimated that the countrywide energy use of old-fashioned lightbulbs amounted to as much electricity as a large state-of-the-art power plant. What a waste! If we could somehow switch out the Edison-style bulbs for the new bulbs, then the government could potentially reduce demand by several hundred megawatts and save several hundred million dollars! And in the case of Iraq's severe energy shortage, improving efficiency of existing appliances was equivalent to adding more generators to the grid— a big step toward energy independence! I went to the Halliburton employee who managed the facilities in the Green Zone.

"Why did you switch out the lightbulbs in the palace?" I asked.

"It made a huge difference with the generators. Oh, and the new ones run cool—we didn't have to use the air-conditioning nearly as much."

"Why does that matter? Don't you guys have a cost-plus contract?"

"Yeah, I know, but this switch just made my life a lot easier. The new bulbs last longer, so we don't have to change them out as much, we burn a lot less diesel in the generators, and the palace is more comfortable. One more thing—it does save the taxpayers some money."

Halliburton? Worried about saving taxpayer dollars? I couldn't believe what I was hearing!

"What would you say if the government of Iraq bought enough lightbulbs for the whole country?"

"It's a no-brainer. They'd save a ton. And they could use the extra power somewhere else. Don't they have all sorts of blackouts here?"

I nodded yes, then complimented the man. "Sir, somebody should give you a medal!"

"I don't know about that, but a vacation would be nice. These mortar attacks have been rough lately."

"Can I have a box of lightbulbs, sir?"

"Sure, Lieutenant. How many do you need?"

"Enough to cover a general's desk."

Since being fired from my job with Captain Cross, I was forbidden by Colonel Mulder to talk to the E-Team. Thomas and George, however, made a point of ignoring Mulder and keeping the back door open. I approached Thomas and asked him to look at my lightbulb estimates, but he was reluctant.

"Chris, this sounds like a good thing to do, but who's going to manage it? We don't have the time."

"Could you look at it and tell me if it seems correct? I promise you that I won't ask you to run the program!"

"All right, all right . . . but just because it's you, Chris."

"You kick ass, Tom. I'm naming my first kid after you— boy or girl."

When Tom got back to me, the news was interesting. "Your numbers are way off, Chris."

I grew tense.

Tom continued, "This would actually work *better* than you think. If you can find a way to do this without bothering me, then I say go for it!"

With the blessing of the State Department, my next stop was getting through Colonel Mulder to General Kim. Even though General Kim was leaving the country soon, I considered him a potentially important ally. South Korea's government had recently implemented a lightbulb exchange program to increase its nationwide energy efficiency. However, Mulder, the gatekeeper to General Kim, refused to give me the time of day.

"I don't have any time to worry about soldiers going door-to-door and handing out lightbulbs," Mulder growled while fidgeting with his iPod. "Oh, hey, check this out! I just downloaded eighty free songs by Carlos Santana!"

I went to Mitch to beg for help. "There's got to be a way we can get fifteen minutes with General Kim!"

Mitchell shook his head, denying my plea.

"Please, Mitch! I'll come to your Bible study. I'll watch your videos on creationism. *Anything!*"

Mitch looked irritated. "Not without going through Mulder first."

"Then we're giving up, Mitch. *We're giving up.*"

"Drop it, Lieutenant. It's over."

I moped into the Green Bean café to get a fix of my only drug—caffeine. By coincidence, Jessica Rabbit was there. We hadn't seen each other since she'd dumped me a few weeks earlier, and she looked incredibly sexy.

"You're a sight for sore eyes."

She asked what I was doing, so I told her, pulling the antique Iraqi bulb from my bulging waist-level pocket.

She smiled seductively, feigning disappointment. "Too bad . . . I thought you were just happy to see me."

I laughed, entranced by her perfume and her resplendent breasts, forgetting about the war for a few seconds.

Jessica shook her head dismissively, then pulled out her dagger while moving in for the kill. "I just don't understand why you care."

Later that day, George recommended that I speak to a British colonel named Alexander Shelton. Alex was a special assistant to Petraeus's deputy, the officer in charge of infrastructure. Alex seemed young for a person in such a senior position, but I would soon learn that his talents far exceeded his years (and even his relatively high rank). Colonel Shelton was one of the few officers in the headquarters with a graduate degree in management, and it showed. He was very knowledgeable, pragmatic, and effective in his work. On his desk sat a vial like the ones the clinic used to draw blood. It was filled with dark black fluid. I introduced myself and told him about the lightbulb plan, which he immediately endorsed as "brilliant."

"Be ready to brief the general. I'll call you soon," he told me.

On my way out the door I pointed to the vial on his desk. "By the way, sir, is that real blood?"

Alex replied coolly without looking up, "Don't be stupid, Leftenant. It's oil. It's why we're here."

The general was Colonel Goodman's boss, a tough-looking Australian who carried a handgun the size of a small cannon. George agreed to come to the briefing to give me top cover. The timing couldn't have been more perfect. In the previous week, Australia's parliament had banned incandescent lightbulbs from being sold on the continent. My presentation was short and to the point: I handed the Aussie the ungainly 300-watt bulb, then promptly dumped out the box of twenty-seven compact fluorescent lightbulbs that the groundskeeper from Halliburton had given me. The comparison was fairly obvious. The twenty-seven new bulbs used less power than the single antique.

"There are millions of these antique lightbulbs in Iraq, and they're sucking the life out of the electrical grid. For thirty million dollars, we can make them all go away."

"How do you plan on doing this, Lieutenant? You don't seriously think we're going to get soldiers to hand out lightbulbs?"

"Of course not, sir! Here's the plan . . ."

I explained how the Iraqi government could buy the first round of bulbs and flood the markets, giving them away. Then the government could subsidize imports on energy-efficient bulbs and ban the old-fashioned ones—just as Australia had done the previous week. The whole plan would take several months to reach its potential as old bulbs burned out and were replaced with the new ones.

"Well, this is an excellent *Australian* idea, Lieutenant."

"It's not excellent, sir. It's *brilliant*," I corrected.

The Aussie general smiled. George and I excused ourselves.

Around the headquarters, word got out that some goofy lieutenant with a lightbulb in his pocket had some good ideas to try. General Kim caught wind of the proposal and ordered a briefing, much to Colonel Mulder's chagrin. Thomas liked my strategy (and he was convinced that he wouldn't end up being tasked with managing the program), so he agreed to participate in the briefing and support my technical analysis. George came again for more top cover on the military side. As a courtesy, I asked Colonel Mulder if he'd like to join the meeting.

"It's a great idea," Mulder began, "but I won't support it."

I furrowed my brow, bewildered by his statement.

"You see, Lieutenant, this is Iraq. If we try some do-gooder crap like this, I just know that it's gonna get corrupted by something."

I stared, motionless, waiting for Mulder's defeatist logic to unfold.

"I just know that if we do this, all the lightbulbs are gonna end up in Iran."

As stupid a criticism as it was, there was a small ring of truth. Two years previously, the minister of electricity had approved of the merits of such a program and attempted to buy a truckload of lightbulbs for an impoverished neighborhood in Baghdad. The truck was stolen, sold, and driven to Iran, lightbulbs and all. But the problem was not that the truck was stolen—the problem was that the ministry was trying to pass out lightbulbs itself instead of letting the markets do the work for it. Though this was a solution to an electrical problem, the Ministry of Electricity had no business passing out lightbulbs—it had power plants to build! I took note of Mulder's point and shrugged him off.

On my way out the door, Mulder changed the subject and remarked with a cool sense of resignation, "When you've been in Iraq as long as I have you'll see that it's all about the money. That's why I'm here."

When Mulder had first joked about the pay being better than fixing toilets, I thought it was a quip or self-deprecating humor. Now, after seeing the man in action, I realized with horror that he was quite serious. I blinked, taken aback by the unscrupulous candor. The Mercenary Plumber found it more profitable to be in Baghdad than back home where business was slow.

You son of a bitch . . .

I walked out of the grizzly's den, repulsed by the beast that lay within.

The briefing to General Kim went splendidly. With Thomas and George at my side, we convinced the Korean brigadier in a matter of minutes. Kim loved the idea because it was a way for the Iraqi government to provide a small but tangible service to every single citizen while simultaneously improving the long-term strategic energy situation. To Kim, my plan was a perfect project to bridge the civil-military divide—the mission of our directorate.

"Make this happen," the general ordered.

"Yes, sir," I acknowledged.

General Kim then directed me to obtain more data about the consumer demand for lightbulbs before setting up an appointment with his boss, Petraeus's chief strategist. I was heartened by the enthusiastic reception for the program, but the challenge of finding hard data left a bad taste in my mouth. *How the hell am I going to get more data on consumer habits in the middle of the war zone?*

A few phone calls later, I found myself talking to the public relations officers who oversaw opinion polling throughout the country. They were two air force officers—a major and a lieutenant colonel. Their polls covered ten major cities in Iraq, with a large enough sampling to ensure extremely accurate results. The polls asked about a variety of topics, including electricity.

"Are you extremely satisfied, satisfied, somewhat dissatisfied, or extremely dissatisfied with the electrical power system?"

Needless to say, the steady decline of Iraqi satisfaction from 2003 till 2007 had some of the best statistical documentation of anything in the war. When I requested to ask some questions about lightbulbs in Iraqi homes, the PR officers laughed at me.

"We don't usually ask about that sort of thing."

"Yes, yes, I see what kind of questions you typically ask: *'How much does your life suck? A lot, eh? Can you be more precise? It's for posterity.'*"

The two officers stiffened defensively.

"Look, guys—do you want to go home knowing how much life sucks here with a 5 percent margin of error, or do you want to get me some information that will actually help to solve a problem?"

Silence. The two officers looked at each other, then slowly shrugged in unison.

"Well, I guess if you put it that way . . ."

The two nodded in agreement. They would help after all.

"But there's just one more question, Lieutenant."

"Yes, sir?"

"What the heck are ten thousand Iraqis gonna teach you about lightbulbs?"

16

McCainery, Chicanery

The origins of April Fool's Day remain ambiguous to the contemporary world. Some historians believe that pagan festivals celebrating the arrival of spring account for this perennial sense of mirth. Dancing around the maypole and bouts of drunken revelry continue to typify the tradition in many countries. The ancient festivals of Huli in India and Hilaria in Rome may not have started the tradition of April Fool's Day, but they nonetheless set the precedent that spring—in any culture—is a good time to cut loose. Other historians trace the origins of April Fool's Day to France's adoption of the Gregorian calendar in 1562, which shifted the start of the new year from April 1 to January 1. As this story goes, some provincial citizens either hadn't heard the news or stubbornly refused to change their habits, continuing to celebrate the "old" new year in April. Nowadays, schoolchildren in France secretly tape paper fish on each other's backs before gleefully exclaiming, "*Poisson d'avril*! April fish!" In Scotland, the still hilarious "kick me" sign is ignominiously taped upon the fool's arse. Another less common but pragmatic explanation is that farmers who typically wait till May to plant their summer crops occasionally plant a month too soon, exposing their seeds to the last killing frost and earning the title of April fools the hard way. It may have been ignorance of history or curmudgeonly refusal to change or even desperation to plant the seeds of his presidential campaign, but when Senator John McCain went shopping in the markets of Baghdad on April Fool's Day 2007, America's maverick became the April fish out of water.

Specifically, McCain and his "closest ally in the Senate," Lindsey Graham, shopped the markets of Baghdad without helmets, then remarked that the scene was incredibly safe and normal. If the cameras had panned back, they could have captured the reason why the unusually idyllic cityscape appeared so normal. A company of American soldiers, a team of well-placed snipers, and several helicopter gunships had locked down the area, permitting only the senator's crew to pass.

Dammit, John! Stop pretending! You're better than this!

I really wanted to support McCain. He was a Naval Academy man—one of our own. In 2000 I wanted McCain to become president without reservation. In 2004 I would even have picked McCain over Kerry if given the choice. But in

In the heavily protected U.S. Embassy compound at the heart of the Green Zone, soldiers could sometimes relax without wearing armor. The Red Zone, however, remained extremely dangerous.

2007 things were not safe in Baghdad, and I couldn't believe my ears when John McCain tried to convince the world otherwise.

A few nights later, I sat outside after dark, smoking a cigar at the picnic tables by my hooch. A sergeant who worked on security for Petraeus's missions joined me for a smoke and some conversation.

"Sergeant, what do you think about that stunt with McCain? Do you think he was endangering our men?"

"Nah . . . it doesn't really bother me," the soldier replied. "We're pretty safe when we go out."

"Yeah, I guess you're right, Sergeant."

Petraeus's detail would be safe so long as it traveled with such a powerful contingent of troops and support vehicles. Still, it irked me that so many troops were tied up guarding a dog and pony show instead of performing serious security missions. But overall, the major problem was not that American soldiers were put at risk by McCain's gaffe or distracted from important missions, but that regular Iraqi citizens were actually endangered. A few days after the visit, many of the merchants in that particular market were murdered, probably on account of doing business on camera with such high-profile Americans. As every Iraqi who worked in the Green Zone understood, any perceived association with Americans was a dangerous liability. Eventually John McCain apologized for overstating the level of safety in Baghdad, but that apology was likely lost upon the families of the Iraqis who literally died in the collateral damage of McCain's public relations bombshell.

Captain Brian Freeman was a civil affairs officer who worked in a tactical unit for provincial reconstruction. Brian's job was extremely dangerous; he coordinated efforts between local tribal leaders, Iraqi government officials, and coalition forces. Occasionally one of Freeman's troops would be killed by an

IED or a sniper. Once when that happened, Brian set up a scholarship fund for his fallen comrade's children. But while his compassion and leadership were wonderful qualities, what struck me most about Brian was his face; he looked like he should be on a magazine cover. He had piercing, brilliant eyes and perfectly smooth skin—almost too perfect to be real. During a particularly violent week in the spring, groups of emboldened insurgents began taking potshots at coalition helicopters. Freeman's Black Hawk was one of those hit and forced into an emergency landing by a hydraulic leak. The insurgents quickly surrounded the fallen bird, compelling the outnumbered and outgunned passengers and crew to surrender. Without hesitation, the euphoric insurgents dragged the passengers from the helicopter and shot them, one at a time, in the back of the head.

Out of the blue, I received a phone call from a familiar voice that I hadn't heard for months. It was Carl, a politically connected neoconservative navy reservist who had worked as a senator's chief of staff before being recalled into active duty. The two of us had met in our Iraqi boot camp, where we debated about politics with friendly regularity. After working in the war's public affairs office, the "hardest job in my life," Carl said, he caught a well-deserved break and became Petraeus's liaison to Congress.

"Chris, there's something interesting about to happen, but I can't talk about it over the phone. Can you meet me in fifteen minutes?"

In the Green Bean, Carl explained in hushed tones that Senator Graham, the Republican from South Carolina, was still in Iraq and that a small group of people could meet with him. Strangely, this visit was no longer part of John McCain's entourage but part of Senator Graham's two-week active-duty time as a colonel in the Air Force Reserve.

"Wow! I didn't know that we had any senators still in uniform! And I can't believe that he's actually *serving* in Baghdad, not just taking a VIP tour!"

Carl shook his head in acknowledgment. "Yeah, it's pretty crazy, isn't it? They actually had to bend the rules to let a reservist come to the war zone. Normally that's against the law."

"I'm sure the rules weren't a problem," I said with a laugh. "He probably knows a few people in Washington."

"Here's the deal, Chris. *Colonel* Graham invited some people to meet him for dinner at 19:00. It's a small group, but we've got another seat. Can you make it?"

I cleared my schedule.

As a subtle response to McCain's trip to the market, I showed up at the dinner in what I considered to be appropriate attire. Upon seeing me, Carl burst into laughter.

"Chris, what's up with the full-body armor?"

"It's Baghdad, my friend. One can never be too careful," I replied, removing my dark ballistic sun goggles and Kevlar helmet.

Carl shook his head in disbelief, then introduced me to his civilian colleagues who were also attending the dinner (in business suits and ties). The civilians introduced themselves as media consultants from the BBC.

"Cool. I love the BBC! Which programs do you consult for?"

The men in suits glanced at each other and paused awkwardly.

You're not from the BBC . . . Who are you guys?

The senator arrived, interrupting our introductions. Carl and I cocked salutes and the senator returned them, then immediately sized up my armor.

"I need that stuff more in Washington than the Green Zone." Graham chuckled in his smooth, charismatic Southern drawl.

I laughed, immediately set off guard by the politician's charm. Despite Graham's being in a war zone, his smile and hair were perfect. And while his hair was a bit long by military standards, the senator's camouflage uniform looked extremely crisp. We shook hands, drew our pistols, cleared the chambers over a barrel full of sand, then walked into the chow hall like a big, well-armed family.

In line for our greasy Halliburton slop, I stood next to the so-called BBC consultants. I asked specifically what they did for the BBC while working in Iraq.

"Well . . . actually, I won an Emmy as a producer, but now I'm with the Lincoln Group."

The deception started to make perfect sense. The Lincoln Group was a highly controversial public relations firm with a $140 million contract for throwing curveballs to the Iraqi media. Among other things, the Lincoln Group bribed Iraqi editors to print fabricated stories as though they were original pieces written by Iraqi journalists. The stories were based upon selective facts, but the modus operandi was a complete lie. Essentially, it was sanctioned propaganda paid for by U.S. tax dollars.

"That's fascinating! What's your job there?"

"I'm the country director, and this is my deputy."

I gulped, somewhat startled at the realization of who was coming to dinner. This was no casual meet and greet but a strategy talk for the top-level media masters and politicos— the soap of the Baghdad spin cycle. As we sat down at the VIP table, there was some confusion about where the senator was to sit. In the shuffle, I ended up across from Graham and next to Major General William Caldwell, the officer in charge of the Iraq war's public relations. I had never seen Caldwell before in person, though I knew his face well from television news. The Goebbels of Baghdad flanked me on my right. I felt immediately uncomfortable, but kept my cool; I was not supposed to be there, but the Republican from South Carolina clearly didn't realize that.

The senator spoke softly, and the rest of the table listened in rapt attention to hear above the din of the crowd. Graham encouraged the media managers before him to capitalize on the successes of places like Anbar Province, where the Marine Corps had actually achieved moderate success. Ironically, Anbar was successful only because the Marine Corps had eschewed the tactics of General Raymond Odierno, the new commander of combat troops in Iraq. Odierno squandered the army's reputation in Anbar by shelling the diffuse enemy relentlessly from the confines of heavily fortified bases, with little regard for the enormous collateral damage his tactics caused. By contrast, the Marine Corps had engaged the Iraqi people in a more human way and empowered them to take important leadership roles. Effectively, the marines implemented a "counterinsurgency" strategy that the army hadn't fully adopted yet.

Graham then shifted gears to his area of expertise, the rule of law. "If Prime Minister Maliki doesn't find a way to bring the murderers of our soldiers to justice, then I'll recommend that we pull out entirely. Iraq has got to learn to respect the rule of law."

The group nodded in approval—even if a well-oiled justice machine was far from functioning in Iraq, who could argue with the rule of law? Certainly not Graham, who had spent his entire military career as a military lawyer. Still, the notion of trying to enforce justice before bringing peace seemed somewhat naive to me. Senior Iraqi officials were being kidnapped, blown up, and shot on a weekly basis, and rarely were any of the murders investigated, let alone followed through with the due process of law that was expected in civilized countries at peace.

"And when are we going to see some trials of these Iraqi terrorists?" Graham continued. "If we don't get some convictions soon, then we're going to continue to face pressure over Guantánamo."

I stiffened, listening intently to what Senator Graham said next. Perhaps because of the crowd's silence, he apparently felt the need to clarify his sentiments.

"We've got to find a better way to detain these guys indefinitely. If we get some convictions in Iraqi courts, we can at least *say* that we're moving forward with due process."

The penny dropped. Graham's real objective was not to uphold the rule of law by ensuring that detainees were given a fair trial, but to give the public the impression of moving forward with justice. Lindsey Graham, the Republican from South Carolina, was filibustering on habeas corpus, one of the oldest and most fundamental cornerstones of the law. I looked around the table once more at the top-level public relations officers and gulped. *I was definitely not supposed to hear that.*

Almost to highlight my discomfort, the senator turned and looked at me, then cocked his head. "I don't recognize you. What is it that you do here?"

"I work in the energy sector, sir."

"Wow. I guess that makes you the most important person here—you actually do something." Graham laughed, looking at the media moguls, who also smiled, their attention now turning toward me.

Seizing my moment in the spotlight, I replied, "I don't know about my importance, sir, but I am doing something. Do you want to do something that could be a public relations win and improve the energy situation for cheap?"

"I'm all ears."

"Lightbulbs, sir. Compact fluorescent lightbulbs."

The crowd looked skeptical as I explained the elevator conversation version of my plan.

The senator smiled broadly and replied, "That sounds like a great idea—why don't we do it? And let's call them Petraeus bulbs!"

Graham was indeed a good politician—he knew how to kiss the asses of the upwardly mobile. The dinner wound to a close. The officers shook hands and posed with the guest of honor under a South Carolina flag as the general's aide snapped pictures. The Lincoln Group's number one remarked, "I hope you don't mind being called Lieutenant Lightbulb."

I didn't mind—the nickname had a progressive, planet-friendly ring.

On the way back to my hooch, the senator's words about the detainees in Guantánamo twisted over and over in my head. An untold number of people had been kept in secret custody for several years by the United States without even being charged with a crime. Many would be released after years of detention without ever facing a single charge or spending a single day in court. I thought of what Giovani had told me from his experience as an attorney, a lawmaker, and an Iraq veteran.

"It's not due process, but it's the process we do."

This is wrong, I found myself repeating over and over. *How can we export democracy without respecting inalienable human rights?* If those people in detention were guilty, then America owed it to the world to prove it in a court of justice. There was one senator in Washington who could make a difference in this problem—a combat veteran who had been tortured as a prisoner of war. More than anyone else in the world, John McCain had the moral authority to end the practices that were giving the United States a bad name and inspiring extremists to hatred. I recalled the speeches that John McCain and Gerald Coffee and James Bond Stockdale had given to the Brigade of Midshipmen at the Naval Academy, excoriating the inexcusable and unjustifiable wrongs of torture. As a teenager in uniform, I was moved to tears when these heroes described how they had resisted their captors while continuing to have faith in American values.

This is your chance, John. Now is the time to do the right thing! Fire your silver bullet! America needs you!

Days after the dinner with Senator Graham, a film director named Alex Gibney contacted me about screening his upcoming film for an audience in Iraq. Alex's previous film *Enron: The Smartest Guys in the Room* told the story of Enron's downfall and was nominated for an Oscar in 2005. His new film, *Taxi to the Dark Side*, documented the practices of detention and torture in the Global War on Terrorism. After agreeing to screen the film before an audience of officials, I quickly invited General Petraeus and the new ambassador, Ryan Crocker.

While Petraeus and Crocker politely declined to attend the screening, the two were nonetheless preoccupied with the very same issues of human dignity and human rights. A recent mental health survey of the troops in Iraq and Afghanistan was published, shocking the sensibilities of our leaders. Of the troops in war, 40 percent thought that torture was acceptable under certain conditions, 10 percent admitted to having been physically abusive with innocent Iraqis, and two-thirds claimed that they would not report a fellow soldier who was abusive to innocents. One public affairs officer in the Pentagon claimed that the survey results showed how our leadership is working—because most soldiers aren't acting upon these violent impulses anymore. General Petraeus made no such excuses, immediately ordering the entire force to discuss the importance of respecting human dignity in our actions.

And so it came to pass that *Taxi to the Dark Side* made its Eastern Hemisphere debut in the presidential palace of Saddam Hussein in the context of an ongoing moral crisis. Gibney and Petraeus seemed to have a lot in common. In Gibney's film, Dick Cheney was quoted justifying "the dark side" of law enforcement where the rules didn't apply because the Global War on Terrorism was a new type of war with an extraordinary and evil enemy. But the exact words that Vice President Cheney used were fresh in my mind for a different reason—something else I had recently read. I flipped through a copy of Petraeus's newly published counterinsurgency manual to find the exact quote. The section was titled "Lose Moral Legitimacy, Lose the War."

During the Algerian war of independence between 1954 and 1962, French leaders decided to permit torture against suspected insurgents. Though they were aware that it was against the law and morality of war, they argued that—

- This was a new form of war and these rules did not apply.
- The threat the enemy represented, communism, was a great evil that justified extraordinary means.
- The application of torture against insurgents was measured and non-gratuitous.

This official condoning of torture on the part of French Army leadership had several negative consequences. It empowered the moral legitimacy of the opposition, undermined the French moral legitimacy, and caused internal fragmentation among serving officers that led to an unsuccessful coup attempt in 1962. In the end, failure to comply with moral and legal restrictions against torture severely undermined French efforts and contributed to their loss despite several significant military victories.

It was chilling to learn that General Petraeus attributed France's loss to the same flawed reasoning and the same tactics that Dick Cheney espoused for the Global War on Terrorism. But even more disturbing to me personally was what I learned from Alex's film about my hero, Senator John McCain. In *Taxi to the Dark Side*, Alex inadvertently revealed how John McCain's efforts to put a stop to America's policies of detention and torture were duplicitous, ineffective, and filled with secretive compromises. In 2005 McCain's Detainee Treatment Act—a bill that passed on John's moral authority—contained an amendment (sponsored by Senator Graham and Senator Carl Levin) that allowed confessions obtained through torture to be admissible in military tribunals while precluding legal recourse for people tortured by the U.S. government. When the Vietnamese held McCain in captivity, they forced the young officer to "confess" against America. Ironically, in 2006 the same absurd logic of McCain's law would turn his forced confessions from Vietnam into treason.

It was a travesty of justice. Worse still, a shifting, legalistic definition of torture permitted abusive and unethical practices to continue under a darker shroud of secrecy. But worst of all, I learned that the Military Commissions Act of 2006 would continue to hide the bodies in the closets of Guantánamo, completely limiting habeas corpus and granting outright immunity to the Bush administration through preemptive pardons.

In my estimation, only one senator wielded enough power to prevent this mockery of justice from continuing. Only one maverick in America had the moral authority and the political clout to lasso an administration run amok. But tragically, when Senator John McCain was given the chance to do what was right, he chose to compromise for the sake of gaining political support in his upcoming presidential bid. Instead of holding the Senate and the administration accountable to the high standards paid for with the blood of American POWs, McCain reverted to his days at the Naval Academy, where the insidious unwritten rule was to protect the brethren who had done wrong, not to "bilge" his classmates.

My childhood hero had sold his soul.

17

Lukewarm Fusion

Fusion is the process of forcing elements together under intense heat and pressure. Fusion brings order by uniting things that were once divided. Fusion starts with a single event, then grows in a chain reaction as long as the heat and pressure remain. But most important of all to the people of Baghdad in 2007, fusion releases massive amounts of energy. For all of these reasons, the arrival of the Iraq Energy Fusion Cell was long overdue.

From the beginning of the war, Iraq was a land whose occupiers were divided from the government and whose government was divided from its people. The separation was much more than physical, though endless stretches of ten-foot-high blast walls with concertina proved to be adequate metaphors for the problem. As General Casey planned his exit from Iraq, the beleaguered officer decided to leave his legacy in the formation of fusion cells. These units were not just military, they were not just civilian, and they were not limited to any specific country. On the contrary, the purpose of these units was to integrate the forces from every government and every agency into multilateral cross-functional think tanks. Casey knew that if Iraq was to succeed, the walls we had spent so many years building would have to be torn down.

This is not to say that there were no diplomatic meetings or cordial consultations during the occupation. But it is to say that something fundamentally important was lacking in the way decisions were made. The Iraqis were simply not treated as equals in important decisions. Organizations throughout the coalition employed Iraqis as translators or functionaries, but never were the Iraqis given the reins of important projects funded by America's massive resources. This was quite different from the Marshall Plan to rebuild Europe after World War II, where France and England had almost complete control over how to spend the American aid money. In Iraq, only Americans were deemed capable of spending the vast sums of American money. By the end of his three-year tour, General Casey wanted something better than this prescriptive attitude. He wanted an actual team, with Iraqi officials working side by side with coalition forces as true equals.

When General Casey formed the first major fusion cell to provide municipal services to Baghdad, an Iraqi official was invited to share the lead as a codirector. After accepting the responsibility, the Iraqi invitee was baffled by the concept of such equality and repeatedly demanded to know which of the codirectors was actually "in charge."

"We both are," replied an American colonel named Simon Phillips who shared responsibility with his confused Arab friend. "It's better to work as a team."

The Iraqi codirector was not convinced, suspecting some sort of dirty trick. Until Saddam was ousted, dictatorship gave the Iraqis trust in hierarchy. Until the end of 2006, Orientalism gave Americans enough hubris to believe that they alone ought to be the ones in charge. Both of these walls had to come down.

The Energy Fusion Cell was the next evolution of cooperation and teamwork, and it was the first such organization to operate nationwide at the strategic level. In addition to being multilateral, with Iraqis, Americans, and Brits sharing important roles, it was interagency. The Energy Fusion Cell brought military and civilian officials to the table from several different organizations: the Foreign Service, the Army Corps of Engineers, strategic military directorates, and most importantly, the Iraqi ministries.

In theory, the Energy Fusion Cell was the wave of the future. In practice, that glorious future of genuine collaboration was a long way off. Some of State's high-priced consultants felt threatened by the new concept of true multilateral collaboration, being quite comfortable at the top of their separate-but-equal technocracy. To the consultants, the idea of sharing power was tantamount to bureaucratic suicide. This was, in fact, correct; the point was to empower the Iraqis until a coalition presence was no longer required. The Department of State was already reshaping its reconstruction office to fill a new collaborative role. Nevertheless, the leader of the collapsing E-Team, Ian, demanded the title of energy czar as a precondition to participation. When Ian's request was denied, he banned his State Department consultants from speaking to anyone in the fusion cell. Needless to say, things got off to a rocky start.

"This place looks like a ghost town," Colonel Phillips declared as he walked into our newly completed office. The two of us had been working for the last month to prepare the office space for occupants, ordering everything from desks and chairs to wall maps. Without a staff yet, the colonel and I found ourselves rolling up our sleeves, moving furniture, and carrying computers. Whenever Simon and I had worked up a sufficient sweat, we would take a rest and talk about black market oil dynamics, private generator usage in Iraqi households, and the logistical challenges of refinery operations in Baghdad.

Colonel Phillips was not supposed to be the man in charge; he was merely the interim director of the Energy Fusion Cell until the real leader, a British general, could arrive. In part because Simon was only a colonel, in part because he was only temporary, and in part because he was completely indifferent to army protocol, the newly formed fusion cell had serious problems with absenteeism. One particularly insipid army engineer, a reservist colonel, snapped at me when I asked why he wasn't coming to work. "I've got much more important things to do, Lieutenant."

"Respectfully, sir, you're AWOL, and you're not even pretending to be otherwise."

The colonel hung up the phone.

My rank certainly didn't help, but Colonel Phillips was unwilling to take a firm stand by mustering his high-ranking troops. Several other high-ranking officers chose not to come to work too, preferring to stay within the comforts and palatial office spaces of their previous jobs. Colonel Mulder, who was assigned to work for Simon, ambled into the office after a week of "taking care of paperwork and stuff."

"I'm probably not coming in for a few more days," Mulder grumbled sheepishly before vanishing for another fortnight of self-pity and lament for lost glory.

By contrast, Colonel Dawson took advantage of the transition in Baghdad by touring the oil refineries and production facilities around the country, gaining fresh knowledge of the situation in his area of expertise. Upon returning, he immediately set to work on improving the fuel situation in Baghdad. One particular problem that stood out in Peter's mind was the shortage of fuel for new power plants that were scheduled to come online in the early summer. The new electrical turbines in Baghdad needed diesel fuel to run, but there was no current supply route to handle the thousands of liters of fuel required for each turbine every single day. In a clean break from our ineffective mind-set of looking at oil and electricity separately, Peter—an oilman—took the lead in solving this electrical power problem. He combined the security, economic, and technical aspects into a concise analysis and plan. Pete's egomaniacal counterpart in State had been let go during the restructuring process, a liberating stroke of luck that empowered the good colonel. Within two weeks, Dawson's plan found its way onto the prime minister's desk.

The plan called for the Government of Iraq to purchase

diesel from Kuwait. This was not a simple exercise in going to the gas station. In a diplomatic sense, Kuwait still harbored some resentment over its treatment by Iraq in 1991, and there was no existing relationship for cooperation in energy. In the physical sense, sending a constant stream of trucks from Kuwait to Baghdad was an expensive and dangerous proposition. But given Iraq's shortage of refined fuels, importing Kuwaiti diesel was actually the most economical choice. After Peter's analysis, the solution seemed so clear that many people asked why it hadn't been done already. It turned out that Iraqi businessmen and politicians considered oil as a "free" commodity in their analyses instead of considering its opportunity cost—the price it would fetch at market. That strange economic misconception led the Iraqis to eliminate the possibility of purchasing any fuels at an international market price. In reality, the Iraqi refineries were so old and inefficient that domestic diesel actually cost the government more than the market rate. When Colonel Dawson explained the correct economics to the Iraqi government, his audience was amazed. The prime minister approved Peter's plan enthusiastically, but was "taken aback" at the market price of diesel fuel. One can only imagine the hilarious naïveté of a petrol state's prime minister realizing for the first time exactly how much it costs for a fill-up.

As Colonel Dawson and I held the fort, we were occasionally reminded of others' nearby hell. Our office window had a narrow view of the hospital and its helipad, where the choppers took off and landed in Kafkaesque rotation. One morning we heard an unfamiliar whirring sound from that direction. A Bradley Fighting Vehicle had driven up and emergency crews rushed to meet it. Seconds later, two of the emergency crewmen raced back toward the hospital, carrying something grotesque. It had once been a human, but from thirty meters away, I could discern only a bloodied arm that hung limp over the side of the stretcher. The rest was unrecognizable. The other arm and both legs were completely gone. The uniform had been torn off and the body painted over with a coating of his own blood. Another soldier on a stretcher followed the first, motionless and naked above the waist. Whether the soldier was simply unconscious or already dead I will never know, but in either case, he was the luckier by far.

"I'd better go donate again," Colonel Dawson stated flatly. By that point in his tour, the man of sixty had given platelets no fewer than fifteen times, leaving his body in a perpetual state of looking slightly anemic.

Still, some things were looking up. When Colonel Dawson's plan for purchasing diesel took hold, so did the concept of the Energy Fusion Cell. The plan managed to solve a problem that wasn't entirely technical, political, military, or economic, but a mixture of all of those—and Dawson did it without spending a single dime of American money. And just as he had catalyzed the improvement of oil security by break-

The emergency landing pad behind Baghdad ER, as seen from my office window in the Energy Fusion Cell. Actual photos of casualties were prohibited by general order #1 to protect the dignity of the wounded and dead. This prohibition also raised questions about freedom of the press.

ing down barriers and forcing disparate organizations together, so did our new unit catalyze the production of energy by promoting genuine collaboration. The chain reaction of fusion had begun.

After this success, it was natural to ask which of Iraq's five neighbors were cooperating to solve Iraq's energy crisis. Turkey was exporting a small amount of electricity to Kurdistan in the north, but there was significant room for improvement. Syria and Jordan had been cut off from the Iraqi grid for years. Saudi Arabia was not only cut off but building a security fence to keep Iraqis out. Iran was not connected to the Iraqi grid either, but two of Iraq's provinces were "islanded"—separated from the Iraqi grid and supplied with reliable electricity from Iran. As I delved into the data on generation capacity and system interconnects, I was shocked to find out that Iraq's neighbors had some spare capacity that could be easily harnessed to help Iraq. If Iraq had been cooperating with its neighbors and importing a fraction of their extra energy and fuel, then Iraq could have cut its energy shortage significantly within a year!

It boggled my mind that Iraq hadn't sought support from its neighbors during its hour of greatest need. But then it hit me—in a flash of embarrassment, I suddenly realized the fatal flaw in America's plans, the plans that I had worked so hard to champion. When I arrived in Iraq, I believed that energy independence was the most important thing that could allow that country to grow and prosper. But only near the end of my tour of duty did I realize exactly what energy independence meant in practice. For Iraq, energy independence meant separating itself from its neighbors, building political walls, and refusing to ask for help. Energy independence meant a denial of cooperation and a denial of teamwork and unity. Amazingly, energy independence had become an ideology of rugged individualism, mistrust, and fear. Through energy independence, Iraq had successfully cut itself off from the rest of the region, transforming itself into a stormy desert island.

A series of unexpected guests arrived at the Energy Fusion Cell to see what the buzz was all about. Our efforts to make a comfortable workplace for senior Iraqi officials paid off when the oil minister dropped by for a surprise visit. Colonel Phillips and I were the only ones left in the office that evening, so we showed Dr. Sharistani the space.

"I want to put my desk here," the minister stated, to my delight. "How long before I can move in?"

Sharistani handed Colonel Phillips his business card, then left, security guards and senior aides in tow.

"Wow, look at this, Chris!" Simon, handed me the powerful politician's card. The e-mail address was "minister_of_oil@yahoo.com." Simon and I looked at each other, then burst into laughter.

"The army gave them a twenty-million-dollar server, and what do they actually use? *Yahoo!*"

"Are you surprised, Colonel?"

"Not really. The army one sucks."

One day I returned from lunch to find Colonel Phillips in the meeting room with the Australian ambassador and an Iraqi official I didn't recognize. The rest of the office was completely empty, so naturally I joined the conversation.

Students of war doctrine know that the Australians have recently developed some of the finest counterinsurgency strategies in the world. Before David Petraeus, Princeton Ph.D., there was the Australian Dr. David Kilcullen, who produced the definitive works on counterinsurgency before coming to Iraq as a senior advisor. I didn't know what connections the Australian ambassador had to Kilcullen and Petraeus, but I did know that one could count the high-ranking Australians in Iraq on a single hand, and this was their number one man in town. Any ideas we talked about could go straight to the top of the food chain, intellectually and militarily.

Colonel Phillips was floundering. He quickly introduced me and remarked, "You're just in time! I was just about to discuss that, uhh . . . thing that you were telling me about the other day . . ."

You have no idea what you're talking about, do you?

"Do you mean the plan for the northern pipeline, Colonel?" I said.

"Yeah! That's it! Would you care to brief the ambassador?"

"No problem, Colonel!" *And thanks for the heads-up!*

The northern export pipeline ran from Kirkuk to a major Iraqi refinery, then westward through Turkey to the Mediterranean. Tragically, the pipeline was under constant siege. As repair teams from the Ministry of Oil scrambled to patch each newly formed hole, two others would appear. When the government restored the flow of oil, the attacks would start again almost immediately. Though the pipeline was designed to export a million barrels per day, the actual exports were reduced to practically zero. And with so many patched holes, the best anyone could hope for was half of the pipeline's design capacity. That year, due to the perpetual damage on this export line, the Iraqi government lost $7 billion of potential revenue—more than the entire Iraqi defense budget.

My colleagues argued for months to build hardened fortifications around the entire pipeline—razor wire, guard towers with machine gunners, et cetera. While I had believed this possible at first, I no longer considered it feasible for an army to provide that level of security. The insurgency proved that a military solution for protecting the pipelines would fail, just as the Turks failed to defend their railroads from Lawrence of Arabia during the Arab revolt of 1917.

Instead of looking for a military solution, I was determined to defeat the attackers in another way—by understanding their true intentions. Throughout Iraq, there are very few natural sources of fuel. One can't go out and chop firewood because there simply aren't enough trees. In the nearby farms of Azerbaijan, farmers commonly burn cow dung to cook their evening meal while rivers of oil flow underground through the Baku-Ceyhan Pipeline buried under the farmers' fields. It was this basic need of a simple energy source that made me question the motives of the attacks. It turned out that the attackers on the northern pipeline were not out to destroy the Iraqi government. The damage came from locals with tanker trucks and power tools who cut holes in the massive pipeline and stole as much oil as possible before the government could detect the leak and shut down the line. Some of the looters took crude oil to micro-refineries; some burned the oil directly in cement factories or smaller operations. Undoubtedly some even found ways to put the oil to use in their homes.

As I looked across the table at Colonel Phillips, the Australian ambassador, and the unknown Iraqi official, I was surprised to see that they were all taking notes. Encouraged, I continued my explanation. The first time I had voiced this theory about the looters to my chain of command in civil affairs, Colonel Mulder had laughed at me and said, "Why the hell would they want crude oil? What are they going to use it in, their Mercedes?"

The ambassador looked up, clearly having heard this for the first time, and asked, "What, then, ought we to do about this if the security measures prove inadequate?"

It was a great question, one that I had been waiting for months to answer.

"We need to start thinking of these people as Robin Hood instead of Osama bin Laden."

"What do you mean?"

"I suggest we reconcile with them. Open a domestic market for crude but sell it dirt cheap or even give it away."

Their eyebrows raised in unison. Giving away crude oil wasn't exactly a typical American economic reform. But as I saw it, a small amount of subsidized or free crude oil would satisfy the needs of local businesses and households and eliminate the rationale for looting. During this time, the government could register the users of the oil, develop a working relationship with them, and stimulate local economic growth. And most importantly, crude oil exports could increase by an estimated $6 billion per year.

The ambassador put his pen down and asked me bluntly, "Are you suggesting that economic reforms could solve this security problem?"

"I'm suggesting, Mr. Ambassador, that we think a little bit more about what the Iraqi people actually need."

"I see your point. Then why haven't we done it already?"

Another excellent question! The State Department and World Bank put enormous pressure on Iraq to liberalize its oil markets before funding any more large development projects. The requirements included raising the price of subsidized government fuel toward the market price as well as taking steps toward privatization of nationalized assets, such as gas stations. Giving away crude oil was a step toward socialism, which the war architect-turned-World Bank president Paul Wolfowitz feared almost as much as Islamo-fascism. Needless to say, the State Department shared this doctrinaire opinion. To me, this conditionality, which placed long-term economic reforms before the counterinsurgency, was a subtle but serious misstep.

"Of course, when the insurgency starts to die down, the Iraqi government can liberalize as fast as it wants."

"Fascinating."

The ambassador thanked me, noting that he had overstayed his scheduled time, then left with his security detail.

"Man, I'm glad you arrived," Colonel Phillips said with a laugh when the ambassador was out of earshot. "I was running out of things to make up."

Simon then put his arm around the Iraqi official, who smiled warmly, putting his own arm on Simon's shoulder.

"Chris, I'd like you to meet my Iraqi brother, Théa!"

"*Sharafna!* Good to meet you!" Théa said.

We shook hands.

"*Tasharafna bik!* Good to meet you, too!" I replied.

Théa was the deputy prime minister's chief of staff. I was floored that such a high-ranking official was so familial with Simon. The colonel then offered with an air of jovial pleasantry, "Anybody up for some Iraqi chai?"

When General Petraeus called to visit the Energy Fusion Cell, I knew that our new unit had reached critical mass. I sent an invitation to our assigned personnel, many of whom still weren't coming to work more than a month after being transferred to our staff. People I'd never met before started showing up to ask when Petraeus was coming and could I take a picture for them? One civilian contractor brought his girlfriend to see the show. Even I got a bit starstruck by the brush with fame. I printed out a copy of Petraeus's new counterinsurgency manual in hopes of snagging an autograph.

"Are you serious, Chris? What are you going to say to him?" Colonel Goodman asked incredulously.

I shrugged, muttering, "Uh . . . I don't know . . . 'I read your book'?"

Two hours before Petraeus arrived, the Army Corps of Engineers swarmed into the fusion cell's office to take charge of "protocol." To my disgust, the one-star general in charge of the engineers had a larger staff for providing milk and cookies than the fusion cell had for everything. The protocol officer—a well-paid administrative assistant (who had an assistant of her own)—waltzed in with refreshments, a seating chart, and freshly printed place cards, for everyone who she had decided should attend. The place cards, with little Army Corps of Engineers logos, positioned the Corps members at the head of the table, relegating the actual fusion cell officials to seats of lesser importance. Several absentee officers who had contributed nothing to our work flooded into the room to hear Petraeus speak.

"What a bunch of breathers and shitters," George grum-

General Petraeus and a British colonel pose for this shot in the newly formed Energy Fushion Cell.

bled about the bloated functionary staff. Regarding the colonels who had been shirking their responsibilities, he complained bitterly, "Too bad these clowns won't come to work when there isn't a celebrity to gawk at."

"Hey, Chris, come here for a second." Colonel Phillips beckoned me over. "Have you ever heard of some guy named Barack Obama?"

"Yeah, Colonel—I listen to his podcasts."

"What's a podcast?"

"Never mind, Colonel. What's up, sir?"

"Obama's office just wrote to us. They have some questions about the energy sector. The army engineers are fielding the questions, but you're welcome to take a look before we send them to Washington."

"Sure, Colonel. I'd love to take a look!"

The senator's questions were follow-ups to written testimony that the Army Corps of Engineers had given to Congress. Obama's questions focused on two main points. First, how involved were the Iraqis in the army's reconstruction efforts? And second, what barriers were preventing the United States from stepping aside? At the time, these were the best questions that anyone had asked us about what needed to be done. But as I read through the army's responses to Senator Obama, I cringed. At best, the answers were half-truths. At worst, the Army Corps of Engineers simply didn't understand the questions (but answered them anyway).

The Corps insisted that Iraqis were being involved in the process as part of its "Iraqi Associates program . . . providing life support, security, construction management, administrative, and technical services." This language was a euphemism for cleaning the toilets, making coffee, guarding the gates, filling sandbags, and pushing all the paperwork that the Americans couldn't read because it was written in Arabic. In reality, the Iraqi associates in the Army Corps of Engineers were more like Wal-Mart associates than anything else—they may have been employees, but they sure as hell didn't have a seat at the boardroom table. The Corps proudly emphasized that it had employed 43,000 Iraqis with its reconstruction efforts. Over three years, the Corps and its predecessor spent $8 billion dollars on the energy sector alone—equivalent to 25 percent of the entire country's annual income. Despite this, the highest employment of Iraqis that the Corps managed to achieve was less than 0.2 percent of the population. Until 2007, the vast majority of funding went to multinational contractors with strong business ties to America.

In the other areas of reconstruction, the Corps selected some good-looking data points to convince Obama that the situation was better than it really was. For example, the Corps highlighted that Baghdad received eleven hours of power in March and that the goal was an average of twelve hours per day. This rosy data point neglected that in March the weather is beautiful—nobody uses heating or air-conditioning, so the overall electrical demand was seasonally low. If the Corps had told Obama the averages during the winter and summer (when power was needed the most), the number reported would have been four to six hours of power, not eleven. This was a blatant lie of omission. Overall, the yearly average was around seven to eight hours per day—not even close to the stated goal.

On the second point, Obama asked what was stopping America from stepping aside. The reply listed a series of day-to-day problems that the Iraqi government faced, but it completely dodged the senator's question of what major barriers *America* faced in getting the Iraqis to take the lead. Every problem that the response mentioned was technically correct, but it completely missed the strategically important things that prevented America from stepping aside.

In the grand scheme of things, America's problems were really quite simple. First, the Iraqi government didn't want to decide what to do with the country's oil until the Americans left. Any oil law passed under occupation would be considered illegitimate by the people and set the country up for future instability. Second, the Iraqi government was unwilling to spend its budget on developing its oil and electricity while insurgents were still rallying against the American presence and attacking the "puppet government's" infrastructure. Finally, with no end in sight to the occupation, there was no incentive for the Iraqis to commit to taking charge of the situation. It was the same problem that the Democrats had in Congress after the 2006 elections; if they took charge, then they would be blamed for the failures that they had inherited from their predecessors. As a caveat, without a clear deadline for troop withdrawal, there was no leverage for Americans to force the Iraqis to take responsibility. For all the money and personnel at its disposal, the Army Corps of Engineers had become so stuck in the quagmire of managing small, over-priced projects that it lost perspective on these major flaws in the coalition's role.

"Colonel, let me write to Obama," I said. "Somebody's got to be straight with him."

"Chris, do you have any idea how many push-ups the general will make me do if I tell Obama what you just said?"

Colonel Phillips was the only officer I'd ever met who was regularly dropped for push-ups as punishment.

"Chris, if we say those things, then I might as well go up to the Corps commander and call him a big fat poopy-pants liar. Trust me, if Barack Obama doesn't like the answers, he'll write back and say so."

Working with Colonel Phillips was a personal battle. On the one hand, I wanted to strangle him for his fatalistic indifference. To me, there was an enormous sense of urgency in our work. To Simon, the "Washington clock" simply didn't exist.

"Sir, if we don't take responsibility, we're going to lose this war."

Simon caught me off guard with a bizarre and unexpected twist of logic. "Don't be afraid, Chris," he replied gently. "Losing this war only bothers you because you think that losing is worse than winning—which of course, it isn't."

I blinked and stared in utter confusion. *How the hell is it possible that you made colonel?*

Simon actually had a good explanation for *that* question. "You're probably wondering how I became a colonel. It's a funny story. Have a seat, Chris. Would you like some Iraqi chai?"

According to Simon, it was a case of mistaken identity. During his stint at West Point, he was dumbfounded by the school's insistence that he retake quantum physics and differential equations—subjects he had mastered in high school. The army had mistaken Simon for his older, less academic brother—another cadet at West Point whose Social Security number varied from Simon's by a single digit. Years later, as Simon was being thrown off active duty for angering a general with his fatalistic philosophies, his older, stalwart brother rocketed through the active-duty ranks. Against all odds, Simon continued to make rank in the reserves at every first eligibility.

On the other hand, Simon was a very different sort of animal, and I actually grew to like him more and more as time went by. Colonel Phillips had an uncanny ability to attract powerful and influential Iraqis on a regular, familial basis. For some inexplicable reason, Iraqis simply couldn't get enough of the man.

"I think it's because I'm looking for a Sunni wife," Simon reasoned one afternoon, sipping a demitasse cup of chai.

"Why Sunni, Colonel?"

"There's more of them. You know . . . they've got a better shot at taking over the world."

Colonel Phillips joked about wanting to take a Muslim wife, but the fact was that Simon's first wife had left him abruptly and he found solace in treating the Iraqis like family. The Iraqis found Simon's attitude endearing, and they quickly adopted him as one of their own. Senior officials from throughout the Iraqi government would drop by simply to share a cup of tea with their American "brother." And despite the fact that Simon spent several hours per day sipping chai, he was extremely effective when something needed to get done. If the problem was important and his Iraqi family could handle it, then a few cups of tea and a little bit of patience was all it took.

"You may have noticed that I don't actually do very much," Simon explained to me one morning. "If it's really important, it'll get done—someone will make sure of that."

"*Who?*" I insisted with impatient disbelief.

"*Someone,* Chris. You'll see. Someone always does."

18

A Thousand Points of Light

When the conditions are just right in the cloudless desert skies, the dust settles and the stars come out to shine upon Iraq. It doesn't happen as much as one might think—if it's a bit too dry (which it almost always is), the fine-grained sand blankets the sky, blurring and then obscuring the piercing lights. But when the stars come out, without the light pollution of electrified streets, the skyscape is breathtaking. Not only did the stars come out, but the stars actually aligned above me in Baghdad that June. First, a British one-star general named Richard Cripwell took charge of the Energy Fusion Cell, arriving several weeks behind schedule. Second, my relief, a navy helicopter pilot named Matt, arrived several weeks ahead of schedule. Third, the two of them arrived on the very same day that I was scheduled to present my light-bulb proposal to a dozen stars' worth of generals.

In his 1989 inaugural address, President Bush Senior spoke of "a thousand points of light, of all the community organizations that are spread like stars throughout the Nation, doing good." The president spoke of "work[ing] hand in hand, encouraging, sometimes leading, sometimes being led." Above all, the president spoke of "go[ing] to the people," seeking out "the brighter points of light," and "ask[ing] every member of [his] government to become involved." In rhetorical terms, what President Bush described was exactly what I was about to do, with one minor exception—a thousand points would no longer cut it. Iraq needed 26 million.

The circumstances were anything but typical. To my knowledge, Matt and I were the first U.S. naval officers ever to serve as aides to a British general in war. In any case, generals and admirals usually arrived with staff from their own countries. It was my last month in Iraq. The British colonel, Matt B., who had already left for home, impressed upon me that my sole purpose was to impart every bit of knowledge I had unto the brigadier and my relief. I was determined to do better than what had been done for me; dropping the ball was not an option.

After midnight, the general's Puma helicopter touched down, practically invisible in the cover of darkness. I saluted, he smiled, shouting above the helicopter, "Leftenant Brownfield, I presume?" We loaded his gear into my bulletproof Suburban and drove to the palace. Ironically, the Peruvian guards denied us entry to the palace grounds—only Americans were allowed inside at night without a special embassy badge. My fast talking in Spanish turned out to be slower than necessary, and the guards weren't going to let the general through the checkpoint. Embarrassed by our own regulations, I asked the general to wait while I went to find the captain of the guard. Richard looked annoyed but, to my relief, pulled out a pack of cigarettes. Smokers, it seems, are much better equipped to cope with life's inevitable hiccups.

"Right, then. I'll have a fag and you sort this out."

After I begged the security supervisor and surrendered the general's passport, the guards finally let us through the gate. I took the general to his hooch, which, embarrassingly, was no better than mine (and a big step down from Jessica Rabbit's desert island getaway).

After a few hours of sleep, I whisked the general around the embassy, where he completed a stack of standard forms— the same administrivia required of me ten months earlier. When we arrived at the fusion cell's separate compound, the

Nepalese security guards denied us entry. I argued with the guards, convincing them that our British friend was not really a security threat and that he should be allowed to enter. They acquiesced with great suspicion, and only after taking Richard's British Army ID, leaving the man without any form of identification.

According to Les Dixon, the senior-most civilian in the Army Corps of Engineers, the United States had "created a condition of apartheid in Iraq." The previous week, I had escorted an Iraqi major general to my office for a meeting. Noting that I was American, the guards waved me by, but insisted upon searching the Iraqi general. Embarrassed, I put my arms up and insisted that the guards search me, too. The Gurkhas declined. "Do it," I muttered to save face for the senior Iraqi officer. At the next checkpoint, the guards tried to confiscate the general's cell phone—Iraqis were not permitted to have them on the U.S. bases. I put the phone in my pocket and gave it back to the general as soon as we were through.

The Energy Development Committee convened promptly at ten o'clock, with all of the generals and energy-sector and economic power players in the State Department present. It was the highest-ranking meeting I'd ever attended, and it was more than a bit intimidating. Still, I had a responsibility to the Iraqi and American people, and I was not about to let them down.

The proposal was simple. The Iraqi government would buy $20 million worth of energy-efficient lightbulbs, one bulb for every Iraqi citizen. These 26 million points of light would be distributed to the people through the Trade Ministry's in-place food-basket program, used by the vast majority of Iraqi households. Using the food-basket program was key—while my original plan involved a business model for distribution, the real possibilities awakened when Colonel Phillips recognized what the Iraqis could do already and changed my plan to meet them on their level.

The briefing went splendidly. There were charts showing

the demand for lighting on the national electrical grid. The survey data, which took two months to come back from around the country, confirmed my final estimates within 5 percent. There was a big-picture economic analysis that showed how the government would save $300 million in three years over the alternative of building more power plants (and this was a conservative estimate). There was a microeconomic analysis that showed how much money the average Iraqi household would save on gray-market power costs by using the energy-efficient bulbs. Adjusting for Iraq's economic conditions, the savings were about the equivalent of George Bush Junior's tax rebate checks. In short, the plan made good business and political sense, it was easy to implement, and it would be a small strategic step toward improving the lives of the Iraqi people.

The audience loved it, including the two-star Iraqi general in attendance. At the time, my proposal was the most cost-effective way to improve the Iraqi electrical grid's performance, and if it were started in June, it could show results by the peak of the surge.

"Senator Graham had the excellent idea of calling these 'Petraeus bulbs,'" I said, "but that's not our general's style. I think that General Petraeus would prefer to call them by an Iraqi name, like Maliki bulbs."

The audience nodded in agreement, a bit surprised that the senator had weighed in on my plan. But still, I had one concern about the program, which I voiced before the entire audience.

"There is an essential question whose answer will determine whether this program will succeed or fail. Unfortunately, to this date, I have been completely unable to find the answer, and there is no existing data on the topic."

The audience looked perplexed. I had just delivered one of the best performances in my life. Why would I reveal my program's potentially fatal weakness?

"Gentlemen, the single unknown question that will determine whether this program succeeds or fails is this . . ."

They hung on every word. I paused dramatically. The suspense was killing them.

"What is it, Lieutenant?!"

"We have absolutely no idea . . . How many generals does it take to change a lightbulb?"

The audience gasped. Feet actually left the floor as the generals started up from their papers with shocked and incredulous smiles. Petraeus's director of strategic operations, General Fastabend, pushed his glasses back onto his nose, regained his composure, and replied in a cool, mechanical tone, "Thank you, Lieutenant. Your presentation was thirty seconds too long."

There was a roar of laughter. After the committee adjourned, I received a dozen congratulations and even a job offer from the president of a major U.S. utility corporation. Their congratulatory remarks seemed premature to me—we hadn't actually helped any Iraqis yet. But to me, the important thing about the lightbulb proposal was not that it would save the Iraqi government several hundred million dollars and provide a small service to the people. The major win of the lightbulb program was the proof that energy wasn't just a problem for the oil and electricity ministries—it was a problem that everyone could address in some way. Just like President Bush Senior had called upon every member of his government to help, so could different parts of the Iraqi government join together to solve their common problems.

At the morning briefings, General Petraeus immediately asked some very tough questions of Richard. Unlike Cross, Mulder, and the strangely silent Kim, Richard seemed to take the responsibility personally, and he took it like a man. Afterward, we rendezvoused at the Green Bean, where I cheerfully greeted him.

"Good morning, General! How are you today?"

I knew full well that he had just been verbally lashed. Richard's brow furrowed in concentration, and with a uniquely British air, he issued a remarkably minimalist order. "Latte."

I smiled and fetched his coffee. As strange as it may sound, it was refreshing to work for someone who actually knew what he wanted.

With a general comes order. Our absentees started coming to work. The colonel who had hung up on me the month before was doing his best to kiss the general's ass. Our meetings had professional agendas with clear objectives and adequate notice of important decisions. A secretary actually took minutes. We had to make a spreadsheet just to keep up with the plans we were making, and they were good plans, too. As more and more senior officers attended our meetings, I made more and more coffee, and even learned how to make Iraqi chai.

"Just remember, Chris, Iraqis like it with copious amounts of sugar," Colonel Phillips reminded me often.

But life wasn't all spoonfuls of sugar. Dr. Karim's son was viciously attacked while attending high school. A bomb had been placed inside his locker, and when it exploded it tore off the teenager's foot. Though the boy survived, his best friend was blown to unrecognizable bits. A pretty and intelligent twenty-five-year-old Iraqi translator who worked with us fled to the Green Zone in abject terror. Two of her in-laws had been murdered by the militia. The killers hovered over the corpses of the dead women, lying in wait for the family to return home. Colonel Phillips tried to send coalition forces to investigate the crimes, but his gesture was little more than courtesy. He didn't control any combat troops, and there was little we could do to help.

Colonel Mulder's extension was approved. He would be staying in Iraq for another year of high-paid vacation from his plumbing job.

Richard, however, was instantly put off by Mulder's lack of usefulness. "The sooner we have that man managing staplers and pencils instead of people, the better."

I respected Richard, not only for his shrewd skills but because of his willingness to stand up for the right thing. While he lamented the loss of his country's "perfectly service-able empire," he had become a fish out of water himself by speaking words of dissent in the chambers of the Pentagon. After an unnamed undersecretary of defense failed to convince his audience that the Global War on Terrorism should be renamed the "War on Civilization," the topic of Abu Ghraib surfaced instead.

"The problem with Abu Ghraib is that they let those guys have cameras," the undersecretary stated.

The room was silent, except for a few chuckles.

Richard, then a mere colonel, responded, "I beg your pardon, sir, but isn't the real problem that Abu Ghraib happened in the first place?"

The silly Brit was then escorted out of the room and censured for addressing a high-ranking official in such a disrespectful manner.

With Richard in the lead, our fusion cell had become a legitimate multilateral energy consultancy for Iraq. Our primary purpose was to integrate the oil and electrical sectors under a coherent and actionable strategic energy plan.

"Why do you suppose they picked me for this job when they already have the State Department and the Army Corps of Engineers?" Richard asked me one evening as we drove home from the office in our bulletproof Suburban.

"Sir, America doesn't have a real energy policy. Your country's already grown up a bit; you can actually make this work."

The closest I ever came to death was sitting at my desk while making a PowerPoint presentation. I don't blame Microsoft

Richard, the British brigadier general who took command of the newly formed fusion cell. A delay in his arrival almost dealt an early death blow to the unit, though he managed to pull things together admirably as the surge got under way.

Windows (which I associate only with the death of the human soul). Bill Gates had nothing to do with the mortar that landed eleven meters away from me.

Crack! I fell out of my chair, flat onto the floor. *Holy shit!!!* There was no warning, no electronic sirens, no whistle of the incoming shell, and my ears were in pain. The shell landed right outside the brigadier's office! *Is he okay?* I looked up to see the general running through his door. His office windows were blown open and a cloud of dust filled the air. Our colleagues ran into the hallway, Colonel Mulder barreling ahead of the pack with a well-honed reflex of self-preservation. *Who knew that a grizzly bear could move so fast?* Several other rounds hit in succession as we waited in the hallway. The walls shook a bit, but the shots were off the mark. Like every mortar attack on the Green Zone, it was over as fast as it had started, the assailant undoubtedly fleeing the launch site with mortar tube in hand. After a few minutes of silence, we went back to the office, the general rubbing his ear in pain (the shell had impacted only five meters from him). Richard's desk was covered in a fine layer of dust. A chunk of concrete the size of a shoe had been knocked out of his wall and onto the carpet. I picked up the rock, took out a marker, and wrote in big block letters, "The mortar stopped here."

The brigadier smirked. "Right, then. It looks like I've got myself a new paperweight."

"How's your ear, sir?"

"It will be fine, thank you."

Relieved that my last fleeting glimpse of life on earth was not wasted staring at a computer screen, I sighed and went back to work. On my desk, nothing had changed except that my computer had dutifully saved the PowerPoint and the screen had turned itself off to save electricity. I flicked the mouse, waking the dancing cartoon paper clip that cheerfully asked whether I needed any help.

Fuck you, Gates, and your goddam paper clips, too.

It was unbelievably hot. At eight in the morning, it was already over a hundred degrees as I walked toward the office. A small puppy, no more than six months old, lay on the scorching pavement, dying. The poor creature tried to lift its head to look at me, but it was so exhausted from the heat that its head fell softly again onto the concrete. I pulled out a bottle of water and cut it open with my knife, forming a makeshift bowl to let the puppy drink. A few drops rolled off the animal's tongue as I gently lifted its head and poured. Sadly, it was too late to help. Later on that morning, I drove past in my immaculate SUV with shrapnel holes in back. Another dog lay dead in the street, its legs sprawled out unnaturally. It hadn't been hit by a car or shot, it had simply died of thirst. The same rail-thin dog had made me feel guilty for not keeping an extra granola bar in my pocket to feed him on my walk home. That same dog had stood in the midst of

After the fusion cell was hit by mortars, the power was out for a few days. Iraqi electricians worked around the clock to repair our building's electrical system, but the workers were slow and somber—one of their friends had been killed in the attack.

spiraling concertina wire, gazing inquisitively at the shiny vehicles racing past through the pleasant warmth of February. In America, we grow up thinking that spring is a time for renewal and rebirth, but in Iraq spring is the time when the weak are culled before the wrath of the summer tests the will and strength of the strong.

For the next several days, the power was out in the Energy Fusion Cell. After my brush with death, another series of mortar strikes barraged our building with alarming accuracy. Two rounds hit the building directly, and another four landed in our compound, making mincemeat of thirty-five cars in the parking lot. The precision was horrifying. Some Iraqi workers were killed, and our building's power lines were cut by the blasts. It was painfully symbolic that our job of fixing the national power lines would be on hold until our local lines got repaired.

Dejected, I walked past the rocket-made craters and shards of automobile glass toward the hospital entrance to see if they needed any blood (they always did). The cool air of the hospital and the four television screens flashing Fox and MTV were a sharp contrast to the dilapidated facade of the Baghdad ER. The clinic closed an hour before I arrived, leaving me without a place to go (except back to my hooch or to the Green Bean, both of which were getting old). I walked into the lobby, where some of the more ambulatory patients were relaxing, wrapped in fresh new bandages or casts. I decided to sit with them and read *Stars and Stripes*. A soldier who sat down next to me was wearing an unmarked uniform—the kind they gave you when your last uniform was torn off by a bomb or a surgical tool. The soldier's rank insignia were taped on, and a large bandage was wrapped around his right hand.

"Is that the latest paper, sir?" the soldier asked, eyeing my copy of *Stars and Stripes*.

"Yeah, take it."

"Are you sure?" The man was being very polite, probably because I was an officer he didn't know.

"Please, take it."

The man's face had several small cuts and a deep gash through his nose. The injuries didn't look too bad, or at least not permanent.

"What happened to you?"

"Sniper got me," he explained, holding up his hands like he was shooting an M-16. He traced the path of the sniper's bullet with his finger while pretending to aim his rifle. The round had torn through the flesh of his right hand and the plastic rifle grip, hitting his armored chest plate. Shards of plastic from the grip and fragments of the bullet splintered outward toward his face, shattering his ballistic goggles and biting deeply into his cheeks. Amazingly, the damage was superficial.

"What kind of round was it?"

"Seven-six-two. Knocked me right on my ass . . . felt like a

camel kicked me in the chest." He smiled, tapping his chest
with his left fist where the bullet had impacted, then wincing
slightly in pain.

"Aiming right for my heart. Not a bad shot, either."

We talked for an hour about the war and politics and what
we missed about the United States. The soldier was angry
about the Democrats' wanting to pull out too early, potentially leaving behind a horrible mess. I asked him what he
would change if he could do one thing.

"Well, I've kicked in a lot of doors, and what I see inside
always amazes me. In one house there's a baby sleeping on a
flattened pair of pants, covered in flies. In the next house,
there's a stereo, TV, an air conditioner . . . So I guess that's
what I'd change—they need better living conditions . . . you
know, running water, electricity—or else we're in [this war]
for the long haul."

19

The Night of Fire

In the days of World War II, American forces fighting their way through Italy discovered the meaning of collateral damage the hard way. When American soldiers accidentally destroyed priceless works of art in the midst of combat, the people of Italy rallied against America. General Dwight Eisenhower responded by ordering that Europe's monuments and artwork be protected to the maximum possible extent. In 1943, a small army of museum curators, artists, historians, and academics donned army uniforms and deployed to Europe on a mission to protect and preserve the Continent's art from the ravages of war. Unlike Bill O'Reilly, these men were *real* culture warriors; they were called "monuments men." As the war raged on, the monuments men worked tirelessly to prevent irreplaceable treasures from being bombed, and they raced to protect the artwork of cities under siege. Most amazing of all was that the monuments men did not do this for the sake of capturing a prize or simply to quell the unrest—they did it because those statues and paintings embodied the fundamental values of European civilization. By safeguarding the artwork in Europe, the United States sent a powerful message that European people mattered. Despite the violence and tumult that ending the war would bring, the people of Europe would not be trod upon. Dignity and respect for their civilization would prevail.

My Iraqi artist friends invited me to lunch one day.

Mohammed arrived late; he was very glad to see me and had
something important to share. I hadn't seen him for a month,
and he was worried that I'd already left Baghdad. He had
been working on an exhibition of paintings for a secret showing in the city. On this day Mohammed was more than disturbed—he looked possessed, seizing hold of my arm,
leaning close, and whispering, "You must see what I have
done." I was haunted by the way he said it. His paintings
were the most trenchant of all I had seen in Iraq, and his
personal history was heartbreaking. Unlike many artists,
Mohammed was unafraid of reality's dark side. He painted
politics, children in war, and suicide bombers, among other
taboo subjects. It was transformative for him to paint such
things, the kind of work that had been strictly forbidden
under Saddam.

When Mohammad was a young man, his family had suffered immensely. Saddam had ordered Mohammed's brother
to be killed. The brother had been the minister of planning, a
talented official whom Jacques Chirac—then the mayor of
Paris—once described as "the brains of Iraq." After Saddam
seized the presidency, he consolidated power by killing his
most experienced cabinet ministers and replacing them with
terrified loyalists.

So Mohammed had a history of traumatic experience, and
it disturbed me deeply to see him so shaken. He clutched my
arm and whispered in a voice that instilled fear in my heart
something that I will never forget, his story of Laylat an Nar,
the Night of Fire. In 2003, while CNN and Fox were trum-
peting the slogan "Shock and Awe," the residents of Baghdad
who lived through the campaign adopted a different transla-
tion of the buzzwords. As coalition cruise missiles impacted,
followed by screeching fighter jets and thousand-pound
bombs, the six million people of Baghdad watched and listened with abject horror. When reporters asked President
Bush where they could go that would be safe for them to
report on the campaign, he responded that if reporters

wanted to be safe when the campaign began, then they should "leave Iraq immediately." For my Iraqi friends, leaving Iraq was not an option; their city was about to be attacked.

Now Mohammed led me to a private room where a collection of paintings stood. There were twenty-five of them, each depicting a scene in Baghdad during the Night of Fire. The tall, thin aspects of the works echoed the Stations of the Cross, though Mohammed had never heard of such a thing. Half of the paintings showed typical residences in Baghdad, with Iraqi faces drawn inextricably to the windows, watching. Some of the homes were on fire. Some of the faces were distorted in the throes of death. The other half of the paintings showed symbols of Iraq. A demonlike face loomed over a skeletal minion, perhaps representing Saddam's murderous first cousin, Chemical Ali, and Saddam himself. An Iraqi flag was slashed open and covered in oily black handprints.

The ruins of the Ba'ath Party headquarters. Three five-hundred-pound laser-guided bombs decimated the innards of the palace but left the structure intact.

Empty chairs evoked the striking absence of those who were killed. Bloodied, dismembered hands casting dice floated around the canvases—a metaphor for bombs in a densely populated city. One canvas showed images of two women, maimed and disfigured. A baby doll was melted into another painting, its charred, innocent face peeking grotesquely from the nightmarish scene. In the central piece, the statue of Saddam Hussein tumbled from its pedestal in Firdos Square. Around the statue, the chaos of Iraq swirled as monkeylike spectators cheered. It seemed peculiar to me that Mohammed showed the spectators this way. After all, they were cheering the fall of his brother's murderer.

"Why do you portray them as monkeys?" I asked in bewilderment.

"Because they also clapped when the statue went up."

I had never seen anything like it. Aside from my surprise at the massive scope of the works, which stood as tall as a man and forty feet wide, Mohammed opened my eyes to a reality that I simply hadn't imagined. Never again could I hear jingoistic buzzwords like "Shock and Awe" without also hearing echoes of the Night of Fire. Regardless of what Saddam had done, in 2003 the six million people of that capital were undoubtedly terrorized.

Still, tragically, the indiscriminate use of force did not end with the Night of Fire.

"I have never in my life seen such willingness to conduct blind counterfire with 155-millimeter artillery shells," a British colonel lamented in frustration before he left Baghdad. "We have no idea who may become the 'collateral damage,' as your country calls it, but we lob away with the rounds."

It simply hadn't occurred to me that the massive American artillery shells that I heard after rocket attacks were landing within a crowded city; all I had thought about was "getting the bad guys." Suddenly I felt ill.

The colonel continued his explanation. "If we had done this in World War II, they would have said 'those monsters'!"

Time after time, I had heard the deadly report of the outgoing shells into the *beladiyahs* of Baghdad. Now, for the first time, I understood exactly what was happening. Within a millisecond of an incoming mortar or rocket launch, our radar systems would pick it up. Split seconds later, sophisticated tracking systems would triangulate the launch point and relay the coordinates to firing computers. Lightning-fast servo motors then directed the massive barrels of our artillery toward the source of the attack. In less than eight seconds—before the enemy's shell even landed—we would shoot back. But while our assailants used small, Soviet-era mortars, our counterfire was conducted with modern artillery possessing several times the destructive force of the enemy's weapons. The deep sound of the outgoing launches and the reports of their blasts absolutely dwarfed the puny insurgent mortars and typically flaccid rockets; the response was completely disproportionate. The insurgents hit fast and ran, firing no more than a few rounds before fleeing for their criminal lives. This hit-and-run tactic became a veritable rain dance, with our automated rain of death shattering like thunder the silence of the streets. The splendor of our technocracy shielded us from the knowledge of whom we killed, and the sound and fury of our response left little room for questioning. As inscribed on a captured cannon—a war trophy on the Naval Academy's grounds—we had become *Ultima Ratio Regum*, the King's Final Argument.

The colonel's revelation shocked me. I was a submariner who didn't know anything about artillery and targeting systems, but he was an experienced army officer on his third tour of duty in Iraq, and I simply could not refute his observations. Slowly I realized that the general who had destroyed the army's reputation in Anbar Province with brutal tactics had expanded his scope to Baghdad, where a quarter of the nation's people now lived in constant fear. In Anbar, Odierno had ordered his troops to fire upon vehicles at the side of the road, even if the vehicles hadn't engaged the passing soldiers. One puzzled army captain who served under Odierno's command and later studied at Yale asked me, "Isn't that a violation of the laws of armed combat?"

With his promotion to corps commander, Odierno had become the new Old Iron Pants, the Curtis LeMay of Baghdad. Of course, the citizens of that beleaguered city also feared the daily blast of suicide bombs, perhaps even more than they feared the U.S. Army. But they did fear the army, and we continued on a daily basis to give Baghdad's people a reason to do so.

Recent accounts of Odierno's service in Iraq argue that he underwent a transformation for the better, abandoning his reckless and brutal side when the strategy of counterinsurgency took hold. But these tactics of shelling the city continued well past the beginning of the surge. Whatever transformation Odierno underwent, his old habits died hard.

As I stood there in the shop with my Iraqi friends, my head was spinning. Here before me was a man whose brother had been murdered by Saddam Hussein, and yet this man was ambivalent about Iraq's liberation because of the uncontrollable duality of violence. Mohammed had every reason to hope for Saddam's downfall, but that sad and irrepressible part of his life did nothing to lessen the blow when bombs fell upon his homeland. Untold thousands were killed during Shock and Awe, the majority of whom were likely just Iraqi civilians. Their lives were not even important enough to be counted in the death tolls on network television, which seemed only to care about American soldiers. What remained of my simple and naive worldview shattered into a thousand fragments.

"Mr. Christopher," Mohammed pleaded, his voice wavering as his grip tightened on my arm, "will you show this to the world?"

A shiver ran down my spine, and my heart pounded as the horror of Mohammed's reality and the weight of his plea set in.

How could I not?

At the Ministry of Defense, I waited in the hallway as Richard met with the Iraqi Army's chief of staff. A soldier approached and started talking about his life in broken English. Ali had witnessed a coalition helicopter opening fire on a home where an insurgent was shooting with an automatic rifle. The helo accidentally gunned down the family that was living inside the home and completely missed the assailant. Ali's hands were shaking so much that he had to ask his friend for help in lighting his cigarette. The soldier wore body armor, but insisted that he was given armor only because of his new job in the ministry. The men outside of Baghdad didn't get armor, he claimed, and they had to bribe their officers to get bullets. Ali was a sniper before coming to the International Zone. With trembling hand and cigarette, Ali recounted how he had shot a woman in the head before she could drop a grenade on his comrade. Ali's gaze darted back and forth and he twitched nervously. Two weeks after Ali shot the woman, his friend was killed in action anyway.

I put my hand on his shoulder. "I'm so sorry . . ."

The poor man started to ramble again about the helicopter and the shooting of the family, asking why it happened and what we were going to do to stop it from happening again. My stomach tightened and my eyes became moist. There was nothing to say.

It was the Fourth of July, and I wondered whether I ought to hate America. I felt awful about wondering that, but as I walked through the palace toward the dining facility where Halliburton had just finished celebratory decorations, I couldn't help asking myself that odious question. I was the only American who had seen Mohammed's *Night of Fire*, and the images weighed horribly upon my conscience. The Green Bean had been closed off for a private celebration of Independence Day. Inside the monstrous café, red, white, and blue banners arced over the party, and white tablecloths graced the normally informal scene. Blackwater mercenaries surrounded the Bean like FBI agents in casual clothing, bristling with clips of machine-gun ammunition, turning away all mortals who dared approach them. An unnamed VIP was visiting for a big speech—no doubt a politician who wanted a golden Fourth of July sound bite from Iraq, under the blanket of impenetrable and exorbitantly expensive security. I walked onward to the main dining facility. Inside, the Nepalese cooks wore paper hats made to look like American flags. More red, white, and blue symbols of every sort were draped from the ceilings of the facility, ensconcing the soldiers themselves as Trophies of Freedom. A massive cake had been baked and bedecked with glistening symbols of the American Revolution. A life-sized statue of Uncle Sam greeted the soldiers, some of whom took great pleasure in posing with it for photos. It was worse than tacky—it was unashamed, unfiltered arrogance. I looked at the Nepalese cooks, practically kids, who tried to smile while soldiers snapped photos of them like tourists in a zoo. They must have been humiliated. I wondered how an American Christian would feel about serving horse meat in Tehran while wearing a paper hat that looked like the Iranian flag on the anniversary of the Islamic revolution for two dollars an hour while foreign civilian mercenaries made fifty times as much money.

An overweight American civilian stood by the buffet line, arguing with a Nepalese supervisor. "Your buffet line only has one low-carb entrée tonight. How am I supposed to lose weight?" The Nepalese man was confused. "Besides," the chubby American continued in accusation, "*your* servers gave me *two* pieces of fish when I *told* them I only wanted one!"

For a moment I decided that I actually did hate America. But no sooner had I made this determination than I saw the man responsible for the travesty of unabashed Americana that lay before me. The source of the brash, ridiculous party was a gray-haired man in his fifties, sporting a red, white, and blue suit that more closely resembled a Halloween costume than formal wear. His starred-and-striped top hat added another foot to his diminutive height. This was the supervisor who had lavished the Green Bean with banners and erected the statue of Uncle Sam. Beneath his ridiculous suit, the man was incredibly average, a regular Joe with the extraordinary combination of bad taste and an unlimited budget.

Upon a moment's reflection, I realized that I was in error; I hated the garish spectacle that my country had produced, but I didn't really hate America. *Someday, this ridiculous behavior will come to an end.* The words of the famous sea captain Stephen Decatur came to mind: "Our country! In her intercourse with foreign nations, may she always be in the right; but our country, right or wrong."

I mumbled a quick apology to the spirit of George Washington and started to love America again.

Warfare has a strange tendency to honor itself. For the defunct civil affairs unit it was Bronze Stars and Legions of Merit. When Colonel Shelton left, it was the prestigious de Fleury Medal. When General Casey left, the entire headquarters received the Meritorious Service Medal (what else could commemorate such resounding success?). Frankly, I wanted none of it, but avoiding an end-of-tour medal would prove to be difficult—it was item #13 on my mandatory out-processing checklist.

The most odious part of the end-of-tour award is that

senior officers often delegate the authoring of the citation to the recipient. Regulations prohibited foreign officers from writing American awards, so Colonel Mulder was assigned to handle mine, an assignment that must have annoyed the shit out of him. Mulder approached me, stating that he needed me to write my own award within the hour. I told him to piss off (in more polite terms). My new "master," Richard, had an important meeting that day with Petraeus, and I wasn't about to waste preparation time.

Mulder left, but returned in a huff a few minutes later. "Fine. I'll write it, but I need some information right now," he growled. "What other medals do you have?"

I couldn't think straight. I didn't even remember what medals I had been given.

"Sir, I *really* don't have time for this."

"Dammit! I need this data! What other medals do you have?"

I put my hands on the desk, leaned toward him, and stated through gritted teeth, "Expert pistol."

Mulder took the hint and left me alone.

The briefing with General Petraeus went very well. At this point I was working myself out of a job and Matt, the helicopter pilot, was taking over. During the briefing, I sat in the luxury waiting room between Ambassador Crocker's and General Petraeus's offices. Petraeus had shelves full of awards, most of which were quite serious, presented by foreign ministers and dignitaries. One award stood out as my favorite. It was the Kashafa Boy Scout patch, presented to my commanding general for "Outstanding Performance and Lasting Contribution to Iraqi Scouts."

The British have long been known for presenting medals only in exceptional cases. As Richard and his entourage walked out of Petraeus's office, the witty Brit waved his hand, proclaiming, "Bronze Stars, all of you." The American colonels' chests swelled with pride.

"Me, too! Me, too, sir!" I squeaked jokingly.

The general snapped, "It's bollocks for you, Brownfield!"

"Yes, sir! Thank you, sir!"

The colonels caught on that the general was only joking, and their egos deflated back to their normal somewhat bloated levels. Back in the office, our little joke continued.

"*Loo*tenant, please print out a copy of today's presentation and bring it to my desk."

I made the copy.

"Well done, Lootenant. Silver Star."

But the general didn't save all the accolades for me. "The refrigerator ought to be commended for the enthusiasm with which it freezes my apples," Richard declared.

"Right on top of it, sir. You'll have the citation on your desk tomorrow. Bronze Star?"

"Of course. It deserves nothing less."

When Lawrence of Arabia rejoined his fellow British subjects, he was showered with honors. Lawrence was made a Companion of the Order of the Bath, awarded the Distinguished Service Order and the French Legion of Honour. The king of England selected Lawrence to be promoted to the rank of knight commander. But to King George's amazement, Lawrence didn't bother to show up for the ceremony. In the king's befuddled words, "He left me there with the box in my hand."

Of course, Lawrence was loyal to England, but there were other loyalties, too. As he fought and led in Arabia, Lawrence remained loyal to the cause of Arab independence and self-determination, which he believed to be completely in line with British objectives for winning the war. It wasn't until Lawrence learned of the Sykes-Picot Agreement that his loyalties came into conflict. With France and England waiting to divvy up their Arabian spoils, Lawrence tried desperately to catalyze the formation of a functioning Arab government that could represent its own interests. This Damascan debacle failed when the tribal leaders, new to global politics, squabbled like provincial bumpkins while the generators sat idle and the lights of Damascus remained out. Lawrence left feeling like a failure while the looming vultures of empire swooped in for their carrion feast.

My time in Iraq was drawing to a close. Matt, the helicopter pilot, took over the remainder of my duties in a very thorough turnover process—the ball was successfully passed. As I walked past Baghdad ER, I glanced over my administrative checkout sheet, now mostly completed. Strangely, the most important things were not part of the procedure. I stopped in the street, turned around, and went back into the blood bank to give platelets one last time. As I sat in the bed with needle in arm, the blood flowing from my veins felt like the only thing I had truly given to change someone's life. I walked back to the art shop, where I hoped to say farewell to my dear friends Muslim and Mohammed. They were both there, and well. The three of us knew that the time would come when I would have to leave Iraq, and we dreaded the thought of losing each other as friends. Kind words were exchanged. We embraced. I promised Mohammed to meet again someday. As I started to leave the shop, I remembered something that I needed to do. I pulled out a compact fluorescent lightbulb from my pocket, making Muslim laugh.

"You brought us a present?"

All great actions are contingent upon their context. Caesar crossing a river would have been unremarkable if the river had not been the Rubicon. With Muslim's help, I stood precipitously on a wooden stool, removed one of the antique-looking 300-watt lightbulbs, and screwed in the new one, a 40-watt energy-efficient bulb with the same brightness. While this was no Rubicon, I couldn't help but feel that changing out that single lightbulb was one of the more important things that I had ever done. I felt dizzy, maybe because of standing on a wobbly stool or maybe because of something deeper. Muslim and I wished each other good luck, and I walked out the door.

On the day I left Baghdad, there was a ceremony to mark my departure. I was supposed to arrive at nine o'clock sharp to receive the medal that Colonel Mulder was forced to propose and whose citation I refused to write. On the way to the office, I took a cappuccino in the Green Bean, dreading the prospect of facing my colleagues. Around the café, some faces were old, some were new, and still, on that particular morning in the summer of 2007, none were Arab. I sipped the delectable foam from the top of the cup, nibbling on the crystals of sugar that managed not to dissolve in the swirling caffeinated goodness. I needed a reason not to leave the Bean. Whether it was Allah or the spirit of Juan Valdez, I'll never know, but someone answered my prayer. The robotic voice shouted, *Incoming, incoming, incoming!!!* I smiled, safe in the hardened structure of that opulent coffee shop; I now had an excuse not to walk to work. After a few more minutes of enjoying my coffee during the mortar attack, I called Colonel Phillips to lower his expectations. Disappointed, he asked me to come by as soon as possible.

As I hung up the cell phone, an army friend walked through the door and joined me. I smiled, and a great weight fell from my shoulders. I decided not to attend my farewell ceremony, where I was destined to be anointed with administrative honors. I didn't deserve any medals—nothing I had done actually helped any Iraqis or made America safer. T. E. Lawrence refused his medals out of loyalty to principle bigger than empire, but I was simply tired, my nerves were shot, and I wanted to see my friends, perhaps for the last time. My army friend laughed about my skipping the ceremony. I laughed, too, imagining him with blue hair, clove cigarettes, and a goatee, opening the letter that had recalled him to active duty.

Later that afternoon I checked out with the medical department by completing a mental health survey on a Palm Pilot. *Have you been exposed to danger which immediately risked your life?* I checked yes. *Have you seen any of the follow-*

ing wounded? I checked the boxes for coalition forces and civilians. *Have you been exposed to sand?* I checked yes, but only because *no shit, Sherlock*, wasn't an option. The survey continued for twenty-seven slides. An army doctor in his sixties took me into a private examination room.

"Would you like to see any specialists when you return home to . . . uhhh . . ." He looked down at the record, where my home address was written. " . . . Connecticut?"

The doctor looked up from the clipboard and blinked with a detached look of routine concern. I wasn't sure what he meant, but the notion that I might have special problems didn't sit well. It was simpler to say no. The doctor was silent as he typed on his computer. It looked as though he was concerned about something—perhaps my record or the Palm Pilot had triggered a warning signal. *Maybe he'll send me to a shrink . . .* But that sort of complication was the last thing I wanted. The doctor's brow furrowed in concern, which made me increasingly nervous. "Dammit," he muttered in frustration.

"What is it, Doctor?"

"Uhhh . . . It's this darned *Connecticut thing*. What's the abbreviation? I can't get 'CN' to work."

I told him the abbreviation and he typed it into the computer, his face lighting up with epiphany before sending me on my way. I left the clinic with all of my boxes neatly checked.

The ride to Baghdad International Airport on the super-stealth bus felt very different from the time of my arrival. My convoys had driven the route time and time again, and I knew it well. As we dimmed our lights and entered the Red Zone, I could see clearly across the city by moonlight. Dozens of houses by the road hung tubular fluorescent lights by their doors, vertically like light sabers, defending the homes against the darkness with a pale glow and fifty-cycle hum. The Corps commander, General Odierno, insisted that Baghdad got plenty of power because of all the lights he saw from his helicopter at night. But these lights were not symbols of power or progress or prosperity—these lights were lit out of fear, at great expense, despite what the powerful and willfully ignorant chose to believe from on high. Aside from the front doors, the rest of the homes were absolutely dark.

The bus pulled into Camp Victory within five minutes of entering the Red Zone. For the first time, I realized that the vast majority of the ride was within the confines of American military bases. For being only a few kilometers away from each other, the embassy and Victory had seemed so far apart. The bus arrived, I hefted my bags full of body armor, canteens, gas mask, and the central painting to the Night of Fire, and waited for my flight out of the Land Between Two Rivers.

In the outdoor passenger terminal of Baghdad International Airport, a couple sat, waiting to go home on leave. They were soldiers who had gotten married after returning home from their first deployment to Iraq in 2004. Their friends sitting around a dusty picnic table bragged about war stories: the doors they had kicked in, insurgents they had killed, and the IEDs that had given them brushes with death. The wife asked them to change the subject, so they talked about sports. She was an MP at the detention facilities, a tough job in its own right, but not so dangerous as what her husband had done in the Red Zone. She told me a story about another soldier-wife in her unit who once witnessed her fiancé getting "blown up" by IEDs, twice. The fiancé's Humvee took two explosions in rapid succession, but the first was a moment too soon and the second a moment too late. Everyone made it out unscathed, at least physically.

I wanted to change the subject to something more positive, so I asked the couple what they planned to do after their tours of duty were over.

He outlined their New American Dream: "I'm going back to school and hitting it hard, at least for six months until my wife gets out of the army. Then we're going to work for Halliburton and [get] rich—probably be back here in Iraq in a year. We'll stay for two or three, until we've saved enough to pay for a couple of houses, then we'll go home. Then I'll probably become a police officer or something."

She smiled in admiration and nodded as her warrior husband spoke. The hope of common men growing wealthy on the fruits of war had not escaped these two American heroes. Their ambitions lay at the roots of what our nation's actions had taught them, and they soaked up every bit of it. *How could they not?*

Afterword

In the twilight of my naval service, I swapped my camouflage for a suit. But unlike the beginning, the break between military and civilian life wasn't so clean. While my classmates at Yale enjoyed our "networking practicum" with wine and cheese in hand, I found myself standing alone, trying to calm down whenever a door slam or an ambulance siren pushed me from the ivory tower. Aside from one classmate, an army captain who had been wounded twice by IEDs, nobody—family, professors, students—seemed to understand what had happened or what was still happening inside my head.

At the same time, Zalmay Khalilzad replaced John Bolten as the U.S. ambassador to the United Nations, swapping contempt for the world with a more palatable type of diplomacy—multicultural nepotism. Every day in business school, Zalmay's words weighed upon my mind: *Make your money, then go for a political appointment.* With all due respect to the chargé d'affaires extraordinaire, I didn't want money, and I couldn't feel at home in a place where "hedge funds" and "private equity" were the most celebrated buzzwords. And so it came to pass that three weeks after starting business school I quit. One year later, world markets crashed, investment banks imploded, and elite financial lingo lost a bit of its luster.

In the fall of 2007, my relief in Baghdad wrote to inform me that the prime minister's office had approved my plan to subsidize energy-efficient lightbulbs. To my knowledge, it was the first "demand-side management" program that anyone in the coalition had successfully proposed to help the Iraqi people. But more than a year later, to the best of my knowledge, none of the program that Prime Minister Maliki's office approved had actually been implemented. This was to be expected; by that time, none of the people who had served alongside me actually remained in Iraq to follow through on any of our efforts.

Nevertheless, it came as a surprise that a prominent man in America had been championing the cause of energy-efficient lighting. When I learned of Senator Joe Biden's efforts to subsidize compact fluorescent lightbulbs, I wrote him a letter expressing my support and offering to help in whatever way I could. Sadly, Joe's efforts on that front came to a halt and my letter went unanswered. More than a year later, I finally heard back from Joe, now the vice presidential candidate. The message wasn't a personal response to me, but a request for campaign donations, which I happily scraped together a few dollars to fulfill.

The Wärtsiläs remained in Jordan for the rest of 2007 before the Ministry of Electricity made an aborted attempt at the ground transporation plan. After some disastrous deliveries of a few engines, the ministry finally abandoned the project, selling the remaining units at a loss. To this day, the people of Samarra remain starved for electricity as their spiritual wounds from the bombing of the Golden Mosque struggle to heal.

An errant Iraqi oil executive started giving out free crude oil to the local people of the north in an effort to satisfy their basic energy needs. Despite my explanation that such behavior was required to solve the problem, the State Department immediately suspected that the official was being intimidated or bribed. "Attacks" on the northern export pipeline declined.

Colonel Phillips married a beautiful young Iraqi woman, and they now have an adorable baby. After seeking approval

Laylat an Nar (*The Night of Fire*), as it was shown in New York City in 2008. This series of twenty-five paintings depicts the time in 2003 that Western media described as "Shock and Awe."

from Ayatollah al-Sistani, the highest Shi'ite religious leader in Iraq, Simon was granted a blessing for his planned conversion to Islam.

"I've always been a bad Christian . . . Might as well be a bad Muslim instead."

The paintings of my Iraqi friends completed their journey, landing in an art gallery in New York City and drawing a great deal of international media attention. The exhibition generated six person-years of income for these artists of Baghdad, who continue to support their families while honing their skills and rebuilding their nation's damaged cultural heritage. Sadly, the leader of these artists was forced to flee Baghdad for a time after sectarian propagandists accused him of "collaborating with the American military and a New York Jew." The hateful and divisive accusations were technically correct, since the gallery's owner was indeed a Jewish Iraqi American Arab who had been exiled from his Baghdad home in 1951. Several months after this artist became a refugee, I flew to Damascus with a fistful of money to give him and a fresh appetite for Kurdish kebabs. In the finest tradition of Arab hospitality, the artist and his friends took me on a whirlwind tour of Syria, starting in the Damascan ghettos—where one million Iraqis live as refugees—and finishing in the canyon-city of Maloula, where thousands of Syrian Christians celebrated the life of Saint Thecla with fireworks, dancing, and whiskey. In Syria I came to understand the broader implications of my country's actions. Every soldier knows that when you treat a gunshot wound, there are always two wounds to treat—the point of entry and the exit wound. This is the case with Iraq as well—the bullet may have entered in Baghdad, but the exit wound is in Syria and Jordan, where nearly two million Iraqi citizens have fled. This refugee problem requires the direct aid of any benevolent political force that wishes to stabilize the region. To this day, repatriating the refugees responsibly and humanely is the single most important area where hearts and minds in the Arab world can still be won.

Iraqi refugees in a ghetto of Damascus. More than a million such refugees lived in Syria in 2008.

My friend Mohammed took this photograph of me next to the temple of Saladin in Damascus in 2008. It was a great relief to meet Mohammed in Syria, away from the violence of Baghdad. The money I gave Mohammed from the sale of his paintings helped to keep his family safe until the insurgency died down. *Photo by Mohammed al-Hamadany*

Around election time in America, the much-talked-about surge appeared to have worked. Iraq was less bloody, at least according to the statistics on the morning slide shows and *Good Morning America*. Still, when testifying before Congress and asked a pointed question, General David Petraeus couldn't state whether securing Iraq would make America any safer. President Bush continued to assert that victory in Iraq was the only way to secure America, a statement as enormous as saying that all terrorists must get their visas stamped in Baghdad. Needless to say, Osama bin Laden remained at large.

Taxi to the Dark Side won the Academy Award for Best Documentary in 2008. But despite the director's enthusiasm for an "Oscar surge," the film was never released in theaters outside of New York and Los Angeles. The distribution company—the same company that released *An Inconvenient Truth*—folded quickly, quietly, and without warning. The Discovery Channel bought the rights to broadcast the film, then inexplicably reversed course, delaying the televised debut for six months until after the November elections. The *New York Times* hailed *Taxi to the Dark Side* as one of the most important historical works of the decade, a documentary that historians would reference when trying to sort out what had gone wrong. Furthermore, with the onset of the financial crisis, Alex's previous film about the energy giant Enron (which lost the Oscar to *March of the Penguins*) gained new significance as the roles of speculation, unsustainable energy policies, and unaccountable business practices came once more into the limelight. Alex now tells me that he hopes to make a film about the current economic crisis, and one hopes it will gain a better reception in America than a flock of small flightless birds did.

Bill Gates deleted the infamous paper clip from the next version of Microsoft Office, and as penance to the world, devoted himself to improving global health. As a single donor, the Bill and Melinda Gates Foundation now accomplishes more in the fight against AIDS and malaria than most industrial sovereign nations.

Senator John McCain, a graduate of the Naval Academy and longtime hero of mine, made his second bid for the presidency. But instead of the uncritical adoration that I gave McCain in 2000, I reconsidered what I thought I knew about the man. My colleague Giovanni, the conservative attorney, had been fired for insisting upon treating detainees like human beings, while Senator Lindsey Graham—McCain's closest ally in the U.S. Senate—made it clear to me that he wanted to prevent detainees in Guantánamo from ever setting foot in a courtroom. The 2006 Military Commissions Act codified Graham's tooth-and-nail filibuster on due

process, but this law was appropriately struck down as uncon-
stitutional in 2008. Even a conservative Supreme Court
couldn't stomach the double standards.

I place so much responsibility on McCain because he
alone possessed the ability to lasso the neck of an administration run amok. John McCain was the only man in America
with enough power and enough moral authority to stop the
infamous practices, but his duplicitous and hollow actions
failed to measure up to his noble and eloquent words. Later
that year several detainees were released without charge after
spending seven years behind bars in a perverse limbo of contemporary American justice. I felt a deep sense of loss because
of McCain's unwillingness to stand up for what was right.
And more than anything else, I felt a sense of loss over the
words of Pope Paul VI, later echoed by Martin Luther King:
"If you want peace, work for justice."

The Energy Fusion Cell went on to more victories in the
following year, but the overall success of the situation remained doubtful. This should not be interpreted as a failure
of the concept; one can't do the right thing after trying
everything else and expect that all will turn out fine. However limited the fusion cell may be in repairing the hope-
lessly damaged cause of Operation Iraqi Freedom, I am
convinced that genuine multilateral collaboration is the best
way to approach future development challenges. Furthermore, I am convinced that development and empowerment,
more than any physical force, are the antitheses of terrorism
and extremism.

Saddam Hussein was a murderous tyrant whose atroci-
ties against his own people were well documented. It was
moral and just to liberate the people who were oppressed by
this murderous dictator. It would have been just to disarm a
rogue state that truly threatened the use of weapons of mass
destruction.

Sadly, history will show that these were not the reasons
why America went into Iraq. It was irresponsible and hypo-

critical for America to remove Saddam under the false casus belli of weapons of mass destruction when an intervention to prevent the genocide of the Kurds would have been justified more than a decade earlier. But contrary to popular liberal opinion, ownership of Iraq's oil was not the objective either. In the world of global markets, ownership is not so relevant as long as the oil is up for sale at a market-driven price. I believe that America's involvement in Iraq had more to do with imposing the stabilizing norms of Western market structures than with any other single factor. This imposition of norms upon a sovereign state is the truly regrettable flaw of the Iraq war—a flaw that threatens the legitimacy of the Iraqi government until American troops have fully departed the country. The intention, I believe, was to guarantee that the United States could continue to grow profitably on cheap foreign oil, just as James Forrestal encouraged after the Second World War. And most important of all, with the guaranteed supply of oil for sale at market prices, America would not have to embrace a fundamental change of its unsustainable behavior. This objective of installing a predictable, market-friendly regime was largely accomplished. And since the collapse of oil prices in late 2008, the world has returned to the point where cheap oil is once again the most economical, useful, and efficient source of energy.

Since I came home from Iraq, the idea of energy independence has not sat well with me. Instead of being a model of behavior that inspires Americans to consume less, waste less, and use renewable sources of power, energy independence has become something entirely different—an insidious ideology of fear and mistrust. Just as the conservative parliamentarians of England argued for energy independence on Sheffield's coal and railed against foreign oil, so have people of influence in America blamed their unsustainable energy problems on foreign tyrants and a bogeyman of "oil addiction" while harking back to rugged individualism and protection for domestic energy. In reality, oil companies are not the problem, and neither are oil cartels or monarchs in petrol states. The problem is our denial that global energy consumption is inherently and increasingly an interdependent behavior. Despite this reality, some people of great influence still bury their heads in the sand by convincing themselves that it is possible and desirable to manage our global energy consumption with conflict instead of collaboration. As long as the nationalistic debates still give credence to the ideology of energy independence, the truly important problems of our time will be left unsolved.

In March 2009 the USS *Hartford* collided with another naval vessel in the Strait of Hormuz, the strategic chokepoint of the Persian Gulf, through which a fifth of the world's oil supplies are shipped every day. Fifteen sailors suffered minor injuries, and thousands of gallons of diesel fuel spilled from the other ship into the narrow strait, sending the price of crude on the world oil market upward until the brief panic subsided. Personally, it breaks my heart to think that after all we learned aboard the *Hartford,* history is repeating itself. But history repeats itself in many different ways. The *New York Times* declared that "the next ten years will see the rise of a massive new industry which will free us from dependence on foreign sources of oil." In spirit, this sounds great, until one considers that the *New York Times* made this statement in 1948. Sixty years later, Thomas Friedman, a man who has never actually worked in energy or defense or economics, has repeated history by preaching the same pithy, marketable statements to millions of "progressive" readers. Are we to believe that if the *New York Times* keeps preaching energy independence, somehow it will come to pass—or that it is even desirable?

It is time for the world to grow up about the way we think of energy and violence. In the summer of 2008 Senator Barack Obama invited citizens around America to host platform meetings on topics of their choosing and report their recommendations to the campaign. I seized upon the opportunity to host a meeting in Washington, D.C., on a topic that is near to my heart: sustainable interdependence. Rather than the divisive and fear-based ideology that energy independence has become, sustainable interdependence is a strategy that recognizes the value of genuine collaboration. Sustainable interdependence is a frame of mind that breaks through barriers and unites people around the world toward common solutions to global problems. Instead of a nationalistic ideology that puts so much faith in the savior of technology, sustainable interdependence recognizes how technology can help us to live better, but that technology alone will not change the world. The nuclear submarine taught me what can be achieved with technology—that it is possible to sustain one's environment and mission independent of oil. But to put so much faith in technology alone is a Faustian tragedy. The submarine force fell short of changing its world because the war it was built to fight could not be ended by technology or weapons. In the end, the war could be stopped only by changing the way humans behaved toward one another.

Now, at the dawning of the third millennium, we have an opportunity to change the way we behave toward one another. I call upon the men of the silent service to break their silence and share their knowledge of how to sustain the balance between clean energy and one's environment. I call upon the admirals of the United States Navy to have the courage not to squander the talents and dedication of our servicemen by inflating the relevance of submarine missions to the problems America must face. I call upon the brilliant minds in the National Nuclear Security Administration to follow in Rickover's footsteps, to work across functional lines, to dispel the lies about nuclear power, to deflate the myth of clean coal, and to catalyze the growth of a more sustainable nuclear industry that propels America forward with the nuclear navy's perfect record of reactor safety. After the atrocious BP oil spill of 2010, I call upon the oil companies around the world to take note of how the nuclear navy has kept itself safe—big oil could learn a lot from the nuclear navy. I call upon the Department of Defense to recognize that the wars of the future will be won or prevented through shaping the positive forces of growth and opportunity, not through imposing the negative forces of violence. I call upon Congress to recognize this truth and to shift defense dollars toward energy and international development *for the sake of national security*. I call upon the State Department to cast off the provincial overtones of its unfortunate title and to behave as the World Department, where leading the way to sustainable interdependence is embraced as the most important goal.

Martin Luther King did not stand before America and say, "I have a nightmare!" King had a dream, and so do I. In reaching this goal of sustainable interdependence, we must have faith that humankind can build a world where everyone has access to electricity and the fuel required for economic growth. We must envision a world where instead of borders and nationalism, we have freedom of movement and trade and ideas. It is the possibility of this vision that motivates me. It is the possibility of a world where interconnectedness and cooperation prove stronger than fear and mistrust that inspires me to action. Sustainable interdependence goes beyond globalism and neoliberalism by offering a world where the true challenges of our time can be fought head-on through global collective action. Sustainable interdependence recognizes the rights of individuals, the rights of sovereign nations, and the diversity of our world's needs and interests. At the same time, sustainable interdependence requires that our traditional ways of thinking about these rights be flexible when facing our common plight.

After the platform meeting that I hosted in Washington, I drafted a memo that summarized what I had learned and sent it to Obama's campaign. Much to my surprise, an official from the campaign contacted me with an invitation to join the campaign's Energy and Environment Committee (ironically, the group was called the E-Team). Though flattered by the offer, I was more concerned with rolling up my sleeves and hitting the books. A month later, I began graduate school once more, this time at the Johns Hopkins University School of Advanced International Studies, where I committed myself to learning about international energy policy and economics. While I was strongly tempted to join Obama's team, I chose to put knowledge and competence first. *Inshallah*, my time will come when I can serve once again . . .

When I left for Baghdad, I wanted to learn the truth about what was happening in Iraq. I wanted to look into the heart of darkness—to see for myself the root of the evil that America faced in the Global War on Terrorism. But instead of staring into the eyes of a terrorist or the evil of an unspeakable menace, I found regular people who were suffering, I found commonality across the cultures of the world, and I found staring back at me in the distorted puddles of oil a strange reflection of myself. In the struggle of managing our unsustainable energy policies with limited violence, Americans have become their own worst enemies. But this is only half of the story, for the industrious spirit and the freedoms and the enormous capacity for change that led America to greatness are also the world's last best hope. It is time for the spirit of America to inspire the leaders of the world once more.

Mohandas Gandhas declared, "As human beings, our greatness lies not so much in being able to remake the world—that is the myth of the atomic age." The greatness of human beings, Gandhi intoned with farseeing wisdom, is our ability "to remake ourselves . . . to be the change that you want to see in the world."

My coming-of-age in the twenty-first century military has shown me that we still believe in the myths of the atomic age, in our ability to change the world. The challenge of my generation is to unravel this myth, to hold ourselves up to the mirror, and to have the wisdom, the honesty, and the strength to change ourselves.

Appendix A

Selected Letters and Correspondence from Iraq

From: c.brownfield@iraq.centcom.mil
Subject: Detainees and Lightbulbs
Date: April 9, 2007 3:45:02 PM GMT+02:00
To: lindsey.graham@iraq.centcom.mil

Dear Colonel,

I wanted to thank you for your company at dinner the other night. You are absolutely right that the positive stories frequently fail to find their way home to the United States. I also agree with your opinion about bringing criminals who have murdered Americans to justice. I would demand the same thing from the Prime Minister if I were in your position. Nonetheless, I wouldn't be honest with you if I didn't mention that your position on the indefinite detainees in Guantánamo seems to contradict your demand for justice from the Iraqi courts, our nation's principles of due process, and even General Petraeus' Counterinsurgency manual. In the Counterinsurgency manual, I found the section on Focoist insurgencies to be particularly relevant in understanding how Guantánamo hurts our efforts in Iraq. In a Focoist insurgency, small acts of coordinated violence are orchestrated to invoke an overreaction from a strong central government. Once the large government acts too forcefully or in a way that is perceived as unjust, the insurgents gain sympathy from the populace. This may not have been planned with the detainees in Guantánamo, but the Focoist-style result is the same—our denial of what is perceived to be a legitimate process has given the Middle-Eastern populace sympathy for the enemy. I believe our country's goal ought to be to promote swift and transparent justice on both sides of this war, not to detain alleged terrorists indefinitely in an Executive-Branch filibuster. To delay further with granting these people legal proceedings will continue to stoke the flames of unrest by providing legitimate reasons for people to harbor hatred against the United States. In retrospect, it was an overreaction for McCarthy to blacklist people as communists. Before our views on detainees become similarly retrospective, I urge you to prevent this overreactive situation from worsening to the detriment of our troops. We are the most powerful nation in history—if these people are guilty, then we are quite capable of proving it and bringing swift justice. I beg you to reconsider your position on this matter for the sake of our diplomatic and military efforts here in Iraq.

On a lighter note, your idea for calling them 'Petraeus-Bulbs' is a great one, though I think General Petraeus would prefer that they have an Iraqi name, such as 'Maliki-Bulbs.' That's his style, and also why he has been so successful as a leader here. I am working diligently to push this program, but a Navy Lieutenant in an Army's war has very little clout. It would take a miracle for it to gain more momentum, but the results could be strategically important. An immediate improvement in electrical performance and services would ensue. By my estimates (confirmed by several engineers), a $50 million investment in this type of sustainable energy would yield the same effects as installing a $500 million power plant, and it could be done by September with a coordinated media campaign (think of the good things that the NY Times and al Jazeera would say about it!). It would also send a strong international message that we care for Iraq's long-term future and that Iraq can provide a meaningful and symbolic service to its people. It's not just the right thing to do—reducing consumer demand this way is a real solution that we could implement very quickly with results that would be anything but facile.

Once again, thank you for your time the other evening, and thank you for your service! Our politics may differ, but the fact that you continue to wear the uniform while serving in the most respected legislative body in the world is truly inspiring!

Very respectfully,

Christopher Brownfield
LT, USN Submarine Service (Nuclear)

MCI: 914.822.1468
c.brownfield@iraq.centcom.mil
c.brownfield@centcom.mcfi.cmil.mil

HEADQUARTERS
MULTI-NATIONAL FORCE – IRAQ
BAGHDAD, IRAQ
APO AE 09342-1400

10 May 2007

Soldiers, Sailors, Airmen, Marines, and Coast Guardsmen serving in Multi-National Force-Iraq:

Our values and the laws governing warfare teach us to respect human dignity, maintain our integrity, and do what is right. Adherence to our values distinguishes us from our enemy. This fight depends on securing the population, which must understand that we – not our enemies – occupy the m high ground. This strategy has shown results in recent months. Al Qaeda's indiscriminate attacks, for example, have finally started to turn a substantial proportion of the Iraqi population against it.

In view of this, I was concerned by the results of a recently released survey conducted last fall Iraq that revealed an apparent unwillingness on the part of some US personnel to report illegal actions taken by fellow members of their units. The study also indicated that a small percentage of those surveyed may have mistreated noncombatants. This survey should spur reflection on our conduct in combat.

I fully appreciate the emotions that one experiences in Iraq. I also know firsthand the bonds between members of the "brotherhood of the close fight." Seeing a fellow trooper killed by a barbaric enemy can spark frustration, anger, and a desire for immediate revenge. As hard as it might be, howev we must not let these emotions lead us – or our comrades in arms – to commit hasty, illegal actions. In the event that we witness or hear of such actions, we must not let our bonds prevent us from speaking

Some may argue that we would be more effective if we sanctioned torture or other expedient methods to obtain information from the enemy. They would be wrong. Beyond the basic fact that suc actions are illegal, history shows that they also are frequently neither useful nor necessary. Certainly, extreme physical action can make someone "talk;" however, what the individual says may be of questionable value. In fact, our experience in applying the interrogation standards laid out in the Army Field Manual (2-22.3) on *Human Intelligence Collector Operations* that was published last year shows that the techniques in the manual work effectively and humanely in eliciting information from detaine

We are, indeed, warriors. We train to kill our enemies. We are engaged in combat, we must pursue the enemy relentlessly, and we must be violent at times. What sets us apart from our enemies i this fight, however, is how we behave. In everything we do, we must observe the standards and values that dictate that we treat noncombatants and detainees with dignity and respect. While we are warriors we are also all human beings. Stress caused by lengthy deployments and combat is not a sign of weakness; it is a sign that we are human. If you feel such stress, do not hesitate to talk to your chain o command, your chaplain, or a medical expert.

We should use the survey results to renew our commitment to the values and standards that ma us who we are and to spur re-examination of these issues. Leaders, in particular, need to discuss these issues with their troopers – and, as always, they need to set the right example and strive to ensure prop conduct. We should never underestimate the importance of good leadership and the difference it can make.

Thanks for what you continue to do. It is an honor to serve with each of you.

David H. Petraeus
General, United States Army
Commanding

Appendix B

Post-Hearing Questions for the Record

Submitted to Major General Ronald L. Johnson
From Senator Barack Obama

"Deconstructing Reconstruction:
Problems, Challenges and the Way Forward in Iraq and
Afghanistan"
March 22, 2007

Question 1:

One of the mistakes made at the outset of the reconstruction effort was not involving enough Iraqis in the process. According to your written testimony, over 75 percent of the Corps of Engineers contracts are to Iraqi contractors. What is the value of these contracts? Who has the remaining 25 percent of the contracts? What is the value of those contracts?

Answer:

Since October 2006 when the Corps of Engineers Gulf Region Division (GRD) formally assumed Army's Iraq Reconstruction mission from the Project and Contracting Office (PCO), GRD has awarded a total of 390 million dollars in contracts for reconstruction work. Of the 390 million dollars awarded, 268 million dollars were awarded to Iraqi contractors and 122 million dollars were awarded to non-Iraqi contractors. Non-Iraqi contractors include multi-national firms comprised of U.S. based companies as well as companies from other countries.

The Army has significantly adjusted our strategy since the Iraq reconstruction mission began three years ago. The initial acquisition strategy for the reconstruction effort involved the use of large prime contractors to provide program management and design/build services for large scale projects. This initial strategy was considered to be appropriate at the time given the magnitude and complexity of the reconstruction program and the contingency environment the Army was working in. Over the last three years however, the Army has steadily reduced the involvement of large multinational firms and increased the number of contracts awarded to Iraqi firms to where today over 75 percent of GRD contracts are to Iraqi contractors.

Question 2:

In your written testimony you mention that over 1000 Iraqis are directly employed by GRD and its contractors. Is this group of employees distinct from the thousands of Iraqis you mention that are employed by the Iraqi contractors who hold 75 percent of your contracts?

Answer:

Yes, the 1000 Iraqis directly employed by GRD I referenced in my testimony are separate and distinct from the Iraqi contractors who are constructing our projects. The 1000 Iraqi personnel who work directly for GRD are part of our Iraqi Associates program and provide life support, security, construction management, administrative, and technical services for GRD's offices throughout Iraq. As of March 2007, there were a total of 43,000 Iraqis employed on all GRD managed reconstruction activities. This number includes the 1000 Iraqi associates employed directly by GRD as well as those employed by Iraqi contractors working for the Corps of Engineers.

Question 3A:

A major recommendation in the recently released Inspector General's Lessons Learned Report and the Iraq Study Group Report is for increased interagency cooperation and a point person for contact to prevent duplicative efforts. Do you support this recommendation?

Answer:

Yes, the Corps of Engineers supports the SIGIR and Iraq Study Group's recommendation for a single U.S. entity to be responsible for reconstruction efforts. A single authority responsible for planning, programming, and directing reconstruction efforts could not only assist in preventing duplicative efforts, but also assist in the coordination of the efforts of the agencies involved in the reconstruction mission to ensure the mission is executed efficiently.

Question 3B:

How is your office cooperating with the new reconstruction point person, Ambassador Carney?

Answer:

The Corps of Engineers is fully committed to supporting Ambassador Tim Carney and recognizes the need for a continued close partnership with the State Department and the Ministries of the Government of Iraq. The Corps of Engineers has worked and continues to work closely with the U.S. State Department's Iraq Reconstruction Management Office (IRMO) and the Government of Iraq (GOI) to develop cooperation strategies and to coordinate reconstruction activities. Interagency cooperation in reconstruction is a key element which the Corps of Engineers fully supports. GRD has been tasked to provide liaisons to embed within the Ministry of Oil, the Ministry of Electricity, the Ministry of Water Resources, the Ministry of Municipalities and Public Works, and the Ministry of Construction and Housing. The mission of these liaisons is to assist the Iraqi Ministries in developing the capacity to manage and execute their budgets and to take over the reconstruction mission once the U.S. Government's mission is complete. This plan is in accordance with the vision and direction given by Ambassador Carney.

Question 4A:

Your testimony mentioned two important enterprises, the reconstruction of the electricity infrastructure and the oil sector. Does the Army Corps of Engineers play the primary role in these reconstruction efforts?

Answer:

The Army Corps of Engineers Gulf Region Division (GRD) does play a primary role in the reconstruction effort of the electric and oil infrastructures. The Corps of Engineers is a key member in a team that identifies, prioritizes, and executes programs and projects that are designed to jump start the Iraqi national electrical grid and the oil and gas infrastructure. This team consists of members of the Department of State, GRD and the Iraqi Ministries of Electricity and Oil.

Question 4B:

The Special Inspector General's January 2007 Quarterly Report indicates that oil production continues to lag below targets and electricity demand still exceeds capacity. What could we have done differently, from the outset of the reconstruction efforts, to increase oil production and electricity capacity?

Answer:

The policy of the U.S. Government (USG) during the early planning and execution stages of the oil restoration mission was to repair and restore the oil infrastructure to a prewar level. Since the oil sector offered the greatest potential for private sector investment, the USG felt that the private sector would provide the large investments required to increase oil production. It was never the USG's intent or policy to increase production above the pre-war level using USG funds.

The U.S. Congress appropriated $1.7 billion in 2003 to support the USG policy for the oil sector. The money provided was considerable but still was only a fraction of the estimated $8 billion needed to increase production and was the minimum needed to maintain production. To help put this in perspective, over the last four years the USG's expenditures in Iraq's oil sector averaged about $400 million per year with another $500 million per year contributed by the Government of Iraq. During 2006, Exxon-Mobil spent $20 billion, Chevron-Texaco spent $16 billion and Conoco-Phillips spent $16 billion on capital investments for their companies. Aramco does not normally share their capital spending with the public, but the Saudi Oil Minister mentioned at a conference last year that their budget for capital investment was $20 billion for 2006.

The original objectives for oil production and export would have been met, if not for the insurgency attacks on pipelines and processing plants in the northern part of Iraq. Attacks on export pipelines in the north have essentially eliminated the capability to export the crude oil being produced in the Kirkuk area oil fields. In addition, a mortar attack in early 2006 destroyed a large stabilization plant in Kirkuk. Since that plant is an integral part of crude oil processing, the Kirkuk oil wells have been shut down until the plant is repaired. Oil production in the southern part of Iraq has been at pre war levels since early 2004.

Electricity demand still exceeds capacity. Demand has increased at a rate of 10 percent per year, primarily due to a growing Iraqi economy and greater access to new appliances. Recent Iraq Ministry of Electricity estimates show that demand will lag capacity until at least 2011. The goals of the Iraq Relief and Reconstruction Fund (IRRF) was to jump-start electricity reconstruction efforts, establish between 10 and 12 hours of daily power in Iraq, and increase generation, transmission, and distribution capabilities. Towards that end, the USG has invested $3.4B into an infrastructure that will require at least a $20–30B investment or possibly more to completely restore. During March 2007 an average of 11 hours of daily power was achieved in Iraq.

While the current plan for restoring the Iraq electric infrastructure is working, the plan conceivably could have benefited from two additions. First, the investment in infrastructure for capturing and processing natural gas would have allowed for gas turbines to be put in service. Second, greater investment in thermal units which operate on heavy fuel oil (HFO) would have been beneficial. Thermal units are easier to maintain and could have helped alleviate the burden of excess HFO at Iraqi Oil Refineries.

Question 4C:

What obstacles are we facing now in our efforts to get the Iraqis capable to oversee and protect these important sectors?

Answer:

There are several obstacles we are now facing in our efforts to get the Iraqis ready to take over the restoration and protection of the electricity and oil infrastructure sectors.

The number one obstacle that the Iraqis must overcome is the sabotage of infrastructure by insurgents. Damage to power lines and towers continue, especially for transmission lines into Baghdad. If not secured, there will be little chance that Baghdad will receive 10–12 hours of power this summer. For the oil sector, continued attacks on export pipelines in the north have essentially eliminated the capability to export the crude oil being produced in the Kirkuk area oil fields. These pipelines must be restored and protected to allow the export of oil from the northern oil fields.

The Iraqi capital budget is another obstacle which will

need to be overcome. The Government of Iraq (GOI) budgeted $3.5 billion for their oil sector capital in 2006, but only spent $0.5 billion. They spent $0.9 billion in 2005. The electric sector data has not been as clear and remains to be determined. With the IRRF program ending, it is very important for the Iraqis to execute their capital budget and provide desperately needed infrastructure investment funds.

Finally, a coordinated GOI energy policy that takes into account competing priorities between the Ministry of Electricity and the Ministry of Oil is needed.

Question 5:

In addition to your work on rebuilding the electricity sector and the oil sector, it is my understanding that the U.S. Army Corps of Engineers was responsible for the Primary Healthcare Centers project, which began in March 2004 for 150 centers. It seems to me that an important part of our effort to win the hearts and minds of the people of Iraq would be our effort to provide some healthcare infrastructure. According to the Special IG, for about two years, little progress was made on this project, despite the expenditure of $186 million. By March 2006, we reduced the number of centers requested to 142. Of those 142, 135 centers were partially constructed, one was placed under a different contract, and only six were accepted as completed by the Corps. The government then terminated the contract for 121 of the 135 partially completed centers. So, out of a 2004 request for 150 centers, we now have a contract for 20 centers. What has the Corps learned from that experience and what will the Corps do differently as a result?

Answer:

The Iraqi Ministry of Health (MOH) requested in 2005 that the U.S. Army construct 142 Primary Healthcare Centers (PHCs). The Army contracted with Parsons Corporation to build 141 PHCs and awarded the contract for one PHC to an

Iraqi construction firm. Parsons substantially completed six PHCs, however was only able to partially complete the remaining 135. Parsons had considerable difficulty in meeting the requirements of their contract and ultimately the U.S. Government terminated their contract because the Government felt Parsons was not capable of successfully completing the work. The U. S. Government only paid Parsons what they were due under the terms of their contract at the time it was terminated.

As of April 15, 2007, fifteen PHCs have been completed and turned over to the Iraqi MOH. Eight of these PHCs are open and providing healthcare to the Iraqi people. The Iraqi MOH is currently staffing and setting-up the other seven PHCs for immediate operation. The Army has contracted with Iraqi firms to complete the remaining PHCs and currently 120 PHC's are under construction by local Iraqi contractors. Of the 120 PHCs under construction, 70 are scheduled to be completed and turned over to the Iraqi Ministry of Health (MOH) by July 2007 with the last PHC scheduled for completion in December 2007.

The Corps has made a number of significant changes as a result of lessons learned from the PHC projects and other reconstruction projects in Iraq. GRD has shifted away from design-build and cost plus contracts to direct and fixed price contracts. GRD has reduced the involvement of large multinational firms and increased work with Iraqi firms that have proven themselves as successful contractors. A strict "cost to complete" system has been instituted to ensure that sufficient funds are available to complete our projects in the future. GRD also learned from the construction of the PHCs that each local community has a unique set of circumstances, and construction must be tailored to meet those needs. In this type of situation, it is more effective to use multiple local contractors rather than one large prime contractor.

The construction of the PHC Program has been especially challenging, however it has also been especially rewarding.

Each of the open clinics has been successfully treating on average over 350 patients a day and is a significant enhancement to the delivery of primary healthcare to the Iraqi people. When the PHCs are all finished and in operation, primary healthcare will be available to thousands of Iraqis, most of whom had little or no access to healthcare previously.

Acknowledgments

(in no particular order):

Thanks to Ralph Franklin, a truly outstanding friend and critic, without whose timely advice my thoughts would have been unpublishable.

Thanks to Vicky Wilson, my editor, whose profound yet brief strategic guidance was like having my own personal Sun Tzu.

Thanks to Alex Gibney, whose work gave me moral support by championing human rights at a dark moment in American history.

Thanks to Simon Samoeil, Jacinto Lirola, Robert Lalka, and Aaron Dalton for their friendship and insight.

Thanks to Hunter Thompson for inventing gonzo journalism and for reminding us that irreverence can *sometimes* be a good thing.

Thanks to my dear friend Laki Vazakas, who persistently reminded me to write while I was in Iraq, even if what I wrote each day amounted to nothing more than a sentence fragment.

Special thanks to Lynn Nesbit, the "invisible hand" of publishing who made this book possible; I will always remember your grace and kindness.

Thanks to Tina Simms and Michael Steger for steering me through the myriad details of the publishing process.

At Skyhorse Publishing, I'd like to thank Tony Lyons for starting the ball rolling, Jennifer McCartney for coordinating the effort with me, Sara Kitchen and Abigail

Gehring for managing the book's production, and Jane Sheppard for the book's cover design. Also, I'd like to send particular gratitude to the innumerable unpaid interns who toiled away in the seamy underbelly of corporate America (in addition to making me some very nice margaritas at the office party). Don't give up, comrades!!!

Thanks to Tim O'Brien for writing the lexicon of all war stories; I am not worthy to lick your combat boots.

Thanks to Nibras, Muslim, Mohammed, Munir, Ahmed K., Corbyn, and Captain "Blue-beard" Mike for creative fuel.

Finally, thanks to my Nepalese, Bengali, Indian, Iraqi, Syrian, Lebanese, Australian, Ukrainian, Bulgarian, Italian, Eritrean, Costa Rican, Russian, European, Jewish, and Palestinian friends at the Green Bean, the Woodland Society, and Giulio's Bar for good conversation, good music, and a seemingly endless supply of caffeine.

Notes

Introduction

3 "a gentleman of liberal education, refined manners": This quotation, which midshipmen are required to memorize, is frequently attributed to John Paul Jones, though it was later proven to have been written by Augustus C. Buell to reflect his view of Jones. My writing reflects my belief at the time. For more information, see "The Best Quote Jones Never Wrote," by Lori Lyn Bogle and Joel Holwitt.

7 "trained to conduct surveillance": See *Blind Man's Bluff*, by Christopher Drew, Sherry Sontag, and Annette Lawrence for more reading on this Cold War topic.

1 / In the Belly of the Beast

15 "the first hybrid vehicle that could sustain its environment and mission independent of oil": Technically submarines use oil for several things like lubricants for bearings and diesel fuel for backup generators. My point is that burning oil is not the normal source of energy that allows nuclear submarines to operate.

16 "a British prospector unearthed the massive oil reserves in 'petroliferous' Persia": The most comprehensive account of the history of oil can be found in *The Prize*, by Daniel Yergin.

17 "the Anglo-Persian Oil Company (later British Petroleum) exploited the unsophisticated Persians": Yergin's account of Iranian oil seems technically accurate, but Stephen Kinzer's recent account of the politics of Iran in *All the Shah's Men* provides a more comprehensive presentation of the forces at work.

19 "world's first naval nuclear reactor came to life": There are several accounts of this historical feat, but the one I find most interesting is *Rickover: A Struggle for Excellence*, by Francis Duncan. This account focuses on Rickover at the center of a bureaucratic, scientific, and engineering struggle to integrate disparate institutions and build the nuclear submarine force.

20 "stacks and stacks of electronic equipment": For a surprisingly serious look at the innards of nuclear submarines, try reading *The Complete Idiot's Guide to Submarines,* or the old standard, *Submarine,* by Tom Clancy and John Gresham.

2 / Nuclear Family Life

26 "I couldn't pass the nuclear qualification exam": Technically, there were two separate written exams, one for basic engineering qualification and one for

supervisory qualification. Officers are required to pass both at approximately the same point in their training.

31 "The nuclear cheating scandal aboard the *Hartford* was but one instance of a fleet-wide problem": This information comes from numerous informal interviews that my colleagues and I conducted at the Naval Submarine School in Groton, Connecticut, from 2006 to 2007. At this point in our careers, my colleagues and I had left our submarines for shore duty and felt more open about discussing the dubious practices. A detailed interview with a Submarine School instructor in 2009 confirmed that the cheating continues, even though one junior officer was recently court-martialed for having used a "study guide" similar to the one on the *Hartford*. The instructor asked not to be identified.

3 / *Damn the Torpedoes!!!*

37 "They couldn't hit an elephant at this dist—": There are differing historical accounts of Sedgwick's death. Some say it was immediately after he made this statement; some say it happened a bit later. In every case, these are generally regarded as his last words and illustrate my point quite clearly.

4 / *Crush Depth*

60 "Captain Richard Gannon and his marines of the Third Battalion were on the move": More information about Richard Gannon can be found at www.rickgannon.com.

5 / *Gunboat Diplomats*

68 "What kinds of intelligence could a submarine gather that other methods couldn't get for pennies on the dollar?": Nuclear submarines cost between $750 million and nearly $3 billion to build, depending on the class. Newer designs typically cost twice as much as older ones, at least until several have been made. Submarines typically cost about $30 million per year to operate.

8 / *The Process We Do*

97 "There had to be a plan somewhere": Eventually I found two strategic plans for energy, one written by a consultancy named Bearing Point for USAID and another written by the Ministry of Electricity. The Bearing Point report was fanciful, planning on financing state-of-the-art gas turbines with carbon credits from the Kyoto Protocol. The ministry's document was equally naive—it simply assumed that security would exist and that investors would line up to finance Iraq's industry. To my knowledge, none of my colleagues in the military had read either of these reports.

9 / *The E-Team*

108 "the responsibility for rebuilding Iraq's energy sector lay between these consultants and my civil affairs unit": The E-Team, my nickname for our

group, technically comprised the Iraqi Reconstruction Management office (IRMO) and the Civil Military Operations Directorate (CMO). The Army Corps of Engineers executed infrastructure projects through subcontractors, and the Strategic Operations Center provided coordination of infrastructure security to the team.

13 / Flying Solo

168 "the ministry's ten-year blueprint for development": These documents from the Iraqi government will generally not be available for public viewing. They are not classified, but I don't consider it proper for me to make foreign government documents available to the public. Requests for information may be directed to the appropriate ministry, such as the Ministry of Electricity, http://www.moelc.gov.iq.

14 / Non Sibi Sed Petraeus

184 *"Dulce et decorum est"*: This phrase is part of the famous saying "It is sweet and fitting to die for one's country." See the poem "Dulce et Decorum Est," by Wilfred Owen.

15 / The Precipitous Pullout

205 *"Halliburton? Worried about saving taxpayer dollars?"*: The company that provided these services was actually KBR, formerly Kellogg, Brown and Root, which was a subsidiary of Halliburton at this time. The name KBR is less well known than Halliburton, so I use the parent company's name for simplicity, even though they are not the same.

16 / McCainery, Chicanery

222 "John McCain's efforts to put a stop to America's policies of detention and torture were duplicitous, ineffective, and filled with secretive compromises": See the open letter I wrote to John McCain, published in the *Daily Beast*, "Why My Former Hero Should Not Be President," October 3, 2008.

17 / Lukewarm Fusion

231 "The army gave them a twenty-million-dollar server, and what do they actually use? *Yahoo!*": The expensive server that was installed in 2003 for the Iraqi government to use worked only in the Green Zone. Its functionality in Arabic was limited, and its American administrators required too much paperwork and vetting for the Iraqis to use the system. Use was actually restricted to officials who had access to the Green Zone, a bureaucratic limitation that made using the server completely impractical.

236 "Obama's office just wrote to us. They have some questions about the energy sector": See appendix A for the correspondence that Colonel Phillips shared with me. This document was presented to me as the official response submitted to Senator Obama's office from the Army Corps of Engineers.

18 / *A Thousand Points of Light*

241 "a dozen stars' worth of generals": The Energy Development Committee was chaired by Petraeus's director of strategic operations and the State Department's top general for reconstruction management. This committee, which included the entire senior staff of the E-Team, fed its recommendations directly to the steering committee chaired by the prime minister.

19 / *The Night of Fire*

253 "'monuments men'": For a captivating account of what the monuments men did to preserve European culture in World War II, see the documentary titled *The Rape of Europa.*

254 "Saddam had ordered Mohammed's brother to be killed": There is a harrowing account of this political purge, titled "Tales of the Tyrant," by Mark Bowden in the *Atlantic.* Mohammed's brother was one of the first among the men who were silenced and murdered in this purge.

255 "There were twenty-five of them, each depicting a scene in Baghdad during the Night of Fire": To see these works, visit www.praxis-unitas.com and download *Oil on Landscape: Art from Wartime Contemporaries of Baghdad.*

258 "the new Old Iron Pants": Thomas Ricks writes comprehensively about Odierno's indiscretions in Anbar in his book *Fiasco,* then follows up with much more detailed accounts of Odierno's transformation in *The Gamble.*

Bibliography

Ahmad, Tha'ir. "Rise of Inflation Causes Failure of Monetary Policy." *Niqash.* 2007. http://www.niqash.org/content.php?contentTypeID=74&id=1705.

Baker, James A. III, and Lee Hamilton. *The Iraq Study Group Report.* New York: Vintage Books, 2006.

Barnes, Joe, and Matthew E. Chen. "NOCs and U.S. Foreign Policy." The James A. Baker III Institute for Public Policy, Rice University, Houston, Texas, 2007.

Beeman, William O. "The House of Chalabi: The Future of Iraq?" *Agence Global.* 2004. http://www.agenceglobal.com/article.asp?id=128.

Berman, Paul, Thomas Friedman, Christopher Hitchens, Fred Kaplan, George Packer, Kenneth M. Pollack, Jacob Weisberg, and Fareed Zakaria. "Liberal Hawks Reconsider the Iraq War." *Slate.* 2004. http://www.slate.com/id/2093620/.

Bogle, Lori Lyn, and Joel I. Holwitt. "The Best Quote Jones Never Wrote." Annapolis, Md.: Naval History.

Bowden, Mark. "Tales of the Tyrant." *Atlantic.* 2002. http://www.theatlantic.com/doc/200205/bowden.

Brownfield, Christopher J. "How America Blew It in Syria." *Daily Beast.* 2008. http://www.thedailybeast.com/blogs-and-stories/2008-10-28/americas-mistake-in-syria/.

———. "Why My Former Hero Shouldn't Be President." *Daily Beast.* 2008. http://www.thedailybeast.com/blogs-and-stories/2008-10-07/why-my-former-hero-shouldnrsquot-be-president/.

Bryce, Robert. *Gusher of Lies: The Dangerous Delusions of "Energy Independence."* New York: PublicAffairs, 2008.

Carter, Jimmy. *Our Endangered Values: America's Moral Crisis.* New York: Simon and Schuster, 2005.

———. *Palestine: Peace Not Apartheid.* New York: Simon and Schuster, 2006.

Charpak, Georges, and Richard L. Garwin. *Megawatts and Megatons: A Turning Point in the Nuclear Age?* New York: Alfred A. Knopf, 2001.

Clancy, Tom, and John Gresham. *Submarine: A Guided Tour Inside a Nuclear Warship.* New York: Berkeley Books, 2003.

Cohen, Roger. "America Needs France's Atomic Anne." *New York Times.* 2007. http://www.nytimes.com/2008/01/24/opinion/24cohen.html?ref=opinion.

Crocker, Ryan C. "Statement of Ambassador Ryan C. Crocker, U.S. Ambassador to the Republic of Iraq to a Joint Hearing of the Committee on Foreign Affairs and the Committee on Armed Services." Washington, D.C., 2007.

DiMercurio, Michael, and Michael Benson. *The Complete Idiot's Guide to Submarines.* Indianapolis: Alpha, 2003.

Drew, Christopher, Sherry Sontag, and Annette Lawrence. *Blind Man's Bluff: The Untold Story of American Submarine Espionage.* New York: PublicAffairs, 1998.

ElBarredei, Mohamed. "Nuclear Energy: The Need for a New Framework." International Conference on Nuclear Fuel Supply: Challenges and Opportunities. Berlin, Germany, 2008.

———. "Towards a Safer World." *Economist* p. 16, October 2003.

Fagen, Patricia Weiss. *Iraqi Refugees: Seeking Stability in Syria and Jordan.* Doha, Qatar: Institute for the Study of International Migration: Center for International and Regional Studies, 2007.

Faraj, Maysaloun. *Strokes of Genius: Contemporary Iraqi Art.* London: Saqi Books, 2001.

Ferguson, Charles. "No End in Sight." New York: PublicAffairs/Perseus Books, 2008.

Francis, Richard. *Judge Sewall's Apology: The Salem Witch Trials and the Forming of an American Conscience.* New York: Fourth Estate, 2005.

Frank, Robert H. *What Price the Moral High Ground? Ethical Dilemmas in Competitive Environments.* Princeton, N.J.: Princeton University Press, 2004.

Fukuyama, Francis. *America at the Crossroads: Democracy, Power, and the Neoconservative Legacy.* New Haven, Conn.: Yale University Press, 2006.

Galbraith, Peter. *The End of Iraq: How American Incompetence Created a War without End.* New York: Simon and Schuster, 2006.

Gibney, Alex. *Enron: The Smartest Guys in the Room.* 109 minutes. Think Film, USA, 2006.

———. *Taxi to the Dark Side.* 106 minutes. Think Film, USA, 2008.

Glanz, James. "Iraqi Insurgents Starve Capital of Electricity." *New York Times,* December 19, 2006.

Hagan, John, and Ruth D. Peterson. *Crime and Inequality.* Stanford, Calif.: Stanford University Press, 1995.

Hiro, Dilip. "Concessions in the Pipeline: Nouri al-Maliki's Government Plans to Grant Big Concessions to Western Oil Companies—But in Reality, It Lacks the Legitimacy to Do So." *Guardian* (Comment Is Free . . .). 2007, http://commentisfree.guardian.co.uk/dilip_hiro/2007/01/running_on_empty.html.

Huntington, Samuel P. *The Clash of Civilizations and the Remaking of World Order.* New York: Simon and Schuster, 1996.

Ignatieff, Michael. "Why We Are in Iraq." *New York Times Magazine,* September 7, 2003.

International Atomic Energy Agency (IAEA). "Talks Proceed on Proposed International Uranium Enrichment Centre." 2007, http://www.iaea.org/NewsCenter/News/2007/russiatalks.html.

Khalilzad, Zalmay. "Statement by U.S. Ambassador to Iraq Zamay Khalilzad on the Hydrocarbon Law." 2007. http://iraq.usembassy.gov/iraq/20070226_hydrocarbon_law.html.

Kinzer, Stephen. *All the Shah's Men: An American Coup and the Roots of Middle East Terror.* Hoboken, N.J.: J. Wiley, 2003.

Kolko, Gabriel. *Another Century of War?* New York: New Press, distributed by W. W. Norton, 2002.

Lawrence, T. E. *Seven Pillars of Wisdom: A Triumph.* London: J. Cape, 1935.

Leslie, Russel. "The Good Faith Assumption: Different Paradigmatic Approaches to Nonproliferation Issues." *Nonproliferation Review* 15, no. 3 (2008).

Lewarne, Stephen, and David Snelbecker. "Lessons Learned about Economic Governance in War Torn Economies: From the Marshall Plan to the Reconstruction of Iraq." USAID (under contract of the Office of Development Evaluation and Information Bureau for Policy and Program Coordination), 2006.

Marks, Anne, ed. *NPT, Paradoxes and Problems*. Washington, D.C.: Arms Control Association, Carnegie Endowment for International Peace, 1975.

Mayer, Jane. "The Black Sites: A Rare Look Inside the CIA's Secret Interrogation Program." *New Yorker,* August 13, 2007.

McCain, John, and Mark Salter. *Faith of My Fathers: A Family Memoir*. New York: Harper Perennial, 2000.

McClellan, Scott. *What Happened: Inside the Bush White House and Washington's Culture of Deception*. New York: PublicAffairs, 2008.

McNamara, Robert. "Inviting War." *New York Times,* September 15, 1983.

Micklethwait, John, and Adrian Wooldridge. *The Company: A Short History of a Revolutionary Idea*. New York: Modern Library, 2003.

Ministry of Electricity Office of Planning and Studies. "Ministry of Electricity Plan 2006–2015." Ministry of Electricity. Baghdad, Iraq, 2006.

Morris, Errol. *The Fog of War: Eleven Lessons from the Life of Robert S. McNamara*. 95 minutes. USA. 107 minutes (theatrical version). USA, 2004.

Muttit, Greg. "Is Iraq Pressured to Sign Unfair Oil Contracts?" *Niqash*. 2006. http://www.niqash.org/content.php?contentTypeID=171&id=1617.

———. "Of Oil, War, and Power—Learning from History." *Niqash*. 2006. http://www.niqash.org/content.php?contentTypeID=171&id=1314.

Noriega, Manuel Antonio, and Peter Eisner. *America's Prisoner: The Memoirs of Manuel Noriega*. New York: Random House, 1997.

Noujaim, Jehane. *Control Room*. 84 minutes. USA, 2004.

Nye, Joseph Jr. "US Power and Strategy After Iraq," *Foreign Affairs* 82, no. 4 (2003): 60–73.

O'Donnell, Tom. "The Political Economy of the US-Iran Crisis: Oil Hegemony, Not Nukes, Is the Real Issue." *Z* Magazine, 2006.

OPEC Secretariat. "OPEC World Oil Outlook 2008." Organization for Petroleum Exporting Countries, Vienna, Austria.

Open Society Institute. "Open Letter on the Oil and Gas Wealth in the Draft Iraqi Constitution. To: The Speaker of the National Assembly and Its Esteemed Members and the Future Speaker of the House of Representatives and Its Members. New As Sabah, Az Zaman, Al Mutamar, Baghdad, Iraq, 2005.

———. "Policy Recommendations from Discussions at the London Conference." *Iraqi Oil Wealth: Issues of Governance and Development*. London: Open Society Institute and London School of Economics, 2005.

O'Reilly, Bill. *Culture Warrior*. New York: Broadway Books, 2006.

Petraeus, David. "Letter from the Commanding General. Sailors, Soldiers, Airmen, Marines and Coast Guardsmen Serving in Multi-National Force, Iraq." Baghdad, Iraq, 2007.

———. "Report to Congress on the Situation in Iraq. Commander, Multi-National Force—Iraq." Washington, D.C., 2007.

Petraeus, David, and James Amos. "Counterinsurgency." *FM 3–24*. Washington, D.C.: Headquarters, Department of the Army, 2006.

Place, Jean-Michel, ed. *Bagdad Renaissance: Art Contemporain en Irak*. 2006.

Powell, Colin L., and Joseph E. Persico. *My American Journey.* New York: Ballantine, 2003.

Republic of Iraq. The Constitution of the Republic of Iraq. Baghdad, 2005.

Ricks, Thomas E. *Fiasco: The American Military Adventure in Iraq.* New York: Penguin, 2006.

———. *The Gamble: General Petraeus and the Untold Story of the American Surge in Iraq, 2006–2008.* New York: Penguin, 2009.

Rockwell, Theodore. *The Rickover Effect: The Inside Story of How Admiral Hyman Rickover Built the Nuclear Navy.* New York: John Wiley, 1995.

Sachs, Jeffrey. *The End of Poverty: Economic Possibilities for Our Time.* New York: Penguin, 2005.

Said, Edward W. *Orientalism.* New York: Vintage, 1979.

Salih, Asso. "Kirkuk: Between the Politicians' Games and the Citizens' Suffering." *Niqash.* 2006. http://www.niqash.org/content.php?contentTypeID=165&id=1731.

Schelling, Thomas C., Morton H. Halperin, et al. *Strategy and Arms Control.* Washington, D.C.: Pergamon-Brassey's, 1985.

Sen, Amartya Kumar. *Development as Freedom.* Oxford and New York: Oxford University Press, 2001.

———. *Identity and Violence: The Illusion of Destiny.* New York: W. W. Norton, 2006.

Stephenson, James. *Losing the Golden Hour: An Insider's View of Iraq's Reconstruction.* Washington, D.C.: Potomac Books, 2007.

Tavernise, Sabrina. "Iraq Ends Security Company's License After 8 Deaths." *New York Times,* 2007. http://www.nytimes.com/2007/09/17/world/middleeast/17cnd-iraq.html?_r=1&hp&oref=slogin.

Timberg, Robert. *The Nightingale's Song.* New York: Simon and Schuster, 1995.

United States Government Accountability Office. *Rebuilding Iraq: Integrated Strategic Plan Needed to Help Restore Iraq's Oil and Electricity Sectors. Report to Congressional Committees.* Washington, D.C.: Government Accounting Office, 2007.

VanDeMark, Brian. *Pandora's Keepers: Nine Men and the Atomic Bomb.* Boston: Little, Brown, 2003.

Wilson, Joseph C. *The Politics of Truth: Inside the Lies That Led to War and Betrayed My Wife's CIA Identity. A Diplomat's Memoir.* New York: Carroll and Graf Publishers, 2004.

Wright, Lawrence. *The Looming Tower: Al Qaeda and the Road to 9/11.* New York: Alfred A. Knopf, 2006.

Yergin, Daniel. *The Prize: The Epic Quest for Oil, Money, and Power.* New York: Simon and Schuster, 1991.

Yingling, Paul. "A Failure in Generalship." *Armed Forces Journal.* 2007, http://www.armedforcesjournal.com/2007/05/2635198.

Zorpette, Glenn. "Re-Engineering Iraq." *IEEE Spectrum.* 2006. http://www.spectrum.ieee.org/print/2831.

INDEX

Page numbers in *italics* refer to illustrations.